PUBLIC ADMINISTRATION
The Execution of Public Policy

THE LIPPINCOTT SERIES
IN AMERICAN GOVERNMENT
under the editorship of
WILLIAM C. HAVARD
*Virginia Polytechnic Institute
and State University*

PUBLIC ADMINISTRATION
The Execution of Public Policy

DON ALLENSWORTH

J. B. LIPPINCOTT COMPANY
Philadelphia
New York   Toronto

ISBN 0–397–47272–2

Printed in the United States of America

Cover design by Smudin Studio

1 3 5 7 9 8 6 4 2

Library of Congress Cataloging in Publication Data

Allensworth, Donald Trudeau, 1934-
    Public administration.

    Includes bibliographical references.
    1. United States — Politics and government. 2. State governments.
3. Local government—United States. 4. Public administration. I. Title.

JK421.A58   353   73-2918
ISBN 0–397–47272–2

CONTENTS

FOREWORD

The opening chapters of this book contain an examination of public policy. They focus on the administrative aspects of governmental policy-making processes. The policy areas covered—housing, urban planning, transportation, and environment—are objects of the many policies of American governments. Each area involves all the levels in the federal system, and each clearly indicates the intergovernmental nature of policy execution in this system. A final chapter in this section looks into the problem of coordinating policy administration, both on an intergovernmental scale and within a given level of government.

Thus, the first part of the book deals with the practical side of public administration. It studies actual cases which portray the practice of administration and calls attention to the many constraints, pressures, decisions, and problems facing administrators as they attempt to provide a wide variety of public services.

The second part of the book turns to the theoretical underpinnings of public administration. It begins with a discussion of administrative thought in political theory and continues with a review of the early efforts to establish the principles of administration and a theory of administrative organization. A study of the recent assault on orthodox thinking in public administration and a discussion of the most recent trends in administrative theory follow. The concluding chapter in this section explains the methods and approaches to the study of public administration. Because of its complexity, this subject is treated only after the reader has had an opportunity to comprehend some aspects of the actual workings of administration and has become acquainted with some of the ways in which students and practitioners of administration have interpreted its workings.

The text closes with a presentation of some contemporary principles of public administration, principles as reflected in current operations of administrative agencies. The final chapter examines the role of administrative bureaucracies in fostering political and social change.

1

INTRODUCTION

MEASUREMENT OF ADMINISTRATION

As a text on public administration, this book is concerned with the administrative activities of government and turns its attention to the executive branch. It does not cover the national government alone, because this government is only one element in the federal system. In fact, administrative processes at the state and local levels may represent a greater part of total government activity than those carried on in Washington. We can attribute this phenomenon to the essentially administrative nature of most state and local responsibilities.

One way of understanding administrative activities is to study the pattern of governmental expenditures. Another method is to study the volume and distribution of government employment. Both of these measures help us comprehend the scale and magnitude of administration.

Government Expenditures

By any standard, government in the United States is big business. This becomes especially apparent in the accelerating pace of public spending. Government expenditures represent an important part of all outlays in the country. Governments at all levels are spending at rates exceeding previous record highs, and the budgets of national, state, and local governments continue to soar each year.

Nearly all government expenditures are for administrative activities (outputs). This means that almost all government money is spent by administrative agencies in the executive branch; only a fraction, less than one percent, is used by legislative and judicial units for their internal operations.

The extent of government outlays dazzles many. In 1972, governmental units in this nation spent over $350 billion. The federal government spends most of this money; nevertheless, state and local government expenditures now run in the neighborhood of $150 billion a year, thus representing a significant portion of the total.

Total government expenditures amounted to $308 billion in 1969—up sharply from $70 billion in 1950 and twice the figure for 1960 (see Table 1.1). From 1950 to 1969, federal outlays rose from $42 billion to about $177 billion, while those at the state and local level jumped from just under $28 billion to over $131 billion.

During this period, local expenditures had increased at the fastest pace, moving up almost fivefold. Also, the rise in state spending has been almost as rapid. Although federal spending is currently four times the 1950 level, the national government's portion of all government outlays has dipped slightly, from over 60 percent in 1950 to about 57 percent in 1969. Federal grants to subnational governments in the early 1970s amounted to over $30 billion annually; in recent years, this assistance has risen much faster than total state-local expenditures and now

TABLE 1.1

Expenditures of Federal, State and Local Governments, for Selected Recent Years

(billions of dollars)

Year	All Governments	Federal	Federal as % of Total	State and Local Total	State	Local
1950	$ 70.3	$ 42.4	60.3%	$ 27.9	$10.9	$17.0
1955	110.7	70.3	63.5	40.4	14.4	26.0
1960	151.3	90.3	59.7	61.0	22.2	38.8
1965	205.6	119.0	57.9	86.6	31.3	55.2
1966	224.8	129.9	57.8	94.9	34.2	60.7
1967	257.8	151.8	58.9	106.0	39.7	66.3
1968	282.6	166.4	58.9	116.2	44.3	71.9
1969	308.3	176.7	57.3	131.6	49.5	82.2

SOURCE: Adapted from U.S. Bureau of the Census, *Statistical Abstract of the United States: 1971,* 92nd ed. (Washington, D.C.: Government Printing Office, 1971), p. 396.

accounts for a substantial portion of all subnational spending. Not only will nearly every dollar of this money pass into the coffers of administrative agencies; but these agencies will have a key voice, perhaps the decisive one, in determining the specific uses of this money. Legislative budget authorizations often grant considerable discretion to executive departments, subject to certain conditions, limitations, and constraints. As a result, government administrators frequently have wide options over the ultimate and precise disposition of public funds. Consequently, administrative determinations in the area of fiscal management can have far-reaching political and economic effects.

Government Employment

Employment figures also demonstrate the importance of public administration. As shown in Figure 1.1, government civilian employment totals over 13 million. The addition of about 3 million federal military personnel (1970) raises this figure to 16 million. By 1973, government civilian employment is expected to jump to almost 14 million and, assuming no change in the military, this will bring the total to 17 million.

FIGURE 1.1: Government Civilian Employment

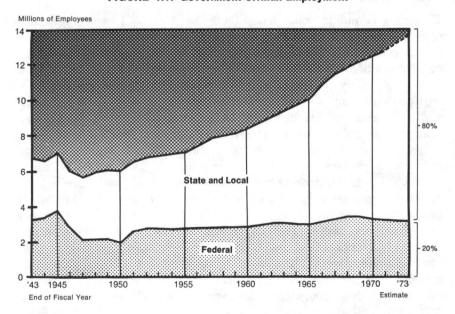

SOURCE: U.S. Office of Management and Budget, *Special Analysis of the United States Government, Fiscal Year 1973* (Washington, D.C.: Government Printing Office, 1972), p. 113.

This figure represents about one-fifth of the work force in the United States, a force which numbered 84 million in 1971.

Although federal civilian employment has leveled off in recent years and currently stands at just under 3 million, state and local rolls have increased sharply. Subnational governments now employ about 10 million people; compared to 4 million in 1950, this represents a 250 percent increase. At present, nearly 80 percent of all government civilian workers are in state and local governments; furthermore, local governments account for about three-quarters of subnational employment.

As with expenditures, employment has significant implications for the administrative branch. This is because nearly all government employees work for administrative agencies. For example, of the 3,076,000 federal civilian employees in 1969, 3,040,000 were assigned to the executive branch; of the remainder, slightly over 30,000 were employed by Congress and 6,000 by the judiciary. Although the number of legislative and judicial officials in state government is correspondingly higher than at the federal level, the overwhelming majority of state employees are in executive agencies. This pattern is also repeated at the local level, in municipalities, counties, townships, and even smaller local units.

PUBLIC ADMINISTRATION AND PUBLIC POLICY

The study of public policy has recently been given a new emphasis in political science. In public administration, the concern for public policy has deep roots; this concern has been evident particularly at the municipal level, where public administrators have long worked for civic improvement. Early public administrators were municipal reformers, and part of the reform package was expanded park systems, better housing, and comprehensive city planning. Parks, housing, and city planning are examples of public policy: a city's park system represents its parks policy, its housing program its housing policy, and its planning activities its planning policies.

Public policy has a number of dimensions. Wade and Curry discuss policy in terms of the benefits it bestows, its costs (taxes), and its effects (regulation of private activities).[1] Lewis Froman views it in terms of its substantive content (education, transportation); the relevant government institution (Congress, bureaucracy); the targets of public policy (low-income residents, bankers); its time periods (when policy was enacted or made an issue); its ideological perspectives and the values associated with it; the extent of support for it; and the level of govern-

[1]L. L. Wade and R. L. Curry, Jr., A Logic of Public Policy: Aspects of Political Economy (Belmont, California: Wadsworth Publishing Company, 1970), Chapter 1.

mental activity involved.[2] Ira Sharkansky considers the different aspects associated with it; government action ("policy"); service levels ("policy outputs"); effects of the service ("policy impacts"); and the environment (the economic, social, and political forces surrounding policy).[3]

Public policies can be examined in other ways. For example, policies may provide either or both "material" or "symbolic" satisfactions; the former would involve tangible resources or substantive power, and the latter would serve psychological or moral ends. Furthermore, policies may be distributive, regulatory, or redistributive. The first are illustrated by the allocation of government resources on a "give-away" basis (e.g., farm or rent subsidies); the second, by those policies that restrict private alternatives (e.g., acreage allotments, zoning); and the third, by policies that shift resources from one group to another (e.g., the progressive income tax).

We can also study public policy by considering the processes by which political and administrative policies are determined, implemented, and adjusted.[4] This process will involve a number of steps but, at a minimum, it includes the following: the perception and identification of problems or issues; the presentation of them to government; the formulation of possible courses of action by government; the determination of government action to be taken; the execution or implementation of this action; evaluation and appraisal of this action; problem or issue resolution; and proposals for new action. As delineated above, the policy process encompasses the totality of political activity.

When narrowly viewed, administration belongs only to the execution part of this process; however, in reality, it extends to the entire political process. Administrative agencies may identify problems; make others—such as interest groups, legislative committees and other bureaucracies—aware of these problems; formulate courses of action or help others to do so; help determine needed government action; administer the action; react to, evaluate and appraise this action; resolve problems; and propose new courses of action. Only when viewed in this broader perspective can the complexity of administration be fully apprehended.

The specific issue areas covered in the consecutive four chapters

---

[2]Lewis A. Froman, Jr., "The Categorization of Policy Contents," in Austin Ranney, ed., *Political Science and Public Policy* (Chicago: Markham Publishing Company, 1968), pp. 41–52.

[3]Ira Sharkansky, "Environment, Policy, Output and Impact: Problems of Theory and Method in the Analysis of Public Policy," in Ira Sharkansky, ed., *Policy Analysis in Political Science* (Chicago: Markham Publishing Co., 1970), p. 63.

[4]For a detailed discussion of the policy process, see Charles O. Jones, *An Introduction to the Study of Public Policy*. (Belmont, California: Wadsworth Publishing Co., 1970).

were selected because of their timeliness and because they are well-suited to illustrate the key role that administrative agencies play in the public policy processes. We have had much experience in the areas of housing, planning, and transportation because there has been considerable governmental activity in each of these areas for decades. We have chosen air and water pollution control because it is more of an emerging policy matter, one in which experience is somewhat limited. Much can be learned from watching an administrative process grow and mature.

In the final policy chapter (Chapter 6), we have concentrated on administrative coordination, a significant consideration in view of the increasingly wider range of policy issues facing government administrators at all levels in the federal system. In Chapters 2 to 5, we focus on the substance of public policy; the politics of decision-making in particular policy areas; and the administration and management of public policy.[5]

---

[5]General sources on policy administration include Michael D. Reagan, ed., *The Administration of Public Policy* (Glenview, Ill.: Scott, Foresman and Co., 1969); Charles E. Jacob, *Policy and Bureaucracy* (New York: D. Van Nostrand Co., 1966); and Francis E. Rourke, *Bureaucracy, Politics, and Public Policy* (Boston: Little, Brown and Co., 1969).

General works on public policy include Charles E. Lindblom, *The Policy-Making Process* (Englewood Cliffs, N.J.: Prentice-Hall, 1968); Yehezkel Dror, *Public Policy-making Reexamined* (Scranton, Pa.: Chandler Publishing Co., 1968); Raymond A. Bauer and Kenneth J. Gergen, eds., *The Study of Policy Formation* (New York: Free Press, 1968); Randall B. Ripley, ed., *Public Policies and Their Politics* (New York: W. W. Norton and Co., 1966); John C. Donovan, *The Policy Makers* (New York: Western Publishing Co., 1970); Allan P. Sindler, ed., *American Political Institutions and Public Policy* (Boston: Little, Brown and Co., 1969); George S. Masannat, ed., *Basic Issues in American Public Policy* (Boston: Holbrook Press, 1970); Abraham Kaplan, *American Ethics and Public Policy* (New York: Oxford University Press, 1958); Norman R. Luttbeg, ed., *Public Opinion and Public Policy* (Homewood, Ill.: Dorsey Press, 1968); and Joyce M. and William C. Mitchell, *Political Analysis and Public Policy* (Chicago: Rand McNally & Co., 1969).

2

THE ADMINISTRATIVE PROCESS & HOUSING POLICY

THE HOUSING PROBLEM

Although most people in the United States enjoy decent, safe and sanitary housing, many do not. About 20 million citizens live in housing that is below the minimum standards that have been established for human habitation. Conditions are worse in some sections of the country than others; housing is particularly bad among nonwhites; and rental housing is more apt to be substandard than owner-occupied units. Well over 50 percent of rented housing units in the metropolitan areas occupied by nonwhites is unsound, and the percentage rises to alarming heights in the South.

HOUSING PRODUCTION

Private enterprise has produced most of the housing in America. Government has put up only a small portion of the nation's dwellings. Furthermore, direct government action accounts for only a minor portion of the new housing starts each year. In 1969, private expenditures for residential construction amounted to $30 billion, compared to $1 billion spent by all levels of government.

The homebuilding industry is an important one. Michael Sumichrast, a housing economist, indicates that the impact of new construction alone was approximately $50 billion in 1969; this amount includes the effects of the new dwelling units on schools and other community facilities and service industries. In other terms, new housing construction accounted for $1 of every $18 of the gross national product for 1969.

The homebuilding industry constructs single-family dwellings, apartment houses, townhouses and other types of units. Building firms may also engage in land development, shopping center construction, and the development of new towns.[1] The building industry also handles the actual construction of public housing (housing which is planned, financed and owned by governmental units).

The homebuilding industry is dominated by small builders. About one-half of the over 100,000 builders in the United States belong to the National Association of Home Builders. The vast majority of builders do less than $5 million worth of business a year, and many are in the under $500,000 category. The largest builder is Levitt and Sons, a subsidiary of International Telephone and Telegraph; Levitt did $123 million worth of business in 1968.

HOUSING POLICY

The area of housing policy covers a wide variety of programs and activities in American governments. Housing policy includes governmental actions in the areas of land-use regulation, building and housing codes, public housing, urban renewal, model cities, mortgage guarantees, and different programs for the stimulation and subsidization of the housing market. Many programs are found in these areas at all levels in the political system, and it would be impossible to cover all of them. Housing policy includes government expenditures, loans, grants, controls, direct ownership and other actions designed to affect the production, location, supply and availability of housing.

Administration of Housing Policy

All three levels of government share in the administration of housing policy; nevertheless, local and national governments have the most im-

[1]See Michael Sumichrast and Sara A. Frankel, *Profile of the Builder and His Industry* (Washington, D.C.: National Association of Home Builders of the United States, 1970).

portant role in housing. Furthermore, it is fair to say that the day-to-day administration of housing policy is mostly a matter for local government and that the basic power over housing policy is about equally divided between Washington and community governments. Patterns, however, vary according to the particular housing field considered.

ADMINISTRATION OF HOUSING POLICY IN LOCAL GOVERNMENT

There are more than 80,000 local governments in the United States and some of them have housing duties. Because local governments generally operate within the confines of state law and constraints, they must seek state authorization to embark on certain programs. The actions of the national government also affect local governments. Both the state and national governments shape local housing activity, including administrative patterns and operations.

LAND-USE, BUILDING AND HOUSING REGULATION

The key land-use, building and housing regulatory powers reside in local agencies. These powers have a significant bearing on housing and building activity and, therefore, should be considered as a part of the housing policy picture. They affect the costs of housing and may well determine who will and will not be able to afford certain housing; they may also dictate residential living patterns and the location, existence and extent of important community facilities and services. Their effects on development patterns and the general environment can scarsely be underestimated.

All told, over 14,000 local governments have land and building regulation powers: nearly 11,000 have planning boards (treated in the next chapter); over 9,500 have zoning ordinances; 8,000 have subdivision control regulations; 8,300 have building codes; 5,000 have housing codes. About 14,000 have one or more of these powers or a building permit system.[2]

The most important of the land-use controls is zoning and subdivision regulation; another land-use control is the official map. Zoning covers such matters as type of land use (residential, commercial, single family), lot size minimums (one-half acre, one acre), residential densities, setback requirements (distance from the road or other lots), minimum house sizes (in square footage), and building height. The key zoning policy is the designation of the type of land use, for this de-

[2]Allen D. Manvel, *Local Land and Building Regulation* (Washington, D.C.: Government Printing Office, 1968), p. 4.

termines the nature of basic community development. Subdivision regulation refers to control over particular developments; it includes control over the layout of streets, lots, curbs and gutters, the dedication of land for public purposes (roads, parks), the provision of certain community facilities (sewer, water) and the payment of fees for government uses. Because subdivision regulations apply to developers of large tracts of land and because subdivision policy must work within the general framework set by zoning policy, subdivision policy has a somewhat more limited impact than zoning policy. The official map is used to reserve private land for future public use.

Building and housing regulation refers to local government codes that govern construction and maintenance matters. Building codes apply to new construction and set standards which include stipulations on materials and building technique. Housing codes apply to existing structures and include standards designed to protect the health, safety, and welfare of the occupants.

In American government, land-use, building and housing controls are largely administrative matters. Although local legislatures enact these controls, state legislatures must authorize their enactment in some manner. However, once they are enacted, the implementation of these regulations becomes chiefly an administrative task. The one possible exception to this is rezonings, or the changes in official land-use designations. Generally, rezonings fall within the scope of local governing bodies—elected city, county or town councils or boards; however, the trend has been toward shifting the rezoning power from elected to appointed officials—that is, from the legislative to the administrative branch. Many communities now have zoning boards or zoning administrators (zoning examiners) for making basic zoning or rezoning decisions.

Although administrative patterns in the area of land-use, building and housing regulation vary by community, important zoning power will normally reside in the community planning commissions. In addition, these commissions usually administer subdivision regulations. Community and professional people make up planning commissions, and they are both likely to have some voice in making zoning decisions. Both may participate in drawing up the zoning ordinance, and both usually serve in an advisory capacity on proposed changes in the zoning ordinance and its application. The final zoning authority normally rests with the legislative body. Responsibility for the administration of building and housing codes may rest with various agencies or departments: a building and housing department, a building department, a public works agency, a public safety department, a licenses and inspections department, a health department, or a planning and urban development department. Even within the same city or county, different codes (such as plumbing, electrical or heating) may be administered by different agencies.

Political Patterns

The political patterns in the area of land-use and housing and building regulation vary according to the public power involved. The politics of zoning administration often pits the single-family homeowners against the real estate forces; both may be organized into interest groups, the former into neighborhood citizens' associations and the latter into developers' associations. In land-use policy, the citizens' associations favor strict government controls on development and developers; the developers lean toward a free market policy. Each group presses administrators for favorable decisions; developers are usually more effective with executive branch officials, and citizens' associations are more successful with elected officials. Administrators make key interpretations of the zoning ordinance, may make specific zoning decisions, and give advice and technical information to legislative bodies, which make the final determinations. If citizens or developer groups are not satisfied with local administrative or legislative decisions, they may appeal these decisions to the courts (for cause) or seek to bring state or federal pressure to bear on local authorities. (We will return to the politics of zoning administration in the next chapter.)

Administrators nearly always handle subdivision regulations. Consequently, the politics of subdivision control administration will rarely involve elected officials and is generally a matter between the administering agency (usually the planning commission) and private developers. Subdivision ordinances normally permit considerable discretion in the administrative process, and much political bargaining goes on between the municipal staff and the developer. Nevertheless, this discretion does not allow a deviation from the basic pattern of development required by the zoning ordinance. Municipal officials typically attempt to convince the developer to make generous land dedications to the community and, as the developers give the dedications gratis, there are often misunderstandings between the two parties. Developers complain that municipal administrators are not sensitive to time restrictions and deadlines and, therefore, unnecessarily delay approval of subdivision plans. They also feel that municipal agencies often lack sufficient technical expertise.

The politics of building codes administration are somewhat invisible. Building codes officials, labor unions and private builders are key interests and, all attempt to shape the building codes process. National organizations of building codes officials develop model codes and standards that certainly have some influence over the provisions in building codes and administrative decision-making at the local level. Labor unions which represent the building and construction trades are active participants in the politics of building codes; they oppose codes policy that might eliminate jobs, including the easing of the codes to permit factory-built housing. Unions are organized through the AFL-CIO which has councils in the larger metropolitan areas.

Private builders commonly favor an easing of building codes restrictions; they want policies that reduce building costs and permit a wider choice in the use of building materials and construction techniques. Builders may also support a shift in the administration of the building codes from a municipality to a higher governmental level—or to a local government with broader geographical jurisdiction, such as a county or a metropolitan-wide government. We should note that building codes are frequently quite restrictive, prohibiting the use of materials or assembling processes that could substantially reduce housing costs; these restrictions are grounded in tradition and are reinforced politically. Also, in any given metropolitan area, builders may have to contend with dozens of codes, perhaps as many as there are general local governments; for instance, a builder in greater Cleveland or Chicago must comply with 50 different building codes, a builder in Minneapolis with 30. These codes differ in content from municipality to municipality and thus make techniques of standardization, industrialized housing, and assembly-line production impossible.

Nevertheless, builders are split as to their degree of dissatisfaction with current building codes administration. The major builders' organization is the National Association of Home Builders, which has local branches or affiliates. Small builders dominate this organization. Larger builders belong to the Council of Housing Producers. The National Association of Home Builders and its local affiliates can be expected to lend their political weight to *some* codes changes, but the Council of Housing Producers favors more massive ones: administrative and substantive measures designed to facilitate large-scale housing projects.

Housing code administration is becoming an increasingly visible matter in some cities, especially the larger ones. Political forces in this area include the codes officials who are organized at the national level, civil rights groups, health and welfare councils, apartment owners' associations, tenant organizations, and real estate firms. In some big cities, landlords have complained that housing codes are enforced selectively, sometimes on political and racial grounds. Civil rights groups insist on strict enforcement, while white real estate interests believe this may result in black ownership. With the passage of a 1965 law, the national government now provides grant assistance for local housing codes; in cities receiving such assistance, federal officials must be considered important participants in the housing code process (the national government already had some influence over community housing codes through a 1954 enactment which applied to localities receiving certain kinds of federal housing assistance).

Management Issues

Standard-setting is one management problem that is common to the land-use, building and housing regulation policy area. In zoning, administrators are continually searching for new and improved standards that can serve as bases for decisions about amendments to zoning ordinances, changes in zoning for particular pieces of land, and the application of zoning categories to undeveloped areas. These standards have to be related to the question of "good land use." Zoning decisions cannot rest on value judgments or be left to elected officials or to the public. There may be considerable conflict over the matter, and experience shows that few elected officials will always hand down definitive standards. Consequently, administrators have had to step into this decision-making vacuum and set standards. Therefore, administrators and executive branch officials have roles in zoning, and they must make decisions, advisory or final.

In subdivision regulation policy, administrators must decide a myriad of questions: what constitutes a reasonable dedication? what concessions can the community demand and expect from the developer? should developers contribute land for community facilities other than the typical ones? what about school sites? The law may or may not cover these matters; in any event, administrators must make implementing decisions, they must rely on standards. Those involved in building or housing codes must answer similar questions and, in general, codes officials must decide whether to support amendments to codes or whether to support changes called for in model codes. Answers to these questions require standards.[3]

---

[3]On the administration of housing codes, see Barnet Lieberman, *Local Administration and Enforcement of Housing Codes* (Washington, D.C.: National Association of Housing and Redevelopment Officials, 1969). On building code administration, see Advisory Commission on Intergovernmental Relations, *Building Codes* (Washington, D.C.: Government Printing Office, 1966). On zoning and subdivision control administration, see William I. Goodman and Eric C. Freund, eds., *Principles and Practice of Urban Planning* (Washington, D.C.: International City Managers' Association, 1968), Chapters 15 and 16.

PUBLIC HOUSING

Public housing refers to governmental provision, ownership and management of residential dwellings for the needy. The federal Housing Act of 1937 set up the national public housing program. Although public housing was a national program, local governments were to administer it through local housing agencies (LHAs). Public housing was backed by New Deal Democrats, including the Roosevelt administration and the majority of Democrats on Capitol Hill.

Public housing is a local matter. The national government provides financial assistance and guidelines, rules and regulations; also, local public housing policy must be consistent with federal law. There are between 1,500 and 2,000 LHAs throughout the United States. LHAs operate independently of general purpose local government; they are governments in and of themselves and are called special districts.

Political patterns in the administration of local public housing agencies have shifted somewhat over the years. In the early days, liberal community forces had much to say in these agencies. Middle and upper-middle class liberals and reformers were commonly excluded from the city machine government. However, as supporters of the national Democratic party, local liberals were "rewarded" by being given control over public housing. The reasons for this were mixed. Liberals wanted more influence at the community level, and a public housing program, located outside the local power structure and subsidized by Washington, would further this goal. However, the early liberals wanted more; they wanted decent housing for the poor, and they were convinced that city hall would not direct the program toward this end. Consequently, they wanted the program "out of politics." With the backing of Washington, they made sure it was independent.

With missionary zeal, early reformers built an ambitious public housing operation and set up representative mechanisms to assure a voice for the poor in the program's management. As time passed, ideology gave way to administration, and the LHAs curtailed the role of the poor. By the 1950s, power over the program rested almost exclusively in the LHAs' management and board. Agencies discouraged tenant organizations, and some LHAs prohibited them.

In the 1960s, the LHAs reversed themselves—largely because of pressure from civil rights groups and the federal government. The community action agencies of the federal war on poverty appeared to have something to do with modifying LHA political patterns; the community action agencies, also funded by Washington, demanded constituent participation in government programs. For most LHAs, this meant black participation. Ironically, one the first "victims" of the black revolution inspired community action program in the 1960s was the liberal housing bureaucracy rather than the conservative power structure. Black tenant organizations sprang up all over the country, and LHAs had no choice but to share their power with them.

Two issues loom large in the administration of public housing policy: the location of suitable sites for public housing, and the organizational isolation of the LHA. The first one is particularly perplexing, and it is related to the second. The crux of the public housing problem is that most Americans appear to support public housing in principle but to oppose it in their neighborhoods. Many observers have found that the government's commitment to public housing is inadequate and, by objective standards, the supply of public housing falls far below the demand. Public housing waiting lists numbering into the thousands are not uncommon in larger cities and, although over three-quarters of a million public housing units have been built since the program's inception, more are needed.

However, too much of an emphasis on the inadequacy of government commitment to public housing may prove misleading. In the first place, this commitment has increased: in the first 31 years of its operation, the public housing program produced about 20 to 25 thousand units a year; in 1971, the annual rate was 90 thousand. Still, the problem remains, and the real reason is the difficulty in finding politically acceptable sites.[4] Although most vacant land is likely to be found in middle and upper-middle income areas, communities repeatedly turn down LHA requests to put public housing on sites outside the slums. Neighborhood citizens associations invariably oppose public housing in their neighborhood—frequently insisting on supporting it "in principle," but not "here." This and other factors have caused LHAs to seek approval of scattered site public housing, thus avoiding massive housing projects and possible new slum concentrations by locating public housing in small quantities among middle income units. This practice has met with less resistance. Nevertheless, all the money in the world (an expanded federal "commitment") will not solve the site problem. Middle income residents simply do not want public housing near them; they assume (rightly or wrongly) that public housing means black housing and this, they believe, hurts property values.

Although the LHAs are nominally independent of city hall, links

---

[4]For an illuminating discussion of this matter in the context of Chicago politics, see Martin Meyerson and Edward C. Banfield, *Politics, Planning, and the Public Interest: The Case of Public Housing in Chicago* (New York: Free Press, 1955).

do exist.[5] Often, the chief executive and/or governing body of a locality will appoint members of the local housing authority board. Also, the general purpose government will typically have considerable authority over LHA site selection, and this is an additional check on the LHA's independence. Furthermore, public administration orthodoxy requires coordination through a single executive and a unified bureaucracy. (See Chapter 8.) For local politics, a single, rather than divided, administrative structure would seem desirable.

Yet, what would the consolidation of LHAs with city hall achieve? City hall has often vetoed sites for public housing and city hall is quite naturally sensitive to majority pressures. In no major city in the United States do *poor* blacks constitute a majority, and middle income blacks are no more anxious than middle income whites to have public housing in their neighborhoods—in fact, they may be less so. LHAs are less sensitive than city hall to majority pressures because their boards are appointed and independent of elected officials. What would happen if public housing were put under the elected city or county council, or under the elected mayor or county executive? In all likelihood, the program would receive additional—and more direct—setbacks. Therefore, if the objective of public housing is housing for the poor rather than administrative simplicity, the LHAs should remain independent.

URBAN RENEWAL

Urban renewal dates to the Housing Act of 1949 ("Title 1" as the program was termed for years). Its background is important. After World War II, significant trends developed in metropolitan areas: middle-income residents were leaving the city for the suburbs; business began to move out; city cores declined and deteriorated economically; and the inner city became increasingly the home for the poor and for blacks. Those with core city investments were disturbed, and they looked for help. However, city hall was controlled by machines or *status quo*-minded organization politicians, and chambers of commerce were conservative, dominated by small businesses, and opposed to an active government. Only one option remained: organize and seek federal aid. Thus, big downtown businesses organized and demanded government action to reverse economic trends.

Civic action groups were formed. Some examples are the Greater Philadelphia Movement (GPM), the Allegheny Conference (Pitts-

---

[5]Advisory Commission on Intergovernmental Relations, *The Problem of Special Districts in American Government* (Washington, D.C.: Government Printing Office, 1964), p. 73.

burgh), the Central Area Committee of Chicago, Civic Progress in St. Louis, and the Civic Conference in Boston.[6] The dominant forces in these organizations were bankers, industrialists, department store executives, members of prestigious law firms, and comparable local business interests. The organizations were not composed of big *national* businesses or small local businesses, only big *local* businesses. These groups wanted redevelopment of city cores; they wanted to improve the business climate and most importantly, to protect their investments.

The strategy of each city's civic action group differed, but they were agreed on one point: a major government program was needed. These groups provided an important support base for the Housing Act of 1949, and this may have accounted for conservative Senator Robert A. Taft's sponsorship of this legislation. One conservative Senator was reported to have said of Taft's support for housing legislation, "The socialists have finally gotten to Bob Taft." These businessmen were scarcely socialists, but they did want government aid—and the federal government was where they ultimately turned. At this point, housing policy took on a complexion which was decidedly that of private enterprise, an orientation which could be contrasted with the earlier social welfare orientation (1937).

Urban redevelopment efforts helped shape local political patterns. In some cities, urban renewal advocates worked with liberal reformers; in others, they found the political machine receptive and prepared to accept change. In Philadelphia, downtown business interests formed a coalition with middle and upper class liberals; the coalition succeeded in crushing the Republican machine. Once in power, the new forces concentrated on inner city face lifting and city planning. They controlled the urban renewal agency and the planning commission, and both were instrumental in carrying out redevelopment programs. "Organization" interests on the city council, representing minority ethnic groups, were often overruled, and physical renewal proceeded. Another pattern was found in Pittsburgh, where the Allegheny Conference businessmen worked closely with the Democratic machine, then led by Mayor David Lawrence.

Urban renewal agencies are officially known as local public agencies or LPAs and, following the earlier pattern, they are independent of city hall, but to a lesser extent than LHAs (some city councils actually serve as the LPA). Some renewal agencies are part of the city government bureaucracy but because political reality has dictated somewhat autonomous operations in this area, many are separate entities. Independent

[6]Edward C. Banfield and James Q. Wilson, *City Politics* (New York: Random House, 1963), p. 267.

operations have facilitated business dominance of LPAs and have most likely led to more "effective" implementation of urban renewal, especially in the early years. Independent organizational status also meant less visible administration and, therefore, more "success." Poor blacks and poor whites who were displaced by urban renewal had no voice in the process; they were not part of the politics of urban renewal administration. Businessmen and administrators controlled the program; it was run to their desires.

However, as time went on, this monopoly on urban renewal began to change. Many discovered to their surprise that urban renewal was not really a housing program after all, that it did not serve the poor; it was a redevelopment program, and it may have hurt the poor. It cleared key core areas of slums; it attracted middle-income residents back to the city; however, it cut into the supply of housing for the poor. It did these things by razing low-income properties and substituting luxury housing. The poor were forced out, but no housing was provided for them elsewhere. Black leaders were alarmed and demanded change. Most urban renewal agencies are no longer insensitive to the housing needs of low-income blacks; and they now provide more low- and moderate-income housing in urban renewal areas. Black and civil rights groups now commonly have a voice in urban renewal, and this has tended to slow down the process. Also, urban renewal has increasingly become subject to central executive direction, and this has brought broader pressures to bear on the process.

Probably the two most pressing management problems in urban renewal today are land disposition and relocation. In urban renewal the private sector, not the government, does the redeveloping. However, urban renewal administrators must select developers and this task requires that they formulate criteria. Which developer is most likely to follow the plan? Developers ultimately take title to the land in urban renewal project areas, and run the development for private ends. It is up to the urban renewal officials to assure that these ends are compatible with the public interest. This means the careful consideration of standards of developer acceptability.

Relocation has been a continuing problem. Federal law requires relocation plans and efforts and, since the enactment of legislation in 1956, federal financial assistance has been provided for relocation. The idea is that persons displaced by urban renewal should be relocated in suitable and decent housing. In the early years, critics charged that little if any relocation assistance was provided; follow-up studies found many former residents to have "disappeared." LPAs have sought to rectify this and, under federal prodding, they now successfully relocate most displacees; nevertheless, finding new housing for these displaced is still no easy task.[7]

MODEL CITIES

Model cities is not wholly a housing program, but it is generally part of the housing policy area and it is administered in Washington by the housing agency. The model cities program can be traced to federal legislation—the Demonstration Cities and Metropolitan Development Act of 1966—but it is run in the community. Specifically, communities wishing to participate must establish City Demonstration Agencies, or CDAs. But, unlike the pattern in the public housing and urban renewal areas, the CDAs are to be completely within the framework of city government. It was early known as the "mayor's program." In fact, it was the mayors' reward from Washington for enduring the dreaded community action program.

The history of model cities is crucial. The federal Economic Opportunity Act was passed in 1964, and it provided for the establishment of community action agencies throughout the United States. Although the national legislation permitted these agencies to be created inside or outside city hall, between 70 and 80 percent were located outside city hall. The Office of Economic Opportunity had determined this administrative pattern, and the practice was continued despite grumbling by the local government lobby in Washington. Community action agencies were typically manned by black and white radicals (or so it seemed to the mayors), and their independent organizational pattern permitted, even encouraged, this. Scores of city officials attributed the mid-1960 city riots to the pernicious influence of the community action agencies and their Washington benefactors. The irony was that most of Washington was controlled by "safe" liberals; Lyndon Johnson was no radical, nor were the vast majority of the bureaucracies that had business with cities.

The mayors were furious. They had consistently produced Democratic majorities for whoever gained control of the national party. Then, they charged, national Democrats subsidized radical blacks, who were challenging local power structures on every front. Mayors demanded an end to this. One mayor called for a "mayor's march" on Washington but, to the mayors' advantage, cooler heads prevailed. First, the mayors

---

[7]For a general discussion of urban renewal, see Scott Greer, *Urban Renewal and American Cities* (Indianapolis: Bobbs-Merrill Co., 1965). For particular cities, see Peter H. Rossi and Robert A. Dentler, *The Politics of Urban Renewal* (New York: Free Press, 1961) and Harold Kaplan, *Urban Renewal Politics* (New York: Columbia University Press, 1963).

and the city bureaucracies were "paid off" with the model cities program. Second, quiet efforts were made to curtail the influence and the independent base of the community action program; this was done through the Green amendment (Edith Green, Democrat from Oregon), and through an administrative "whittling away" of Office of Economic Opportunity power.[8]

In principle, there was little to distinguish the model cities program from the community action program: both had the same general ends, and both represented a coordinated attack on slum problems. However, the important point was that the politics of their administration differed. Under model cities, the local government was to designate a particular neighborhood for improvement. This neighborhood was to be the "worst" area of the city, the area that had the lowest income, the fewest jobs, the least economic resources. The city then developed a plan for neighborhood rejuvenation and, if this was acceptable to Washington, the federal government advanced planning and implementation funds.

In model cities, citizens were to participate in decision-making. Nevertheless, this was not a citizens program; it was a power structure program. No city wanted a repeat of the community action pattern or a citizens' effort. In fact, cynics charged that even the community action program was not a citizens' program, that the name of the citizen was invoked to promote the political power aims of black and white radicals. Citizens boards were to be formed in the City Demonstration Agencies, but their influence was countered by "technical boards" composed of the affected bureaucracies (welfare, health, employment security, and others). The final decisions were to be made by the mayor or the city council or both, not by the citizens.

It is hard to tell how much progress is being made under model cities. The changing of the national administration just as the program was getting underway caused problems. Cities have received their implementation funding, and housing and other programs have progressed. Although it is continuing to finance model cities, the Republican administration elected in 1968 seemed less than enthusiastic about the program as originally conceived. In President Nixon's first term, Housing Secretary Romney announced that the program would cover entire cities, not just a single neighborhood, and some have seen this as an attempt to bring more conservative pressures to bear on the effort.

---

[8]For a discussion of the politics of the community action program, see Daniel P. Moynihan, *Maximum Feasible Misunderstanding* (New York: Free Press, 1969); for a discussion of its administration, see Advisory Commission in Intergovernmental Relations, *Intergovernmental Relations in the Poverty Program* (Washington, D.C.: Government Printing Office, 1966).

LOCAL ADMINISTRATION OF FEDERAL HOUSING PROGRAMS

Some aspects of housing policy are essentially local matters (zoning, subdivision administration) and, although the federal government is not without its influence even in these areas, the basic decisions are made locally. In housing, the local government administers nearly all of the important housing programs; the only major exception to this is FHA, the federal private housing loan guarantee program.

The marked involvement of city government in housing has certain administrative advantages, but it also spells problems. The theory is that although the housing problem is a national one, local authorities are better equipped to determine how the national effort shall be structured in particular communities. In fact, the politics and tradition of the matter are more important than the theory. Traditionally, key housing powers have been assigned to local government, and important political influence serves to reinforce this tradition. Most Americans seem to eventually come to the conclusion that it is not social welfare programs that they do not want; it is just central direction of these programs. This view certainly reflects the position of many mayors and local power structures. Even conservatively inclined mayors did not oppose the community action program; they only fought radical control of it, a control pattern stimulated by a federal bureaucracy. The reason that conservative mayors did not oppose such programs is that they mean money, and few communities refuse money.

The advantages to local administration are that federal programs can be tailored to local needs, that decentralization can cut through red tape and that local support can better be generated with local control. Nevertheless, two questions arise. First, what is to assure that national needs are being met, particularly when local power structures are so often controlled by *status quo*-minded and conservative interests, Democratic or Republican? Second, from the vantage point of the locality, how much discretion do local governments really have in national housing programs? We cannot answer the first question, but strong arguments suggest that national administration may better serve national needs.[9]

There is some question as to just how much authority localities really have anyway. One of the most common complaints of local administrative officials is the burdensome requirements, standards and rules that Washington subjects them to. Some contend that Washington thinks all communities are the same and forces the same set of criteria on every-

---

[9] See Morton Grodzins, "Why Decentralization by Order Won't Work," in Edward C. Banfield, ed., *Urban Government: A Reader in Politics and Administration* (New York: Free Press, 1961), p. 126.

one (housing codes, model cities); conditions vary, and Washington should take this into account. Critics also maintain that the national government requires too many reports, too much paper work, and that this cuts significantly into the time available for program administration. Thirdly, local administrators charge that federal field people are frequently dictatorial. This kind of behavior puts local officials in a bad position because, by offending a federal field administrator, local funds may be endangered. Local governments feel that some process should be developed that allows for a hearing of local complaints of this nature; perhaps, a regularized process of appealing field decisions to departmental secretaries would be appropriate. Some say that this sort of situation is best handled politically—for example, aggrieved local officials should take their case to Congress. Many do, but, there are risks in this practice, let alone its questionable legitimacy.

ADMINISTRATION OF HOUSING POLICY
IN THE NATIONAL GOVERNMENT

The Department of Housing and Urban Development (HUD) administers basic national housing policy. HUD was established by the Housing and Urban Development Act of 1965, and it is the successor to the old Housing and Home Finance Agency (HHFA). Unlike HHFA, HUD is a cabinet-level agency. Key HUD programs include:

1. Urban renewal assistance;
2. Public housing assistance;
3. Model cities assistance;
4. Federal Housing Administration (FHA) mortgage insurance assistance;
5. Urban planning assistance;
6. Community facilities assistance (sewer, water, neighborhood, public facilities); and
7. Open space assistance.

In all of these programs but one (FHA), HUD works through sub-national governments, mostly local governments. Outside FHA, HUD provides financial assistance to sub-national governments and, in these programs, the basic power to run the program rests with the latter. Many HUD decisions are made in its field offices, each of which is headed by a regional administrator; the department has ten regional offices, and each region contains subordinate "area offices" and "insuring offices." A Secretary of Housing and Urban Development directs the department.

HUD seeks to assure effective administration of programs it assists at the local level through enforcement of the "Workable Program for

Community Improvement," usually called simply the "workable program." Each community that wishes to participate in federal urban renewal, public housing, or certain low income directed portions of FHA programs has to comply with the workable program. Under this program, communities must have adequate codes and ordinances in housing, comprehensive urban planning, neighborhood analyses to identify blight, adequate administrative organizations, sufficient finances, a supply of housing for displaced persons (relocation), and citizen participation.

Harold Wolman has discerned a "decision-making elite" in the national housing policy process.[10] This decision-making group includes key officials in the Department of Housing and Urban Development, representatives of key Capitol Hill committees, representatives of private industry, representatives of public interest groups (housing and other city officials), certain state and local government officials, officials of the Executive Office of the President, certain congressional assistants (staff), representatives of other national government agencies, representatives of a government-established housing committee, labor union representatives, the head of a civil rights group, and a university professor. It is instructive to note that the largest single bloc in the decision-making elite came from HUD; this suggests a rather significant role for the government housing agency in policy-making—beyond its formal role of administration.

Any analysis of the power structure surrounding the formation and execution of national housing policy must at least include the following:

1. the Department of Housing and Urban Development, the administrative agency;

2. the Banking and Currency Committees of the House of Representatives and the Senate, the units that draw up substantive legislation in housing (new programs, funding limits). This legislation may be drafted initially by HUD or interest groups;

3. the Appropriations Committees of the House and Senate, the units that make the key congressional decisions in money matters;

4. the National Association of Home Builders, the private interest group that represents the nation's builders and contractors;

5. the National Association of Housing and Redevelopment Officials, a public interest group that represents local housing, urban renewal, housing code, and model cities agencies. It is composed of progressive-minded housing forces, has powerful local clients, has a

[10]Harold Wolman, *Politics of Federal Housing* (New York: Dodd, Mead & Company, 1971), pp. 160–161, 206–209.

talented and aggressive staff, and exercises much influence over housing legislation and administrative practices; and

6. the "cities" lobby—the National League of Cities, a public interest group that represents over 14,000 city governments, and the United States Conference of Mayors, a public interest group that represents several hundred big-city mayors.

Congress as a whole is not included in this listing because the basic housing legislation decisions are made by relevant committees rather than Congress as a whole. We can also assume that the White House influence will be felt in the Department of Housing and Urban Development and will be represented in the department's position. In addition, the two political parties will play a role in the housing policy process in some instances. When it comes to housing policy, the parties are not centrally directed organs, and the presidential and congressional wings of the same party may respond to different interests or differ somewhat over housing policy. The two parties may also differ with one another, and this is usually reflected in Capitol Hill politics.

It is important to point out that groups, not individuals, exert influence over housing policy and its administration. Even state and local officials, HUD's basic constituency, rarely lobby "on their own" (representing only their city, for example), but through one of the public interest groups. The same is true of builders who work through the National Association of Home Builders and of local housing and renewal officials who work through "their" interest group, the National Association of Housing and Redevelopment Officials. In the course of fulfilling their primary objectives, public interest groups spend much time on seeking to keep federal administrative policies and practices from becoming too burdensome to local governments. In addition, the public interest groups work to counteract certain centralizing tendencies in the federal housing policy process. They also provide important feedback to federal administrative officials.

An overview of federal housing policy suggests that it has been most effective in achieving the needs of middle income families. Certainly, FHA policy has had this effect through providing government insured loans with a minimum down payment, favorable interest rates and long-term mortgages. FHA policy has brought housing within the reach of middle income groups; however, FHA and other government housing policy has not served low income groups as well. New one percent interest homeownership and rental programs, introduced in 1968 housing legislation, seem to be providing low income families with decent housing on a scale not known under previous federal housing policy, but a short drive through any big city slum demonstrates how much further the policy will have to go.

Management problems connected with federal housing policy can be summed up in a single phrase: relations with cities. The basic aim of both Democratic and Republican administrations has been the development of a unified housing policy effort at the community level, the level where the services are delivered. HUD has recently revamped its field structure with this end in mind. A single regional administrator will coordinate the different housing functions. Yet, experience suggests that this will be easier to do on the organization chart than in practice. FHA, with its direct-constituent relationship, poses a particular problem. FHA operates somewhat independently within the federal housing bureaucracy and represents a political force in and of itself. This has policy consequences, and FHA was slow to move in the low and moderate income housing area; FHA procedures represent costly delays to builders and nonprofit corporations who seek to provide housing to the poor. Also, FHA has been criticized by local governments for not coordinating its loan programs with city hall.

HUD has recognized the need for coordination of housing programs at the local level. Nevertheless, as a matter of policy, it does not favor metropolitan government or the consolidation of the different housing agencies in local government. Perhaps, neither is needed. Federal housing policy represents a collection of widely varying programs enacted at different times and for different purposes, and this policy has not encouraged a coordinated approach at the community level. One exception to this is in the area of planning and general program review; here, HUD has fostered the metropolitan or city wide viewpoint. However, the practical, operating programs are run by a number of free-wheeling housing bureaucracies spread in piecemeal fashion throughout the metropolitan area.

Housing Policy and the States

The states are only minimally involved in housing. However, the police power (regulation in the interests of the health, safety and welfare of the inhabitants) of American governments resides in the states. What this means is that the national government may legislate only on matters specifically listed in the Constitution or implied from the nature of specified powers; the states, however, possess the power to legislate and regulate for general ends. In the housing area, the states have typically delegated their power to localities. This power can be delegated through state enabling legislation (permitting particular powers to be exercised by local governments or specific classes of local governments) or it can be delegated in a more general manner. This arrangement is not without its political implications. For example, some forces, antagonistic to urban renewal, have lobbied in state capitals against the state's authorizing cities to undertake such a program.

Some states, though, have launched rather ambitious housing efforts. These include the creation of urban development and low income housing corporations or authorities. Some states have also taken steps to strike down local practices that restrict housing to middle and upper income groups, and have made efforts to provide housing relocation assistance. New York, New Jersey and Massachusetts have been particularly active in the housing field.[11]

SUMMARY

This is the first of the public policy chapters. In it, we have examined housing policy, with a special concentration on the administrative aspects of government housing programs, the politics of policy-making and policy execution in housing, and public management problems in this policy area.

We have found that, although the basic powers are assigned to local and national governments, housing policy is an intergovernmental matter. In some housing policy fields, we have discovered that the politics of housing policy is nearly the equivalent of the politics of housing policy administration.

---

[11]See James L. Martin, "Housing and Community Development," in *The Book of the States, 1970–71* (Lexington, Ky.: Council of State Governments, 1970), pp. 443–454.

3

ADMINISTRATION OF URBAN PLANNING POLICY

PLANNING POLICY

In the United States, local governments administer key planning policy. Planning policy refers to governmental action in community development; specifically, it includes activities designed to shape community development and the communities' goals for future development. In the past, planning has had a land-use orientation, and, consequently, the term land-use planning emerged. However, planning now covers both physical (land use) and social development, and the term "comprehensive" is more appropriate. Most planning in this country is done in urban areas—thus, urban planning. Because it has been only in recent years that much planning has been done in rural areas, planning can still be considered primarily an urban phenomenon.

Although all levels of government are involved in planning, there is no national comprehensive plan, and states are just beginning to embark on comprehensive planning programs. However, plans do exist at

27

the community level. About 75 percent of American municipalities, both central cities and suburbs, with more than 5,000 people, have a published plan.[1]

The product of the community planning process can be called a master plan, a general plan or a development plan. Such a plan will often include the areas of private land uses, transportation (highways, public transit), and public community facilities. The plan may also contain study results, data tabulations, maps of present and desired future land uses, and recommendations. The master plan applies to the community, city, county, township or town as a whole; in addition, the locality may have area master plans or neighborhood plans for particular portions of the community.

Community planning policy is directed toward the future, and it may call for certain development patterns for many years into the future. A community master plan will indicate the proposed or desired future land uses in the following areas: commercial, industrial, single family residential, apartment, and other private uses; the planned highway and street network; any planned mass transit systems or extensions; and the planned location of community facilities such as parks, recreation areas, public institution complexes, and school sites. The community plan shows what the locality should look like at some point in the future. The plan will have the greatest meaning in communities with much undeveloped and developable land within their borders; this kind of land is most likely to be found in the suburbs of the typical metropolitan area. In highly developed cities, the master plan may have its greatest meaning in areas designated for redevelopment.

Community planning policy does not enforce itself. The master plan itself does not have the force of law; it serves only as a guide. However, community planning policy may be given considerable legitimacy through the adoption of a plan or portions of it by the community planning commission (normally a semi-independent agency within city, county, or other local government) or by the local governing body which is composed of elected officials. It is likely that most planning commissions throughout the nation have adopted a community plan, although most governing bodies probably have not.

Community governments have several powers by which plans can be implemented. The most important of these powers are the land-use controls which include zoning, subdivision regulation, and the official map. A community government can also promote planning goals and facilitate the achievement of planning policy through the use of sewer

[1]Allen D. Manvel, *Local Land and Building Regulation* (Washington, D.C.: Government Printing Office, 1968), p. 31.

and water lines, urban renewal, mass transit, and the location of local public facilities and parks. The powers, policies, and programs of other governments (those without the planning power) may have a considerable influence on local development and, therefore, on planning policy; examples are the highway powers of the state government, the power of the national and state governments to locate their own facilities and institutions, the public housing policy of independent housing authorities, the mass transit policy of public transportation districts, and the sewer extension or the sewer system creation power of special sanitary districts.

Comprehensive planning is not the only type of planning done by American governments. Another major kind of planning is functional area planning, or planning for particular functions. Illustrations of functional area planning include planning done by highway departments, recreation agencies, health departments, urban renewal authorities, school districts, public works agencies, airport authorities, community action agencies, sewer districts, water departments, and transportation agencies. Although some national functional planning is done (for example, airports and recreation), functional planning is largely a local and state matter since it is these levels at which the basic domestic powers are likely to reside.

Although ideally functional planning and comprehensive planning should be consistent—with the former built on the latter—they may not work for the same ends or in the same direction. In practice, functional planning is more advanced in this nation and is commonly based on criteria and standards in rather narrow policy areas. Thus, planning policy does not necessarily encompass functional planning activities, at least at the moment.

Planning policy, as it is defined in this chapter, need not be explicitly and openly enunciated. Although they have no officially adopted plan many communities have a planning policy; technically, it is even possible for a community to have a planning policy without having formal planning powers and administrative apparatus. This is because the elected and appointed community officials must make decisions on local development; for example, if the community government has the zoning power, it must decide how to use it—and this requires some thought about how the community should be developed. This is not a matter of mere speculation; more metropolitan area municipalities have zoning than a planning board and, in these municipalities, zoning has to be exercised without the benefit of formal planning. The location of a residential or commercial zone suggests that some notion of desirable future development exists, at least among community government officials. Even if community officials are making zoning determinations based on pressure from developers or others (and not on some idealized notion of future development desires), zoning decisions will have to be explained in terms of an acceptable rationale (a community goal). This rationale then becomes the community's planning policy.

Planning policy may simply represent a reinforcement of the private marketplace, and this, to many, means no policy. Nevertheless, planning that is undertaken to reflect the wishes of the private real estate community and to facilitate the workings of the private enterprise system qualifies as planning policy just as much as does planning that is conducted to reflect the wishes of professional planners, "the citizens," a central planning bureaucracy, or some other more legitimate group. Experience has shown that much planning done in the United States is based on the dictates of the private marketplace and the wishes of specialized functional bureaucracies; such planning is no less representative of planning policy than other kinds of planning.

The nature of a nation's economic system will clearly have some effect on its prospects of developing comprehensive planning. In socialist societies, planning is built into the fabric of the economic system, and central planning is presumably easier to effect; furthermore, the socialist economic and political systems are not separate in any basic sense. It is in this light that American planners, who must work in an economy founded on the principle of the private market, have frequently stood in awe of the accomplishments of the planning power in certain socialist countries. These accomplishments have caused many to look unfavorably on capitalism as a system which seems inhospitable to comprehensive planning, and it has led some to consider the socialist alternative as a means of promoting central planning.

Nevertheless, many of the same pressures seem to be operative in both private enterprise and socialist systems, and these pressures may have a similar general effect on planning and planning policy in both types of systems. In the first place, a certain degree of planning is likely to be found under any system. In American communities, a decision by local officials to leave development decisions to the private market does not mean that no planning will occur; private developers in the United States are organized formally and informally, and patterns of influence within the development community will determine to a considerable extent what land will be developed, how, and by whom. Furthermore, these developers work closely with community officials, and what may emerge ultimately as planning policy is apt to be based at least in part (perhaps wholly) on the wishes of private developers.

It is likely that forces of decentralization, special interests, and functional bureaucracies are important in both types of systems. Thus, what may result as planning policy in socialist societies may be little more than compromises and agreements reached after considerable bargaining and interaction among diversified, specialized, and localized interests. In any event, planning policy should be viewed in any setting in the light of its *political* roots; planning policy develops in practical environments containing many pressures and interests. An understanding of the political and practical roots of planning policy should allow us to formulate more appropriate administrative strategies.

Planning has been broadened in recent years in the United States, and this broadening has had its effects on accepted planning policy. Planning now covers the social and economic aspects of the environment, not just the traditional physical preoccupation. In addition, many now feel that planning includes functional planning (transportation planning for example). Although it cannot be said that either is significantly reflective of practice at the community level, these two new stresses represent trends in planning. Both represent current views in the professional planners' association, the American Institute of Planners (AIP).

Other emerging values in planning that may ultimately affect planning policy on a wide scale include advocacy planning, under which planners and planning are active instruments for the promotion of lower income neighborhood and citizens goals; consolidated functional planning, under which planning for different functional areas in government is done by a single planning staff; and the extension of planning beyond the conventional urban framework and its isolated setting.

The last point is a particularly important one and its accomplishment could have the most lasting of impact on planning policy. Herbert Gans suggests that planning is broader than the term urban planning may have implied in the past. To Gans, planning involves problem solving, policy formulation, action programs, and specific implementation decisions; traditional, preordained *urban planning* "solutions" will be of little value in *planning*. Gans maintains that the planning profession has the choice, of becoming *planners*, or remaining *urbanists*. He claims that the pressures of the practical world are in the former direction and that these pressures will require planners trained in policy making, systems analysis, and program development. Gans' proposal, if accepted, would have a revolutionary effect in the planning profession and would carve out a broader base and role for planners in the general political and policy processes. Gans argues that planners may have little choice but to opt for the broader conception.[2]

---

[2]Herbert J. Gans, "The Need for Planners Trained in Policy Formulation," in Ernest Erber, ed., *Urban Planning in Transition* (New York: Grossman Publishers, 1970), pp. 239–45.

ADMINISTRATION OF PLANNING POWERS

Planning is probably the area of American politics in which it is most difficult to distinguish between the making and execution of public policy. Part of the reason for this is that the early municipal reformers who supported planning wanted planning isolated from the general political processes. Planning was seen as primarily an administrative matter, to be divorced from the community's legislative and political functions. In addition, the early reformers assumed that planning would be a power of local government and, to many, local government in the United States is most appropriately viewed as administration.

Although planning has deep roots in American politics, *government* planning does not.[3] The history of urban planning in this country begins in the colonial period with such towns as Williamsburg, Philadelphia, Savannah, and Annapolis. Colonial town plans included a coordinated street pattern with scattered open space sites. After the American Revolution, planning ebbed somewhat and, during the 1800s, little planning was found in communities. However, in the early 1900s, there was a resurgence of planning, and it was a key element in the City Beautiful Movement, a sort of ideological group that called for the creation of attractive civic centers and public structures, the development of boulevards, the stimulation of city park systems, and the improvement of urban housing. Because planning was seen as the instrument by which these and other ends could be achieved, modern comprehensive planning has its base in the City Beautiful Movement.

The City Beautiful Movement was closely linked to municipal reform, and both were directly related to the early stages of public administration. A better city (the City Beautiful Movement), an honestly and ably run city government (municipal reform), and efficient local government (early public administration) were all ends to be advanced by city planning. In this sense, city planning had an early moralistic flavor to it, and it was viewed as the means of promoting the good life.

The first supporters of city planning were distrustful of politics which they associated with corruption and the rule of private interests.[4] Although early reformers intended the planning function to be broadly part of the general purpose city government, they desired to establish

[3]For a discussion of the history of planning in America, see John W. Reps, *The Making of Urban America, A History of City Planning in the United States* (Princeton: Princeton University Press, 1965). For a general history of cities and planning in the world, see Lewis Mumford, *The City in History, Its Origins, Its Transformation, and Its Prospects* (New York: Harcourt, Brace & World, Inc., 1961).

[4]For a realistic discussion of municipal reform in the early years, see Richard Hofstadter, *The Age of Reform* (New York: Vintage Books, 1955); see also Richard Childs, *Civic Victories* (New York: Harper & Row, 1952).

it outside of city hall. The U. S. Department of Commerce's model planning act of 1928 emphasized the isolation of planning from politics and stressed planning as administration. This act, called the Standard City Planning Enabling Act, was to serve as a guide to state legislatures which have the authority to permit localities to engage in planning. The standard act provides for the establishment of an independent planning commission which would then possess the planning power in the community.

The states generally followed the national model in authorizing localities to undertake planning programs; today, as a result, community planning is nearly always a responsibility of a special commission or board that enjoys a certain immunity from the broader political processes. The authors of the model enabling legislation argued that the "planning function" was quite distinct from the "legislative function," reasoning that is somewhat suspect in professional planning circles today. This early distinction between planning and legislative activities is somewhat reminiscent of the distinction between administration and politics (or policy), a central doctrine of early public administration (see Chapter 8).

The administration of planning is a thoroughly decentralized activity in American politics. Normally, at the *local* level, planning is a responsibility of a general purpose government such as a city or county; however, this power may reside in a special district (a form of local government that is independent of the general purpose government). In all, nearly 11,000 communities have planning boards, and this figure represents over half of the local governments that might be expected to have such power. Of this number, nearly all large cities (50,000 or more population) have planning boards; 90 percent of the municipalities in the 5,000 to 50,000 population range also have planning boards. In a typical metropolitan area (a city with at least 50,000 in population plus surrounding counties or other jurisdictions), there will be dozens of local planning commissions, usually one planning commission for each major unit of local government. The basic planning power resides in these local planning commissions and more broadly in the local governments containing such boards.

Planning is also conducted at other levels. All metropolitan areas in the nation presently have some form of metropolitan wide planning, and this form of planning may be conducted by *metropolitan* planning commissions, regional councils of governments, state-created planning boards for a particular metropolitan area, or county planning commissions. Furthermore all *state* governments now have planning agencies or programs, and state planning may be a function of the governor's office or a particular department in the state, including an independent planning agency.

Regional planning is found in some parts of the nation and covers broad areas which encompass more than a single metropolitan area. Regional planning and development commissions have the responsibility for this planning. *Rural* planning is also becoming more popular as time passes; economic development districts and other substate planning districts presently are engaged in rural planning. Finally, *national* planning is done by particular federal agencies. However, unlike planning at the other levels, this planning is not comprehensive, but is done only for certain functional areas.

Let us now turn to a more detailed examination of planning administration at the local, metropolitan, state, regional, rural and national levels.

Local-Level Planning

At the local level, planning boards operate somewhat autonomously within the municipal bureaucracy. Planning board members are typically appointed for specific terms on a staggered, overlapping basis. This appointment process contributes to the independence of the planning commission because planning board member terms do not necessarily coincide with the terms of governing board members or the elected chief executive; incidentally, the model planning law of 1928 stipulated this method. Appointments to the planning board may be made by the chief executive of the municipality or county, or by the elected governing body; executive appointments normally require legislative confirmation.

Planning boards may be composed entirely of lay persons or of lay persons and administrative officials. Such officials may include the director of municipal public works, the superintendent of public schools, or the chief zoning officer; these officials serve *ex officio*. Where it exists, combined public and administrative representation on local planning boards serves further to reflect the intermeshing of political and administrative perspectives in the planning process. In practice, organized community interests are likely to be well represented on the planning board, and the lay members of the board are apt to represent one or another of these interests and to vote accordingly. Lay members commonly owe their appointment to a key community interest, and such members act independently of this interest at their own peril. Administrative officials who serve on planning boards may also be closer to one community interest than another but, more importantly, such officials are likely to represent the interests of specialized municipal bureaucracies which have vital stakes in community planning policy.

Planning boards in cities and towns of 5,000 or more population have an average of 7.5 members, and boards in cities in the 50,000 and above population class have an average of over 9 members. Planning commissions may meet one night every two weeks or so; in addition, their administrative activities may take up much additional time and, in some instances, one member of the board may serve on a full-time basis. Although planning boards are essentially administrative in nature, they perform important policy functions.

The planning board stands at the pinnacle of the typical administrative planning hierarchy. A planning staff is under the board, and this staff may include a director, who may serve as secretary to the board, a deputy director, and divisions or sections concerned with the different planning and land-use control functions. The staff's specific internal administrative structure varies widely from community to community. The planning staffs may include individuals trained in city planning as well as others trained in fields such as engineering, architecture, sociology, geography and public administration. Planning staffs are becoming increasingly professionalized and include those with advanced degrees in planning and membership in the American Institute of Planners. However, most planning staff members throughout the United States probably do not have planning degrees.[5]

The community planning commission has the responsibility for preparing, revising, up-dating and adopting the comprehensive plan for the entire area under its jurisdiction and for particular neighborhoods within this jurisdiction. The planning commission will also render advisory opinions and present recommendations on rezonings, or proposed changes in the zoning map. The rezoning process represents a key political matter in many localities, and the weight given to planning commission recommendations in this process may be considerable; in some communities, a special vote (two-thirds, three-quarters of the governing body) is required to override a planning commission rezoning recommendation. The planning commission will most likely administer the community subdivision regulations, and this is an important power especially in the suburbs. Planning commissions may also draft and recommend proposed amendments to the zoning and subdivision ordinances, prepare and maintain the official map reserving plots of land for future streets and other public uses, and advises municipal departments

---

[5]This discussion is based largely on research done by the Municipal Manpower Commission; see its *Governmental Manpower for Tomorrow's Cities* (New York: McGraw-Hill Book Co., 1962).

on capital budget matters (sewers and public works, for example). Any particular planning commission may have additional or fewer functions than those presented. Some planning commissions prepare the local government's capital budget.

The board's most important planning powers are comprehensive planning and land-use control. Although this power may be generally shared with the elected governing body comprehensive planning is basically the power of the planning commission. The planning commission prepares the plan and has the authority to adopt and change it; the governing body may or may not be involved in this process. The governing body may be the source of standards and goals which serve to guide the planning commission and the planning process; in addition, the governing body may adopt a community wide or area master plan.

Although it is subject to pressures from a variety of sources, the staff of the planning commission is apt to be the key force in the development of plans for the community. The planning commission's board may provide general supervision of the staff in plan preparation and will make the final judgments within the commission on the resulting plan; the board may hold official hearings on a proposed plan or meet informally with community representatives before taking final action. The board is more likely to be sensitive to political pressures than the staff, and the board itself may be composed of representatives of different community factions or interests in the first place. Political pressures and the values of different community, professional and bureaucratic interests are typically built into the process of preparing the plan from the very beginning; planning staffs not sensitive to such pressures and interests may find that the resulting plan lacks the political support necessary for its implementation, and they may also find their own administrative positions in a precarious state.

Planning commissions also have important land-use control powers. The most basic of these is zoning. Even though the typical planning commission has only advisory authority over zoning, this authority can have significant political implications; this is because the planning commission is the custodian of the plan on which zoning is often based and because the planning commission's views may be respected in the community. Although the governing body usually makes the final rezoning decisions, the planning commission may play a key role in setting the stage for these decisions. Proposed rezonings, perhaps more than anything else, thrust the administrative staff into the community land-use processes: it is the staff that must do the research on proposed zoning changes, check such changes against the plan, study the neighborhood in which the proposed change is to take place, and make recommendations to the board of the planning commission; in some areas, the staff recommendations become part of the record that is passed on to the governing body along with the planning commission board recommendations. In the absence of an adopted plan, the planning staff's job is even more complex because they must develop standards for recommendations.

Planning commissions also commonly administer subdivision regulations, another land-use control. The subdivision control process deals with residential developments; its purpose is to assure compatibility in development with the addition of each new subdivision and to guarantee the provision of the necessary public facilities and public improvements. This process is almost entirely an administrative matter; ultimate decisions in this area are usually made within the planning commission, by the staff and the board who work directly with the private developer. The community governing body enacts the ordinance guiding subdivision regulation, and this ordinance operates as the general framework within which subdivision regulations are administered. However, much leeway is typically found in the ordinance, and considerable discretion rests with the planning staff. This discretion is likely to include determination of the precise location of subdivision streets and land dedications for public use; it may also include the amount of land to be so dedicated.

Planning commissions rarely operate programs of their own; their powers are basically limited to planning and to an involvement in the land-use control process. For instance, they do not administer urban renewal programs; this is usually the task of an urban renewal or redevelopment authority or agency (LPA). They do not administer public housing programs, a responsibility of the local housing authority (LHA). They do not carry out the community model cities program, an assignment of the city demonstration agency (CDA). They also do not run the mass transit program, a task of the local transportation authority; the community sewer program, a job of the public works department or a sewer district; the highway program, a responsibility of the state highway commission; the community action program, a project of the community action agency; the building and housing codes program, the responsibility of a building and housing department, a building department or some other agency; or a host of other key programs that are operated by a variety of line departments in the city, county or state government.

Consultation with planners is required at one point or another in many federally aided projects; consequently, planners may sometimes have leverage over operating programs. For example, the federal Department of Housing and Urban Development's "workable program" requires that community comprehensive planning serve as the framework for identifying and eradicating blight; without this, the federal government will not approve urban renewal grants. In fact, planning commissions may or may not play an important role in urban renewal. In Philadelphia, the planning commission, especially its staff director, Edmund Bacon, was a crucial participant in the urban renewal process for years, working hand in hand with the LPA in planning downtown renewal efforts. Nevertheless, Scott Greer found that local planning commissions frequently were "not consulted" or functioned as a "rubber stamp of approval" in urban renewal.[6]

Local planning commissions and administrators are increasingly building ties to departments and agencies in city, county and state governments; they are apparently also working more closely with elected officials at the local level, thus overcoming the institutional blocks to a direct planning-political marriage. Part of this has come by necessity, as planners have been forced out of isolated planning commissions and thrust into the municipal battle; part of this phenomenon is due to the increasing recognition in planning literature of the political and practical roles that planners must play if they are to be successful and to survive in the contemporary environment. Norman Beckman counsels "planner-bureaucrats" to participate in the government hierarchy, to be sensitive to shifts in public policy, to be prepared to revoke or modify key decisions, and to abandon the ivory tower approach; Beckman maintains that these are the marks of an effective planning administrator.[7]

Local planning commissions are constrained by actions at other levels in the political system. For example, if the planning commission is in a metropolitan area, its operations may be affected by a metropolitan planning commission or a metropolitan council of governments; there may also be a metropolitan transportation planning body (it may be part of or separate from a metropolitan planning commission or council of governments). The local planning commission and staff can be expected to have some contact with these metropolitan bodies, and the latter may set the general tone for planning which the local planning agencies should follow. Nevertheless, at this point in history, we should not place too much emphasis on metropolitan planning units because the basic planning power still resides in the community planning commission and the local government, not in any metropolitan agency.

[6]Scott Greer, *Urban Renewal and American Cities* (Indianapolis: Bobbs-Merrill Co., 1965), p. 76.

[7]Norman Beckman, "The New PPBS: Planning, Politics, Bureaucracy, and Salvation" in Thad L. Beyle and George T. Lathrop, eds., *Planning and Politics: Uneasy Partnership* (New York: Odyssey Press, 1970), pp. 108–27.

State planning may also affect the local planning commission and, of course, it is the state that provides the basic authority for the locality to engage in planning in the first place. To some extent, the national government also serves to shape local planning commission operations, largely through the federal urban planning assistance program or the "701" program, initially enacted in the 1954 Housing Act, the urban redevelopment planning provisions of the Housing Act of 1949, and the "workable program" feature of the 1954 act. Federal administrators do not supervise local planning commissions in great detail, but the federal government may have considerable influence over both the nature and extent of local planning.

Metropolitan-Level Planning

Metropolitan planning commissions constitute the next level in planning administration. They serve the metropolitan area as a whole, and their authority extends across local jurisdictional lines. They do not have line authority or any basic legal power over local planning commissions or local governments, and their power over planning is considerably less than that of the local planning commission. The metropolitan planning commission has the authority to develop a metropolitan plan and to make recommendations for this plan's implementation; however, the metropolitan body has no land-use control power and, like the local planning commission, does not operate programs. The metropolitan planning commission is then even more of an advisory body than the local planning commission, and it will seldom enjoy the political base or the prestige of the local planning unit.

Metropolitan planning commissions may be multi-jurisdictional, joint city-county, or county agencies; they may be created by local governments under state enabling legislation (the typical method), by specific acts of the state legislature, by interstate compact, or by statutes based upon the joint exercise of powers. Metropolitan planning commissions report that they receive their chief support from business and citizens groups; it would also appear that the real estate community is usually represented on these bodies.

The boards of the metropolitan planning commission are selected in a variety of ways, including appointment by the county governing board, municipal governing bodies, local planning commissions, and the state government. Both local elected and appointed officials, including local planning board members, may serve on the board of the metropolitan planning commission. Increasingly and mainly in response to federal regulations, local elected officials have representatives on metropolitan planning commissions. The average metropolitan planning commission was created in the mid-1950s, and its board is typically somewhat larger than that of the local planning commission.

Metropolitan planning may also be carried out by metropolitan councils of governments, sometimes called "regional councils." Metropolitan councils of governments are distinguished from planning commissions chiefly in their constituency base; metropolitan planning commission boards have been usually comprised of nongovernmental interests; councils of governments boards are composed of local government elected officials.[8] Where the two have existed in the same metropolitan area, there has been conflict between metropolitan planning commissions and councils of governments; both have sought to become *the* metropolitan planning body. The federal government, in its urban planning assistance program and through other policy, has favored the council of governments approach, contending that it is local elected officials that have the final authority over planning and plan implementation and that these officials should therefore control or have a significant influence over metropolitan planning.

According to one study, metropolitan planning agencies are likely to be concerned chiefly with transportation, housing, renewal, industrial development, open space and recreation, air and water pollution, public utilities and poverty programs.[9] Through the Demonstration Cities and Metropolitan Development Act of 1966, the Intergovernmental Cooperation Act of 1968, and the National Environmental Policy Act of 1969 (as implemented through Office of Management and Budget Circular No. A-95), metropolitan planning bodies have been given new key responsibilities. Now, metropolitan planning units serve as "clearinghouses" for a wide range of federal assistance applications and direct federal development activities; for affected programs, the metropolitan planning body must review and comment on proposed assistance or development actions before a final decision is reached by the appropriate agency, agencies or government. Metropolitan clearinghouses may be metropolitan planning commissions or councils of governments.

The "review and comment" authority given metropolitan planning bodies by the federal government represents the first real, political breakthrough for these agencies. Prior to receiving this authority, metropolitan planning commissions and councils of governments were groping for a political base and, although they still are to some extent, they

---

[8]U.S. Housing and Home Finance Agency, *1964 National Survey of Metropolitan Planning* (Washington, D.C.: Government Printing Office, 1965), p. 5.

[9]The Joint Center for Urban Studies of the Massachusetts Institute of Technology and Harvard University, *The Effectiveness of Metropolitan Planning* (Washington, D.C.: Government Printing Office, 1964), p. 122.

now have a more tangible power by which to build this base. The basic responsibility for this new review and comment authority rests with the staffs of the metropolitan bodies, not with the boards or the elected officials. Metropolitan planners are presently adding to their political capital by bargaining with local, state and federal officials, a process stimulated by the review and comment authority. However, this new authority has also caused problems for metropolitan planners, for few metropolitan planning commissions or councils of governments have definitive plans and standards by which federal assistance and development programs and activities may be judged; this standard setting has been left largely to the staff of metropolitan bodies, and standards appear to be set mostly on an *ad hoc* basis.

State-Level Planning

State governments are important in the planning administration picture in two ways: states authorize localities to undertake planning, and states have planning programs and agencies of their own. The first role of the states has been most commonly recognized; yet, in recent years, states have become considerably more active in direct planning and development. The states, through the enactment of state enabling legislation, have at least been the legal force behind the independent administration of the planning function at the local level, and this local independence has affected the course of planning policy over the years.

The more direct participation of states in planning is now a reality. All states presently have planning programs and agencies of some kind. The state planning function is located administratively as follows:[10]

	Number of States
Governor's office	20
Department of Commerce, Development, Planning and Development	13
Department of Administration, Finance	7
Independent planning agency	5
Department of Community Affairs	3
Other agencies	2
Total	50

[10]Robert M. Cornett, "Planning, Housing and Development," in The Council of State Governments, *The Book of the States 1970–1971* (Lexington, Ky.: Council of State Governments, 1970), p. 441.

Although functional planning has not been uncommon in some state programs, statewide planning is still in the infancy stage. Vermont has realistically initiated a statewide planning effort, which is to serve as the basis for direct state control over major developments.[11] With rare exceptions, exclusive development and land-use control power resides in local governments and not in the states; although some state governments zone for particular purposes (shore line, marsh land, flood plain, wetland, and state building development), only Hawaii and Alaska zone comprehensively on a statewide basis. Statewide planning is an advisory activity and meaningful land-use and comprehensive planning is still rare in state capitals. According to one assessment, there has been only limited success in the central coordinating of the states' own capital projects.[12]

Statewide planning has been given an important boost by the Intergovernmental Cooperation Act of 1968 and by the federal Office of Management and Budget Circular A-95. The former encouraged state coordination of various intergovernmental activities and the latter provided for the designation of state clearinghouses to study certain proposed federal programs, especially federal assistance activities. State clearinghouses, like metropolitan clearinghouses, review and comment on these programs. Effective comment would theoretically require state standards or plans (many states have neither) by which individual assistance applications and development programs could be assessed. The idea is that some central state agency—perhaps in the governor's office but, in any event, responsible to the governor—should judge proposed actions and programs of specific local, state, and federal bureaucracies; this judgment would only be advisory, but it could carry some weight. State planning agencies may serve as the state clearinghouse. The Council of State Governments, the states' public interest group, is currently undertaking an evaluation of the operations and effectiveness of these clearinghouses.

The Regional Level

In some parts of the country, regional planning and development commissions conduct regional planning. A region covers an area broader than a limited set of local jurisdictions and may cover more than a

---

[11]In Vermont, the state controls larger developments, and localities control smaller ones. See Elizabeth Haskell, "New Directions in State Environmental Planning," *Journal of the American Institute of Planners*, vol. 27, no. 4, (July 1971), pp. 253–58.

[12]John N. Kolesar, "The States and Urban Planning and Development," in Alan K. Campbell, ed., *The States and the Urban Crisis* (Englewood Cliffs, N.J.: Prentice-Hall, Inc., 1970), p. 131.

single metropolitan area and more than one state. The Southeastern Wisconsin Regional Planning Commission serves to illustrate this sort of operation. The area covered by the commission includes three metropolitan areas and seven counties; the commission is composed of 21 members, three from each county, of whom two are appointed by the governor and one by the respective county board. The commission conducts studies and performs research in land-use, community planning, transportation, and natural resources. Its authority is only advisory, and local participation is on a voluntary basis.

The different regional development commissions created in the 1960s have also undertaken regional planning. These include the Appalachian Regional Development Commission, created under federal law in 1965, and the Ozarks, New England, Upper Great Lakes, Four Corners, and Coastal Plains Regional Commissions, each of which has planning and economic development implementation powers for its particular region; the latter five commissions were created in accordance with the provisions of the Public Works and Economic Development Act of 1965.

The Rural Level

Rural planning in America has only recently gotten underway, and it lags considerably behind urban planning. Rural planning differs from urban planning in that it is largely limited to economic development; however, efforts are being made to broaden the scope of rural planning bodies. Unlike the situation in urban areas, no single organizational form exists in rural America that has the planning responsibilities and different approaches are used in planning rural development.[13]

The most visible rural planning agencies probably are the economic development districts (EDDs). As of December 31, 1970, there were over 100 EDDs throughout the nation; the EDDs are funded by and tend to be constituent agencies of the U.S. Department of Commerce (Economic Development Administration). The EDDs are not considered governments in and of themselves, and their boards include representatives from a wide spectrum of community interests, including minority groups. Other rural planning groups include the rural areas development committees (RADs) and soil and water conservation districts, both of which normally cover a single county and are sponsored by the U.S. Department of Agriculture. Although RADs are not considered governments as such, the conservation districts are.

---

[13]James L. Sundquist, *Making Federalism Work* (Washington, D.C.: The Brookings Institute, 1969), especially Chapters 4 and 5.

Some states have also been active in forming rural planning organizations. Nonmetropolitan areas will have clearinghouses to review certain federal actions, and these organizations will operate for rural areas in the same manner that metropolitan clearinghouses do in urban areas. Although this process is just starting in many places, it should strengthen rural planning.

The National Level

The national government is prominently involved in community planning. The most important measure in this respect is the "701" urban planning assistance program, under which money is advanced to state and local planning agencies. Initially, the program was somewhat limited in scope, but it has been broadened over the years. Now, urban planning assistance can be made available to cities of any size (until recently, it was limited to those under 50,000), counties, and other local general purpose governments; metropolitan and regional planning agencies; councils of governments; states; and rural agencies. The 701 program is administered by the federal Housing and Urban Development Department.

The national government has also been active in promoting planning in other ways. The clearinghouse network, which is being established with federal prodding, is one example, and perhaps it will have the most far-reaching effects in the long run on state and local planning. In addition, many federal assistance programs (for instance, open space, water, and sewer assistance) have area wide planning requirements.

Nevertheless, the record of the national government in the planning area is mixed. For the basic federal power does not reside in planning or in planners but in operating programs. In this sense, in the carrying out their respective responsibilities, federal bureaucracies have operated essentially independently of each other, of central coordinating mechanisms in Washington, of central officials at the state and local level, and of centralizing forces in Congress. This pattern of operation has not led to or reinforced efforts to develop coordinated or comprehensive planning at any level. The Advisory Commission on Intergovernmental Relations has sought to take the lead in proposing steps toward greater coordination of all governmental inputs, including federal agencies; however, it does not appear that any federal administrative or legislative unit has sufficient strength to put into effect the kind of coordination needed at the national level. Administrative regulations and even laws will not be enough; a political clout will be necessary.

THE POLITICS OF PLANNING ADMINISTRATION

The political stakes in planning vary somewhat according to the level of government involved and the particular arena within any given government. For instance, the actors in local planning are not identical with those in metropolitan planning, and the particular actors concerned with the local planning commission may not be exactly the same as those concerned with the planning decisions of the local governing body. Nevertheless, there are certain basic interests in planning and these interests are likely to have an impact on the planning decision making process at any level and in any arena. The following has the greatest applicability to planning at the community level.

Within the planning agency itself, we can expect to find the following key interests represented:

1. The real estate community, especially developers and builders;
2. Neighborhood citizens associations;
3. Professional planners;
4. The chief executive of the community government;
5. The community legislative body;
6. The planning board;
7. The general business community;
8. The state judiciary;
9. The highway bureaucracy; and
10. Other government bureaucracies.

It is important to note that it is *groups* that have the greatest influence over administrative decisions in planning. These groups do not necessarily have to be formally organized, but they often are. For instance, the real estate community may be organized into a developers and builders association (for example, the Minneapolis Home Builders Association); incidentally, realtors are also organized (boards of realtors), but their interest in planning is less than that of builders. Neighborhood citizens are also organized into citizens or civic associations, sometimes called neighborhood improvement groups. The general business community is organized into the chamber of commerce or board of trade; in some instances, more specialized business interests (other than real estate interests) may also be organized and interested in actions of the planning agency. The Greater Philadelphia Movement, an organization of big downtown commercial interests, is an example. These and other organized groups can be expected to maintain continuing liaison with the planning agency; and the different groups may well be closer to certain different administrative offices or factions in the planning agency than to others.

Each one of the key actors wants the decisions of the planning agency to reflect his view of planning; the views of the different actors are likely to vary somewhat, and it is impossible for the planning bureaucracy to please all interests, particularly to the same extent. It is also true that the different interests may overlap and that permanent or temporary coalitions of two or more interests may occur.

The following are examples of what each of the interests want from the planning agency. The *real estate community* wants a plan that will facilitate development; builders and developers favor community growth and physical renewal and, of course, this is consistent with their economic interests. Developers also want zoning recommendations from the planning staff and board that open new areas for development and increase population density; they also favor a flexible subdivision administration policy. *Citizens associations* usually call for a plan that preserves the *status quo* and that keeps open land from being developed; citizens groups also want planning board and staff zoning recommendations that maintain low residential densities and the integrity of existing neighborhoods. *Professional planners* may have an interest in seeing their professional values reflected in planning decisions and in translating their models into practice; these desires represent forces in planning decision making in the same manner as the positions of citizens associations or builders. Also, professional planners have their jobs at stake, and this may somewhat tailor their views on planning and zoning.

The *mayor, manager, or county executive* may want control of planning decisions to build his political base or for some other reason, such as promoting his conception of the public interest or enhancing his prestige or image. The *community legislative body* could be interested in planning for the same reasons, or it could represent one or more of the other interests in the planning process (it could be a "developers' council" or a "citizens' council"). Of course, under any circumstances, both the chief executive and the legislative body will have certain official powers over planning which they will have to exercise. The *planning board* members may constitute a single collective interest in and of themselves, or they may be split into competing factions, each of which may be aligned with some other interest in the community; the planning board also have formal authority over planning decisions.

The *general business community* will likely favor a plan that is friendly to existing business, that does not introduce too much new economic competition into the community, and that paints a favorable image of the community. In short, the general business community can be expected to work for planning staff decisions that do not bring competing businesses into the area. Through court decisions, the *state judiciary* may provide standards for planning agency decision-making, especially in zoning and subdivision regulation administration; since decisions of the planning agency and the local governing body can be appealed to the courts, the state judiciary is an important force in the planning agency, although its influence is not likely to be exerted in a direct or personal manner.

Various local and some state bureaucracies may be involved directly or indirectly in planning agency decision-making. One of the most important of these is the *state highway or roads commission*. Its interest is to see that general planning decisions are compatible with existing or planned future road networks. Nevertheless, the working relationship between the local planning commission and the roads bureaucracy may not be a particularly close one; the reason for this is that the state highway department can often build roads in the locality without regard to local plans. Pressure has been mounting to contain this highway power, and the planning provisions of the 1962 federal highway legislation were aimed in this direction (see Chapter 4). *Other bureaucracies* that want local plans to reflect their interests and desires include the sewer and water agency, the local roads department, the public works agency, the local school district, the model cities agency, the urban renewal agency, and the public housing authority. In addition, important federal departments may have a stake in local planning agency decision-making; these include the Department of Housing and Urban Development and the Department of Transportation.[14]

MANAGEMENT ISSUES IN PLANNING

To the planning administrator, three issues presently seem to be of utmost importance: the determination of the appropriate administrative posture; the selection of administrative strategies; and the development of administrative standards that can serve as the base for decision making.[15]

David Ranney sees three possible roles for the professional planner operating in a bureaucracy: a political agnostic; a confidential advisor; and a political activist.[16] The political agnostic makes planning decisions

---

[14]A good practical discussion of the politics of planning decision-making can be found in Richard F. Babcock, *The Zoning Game* (Madison, Wisconsin: University of Wisconsin Press, 1966).

[15]For a revealing insightful analysis of planning administration, see Alan Altshuler, *The City Planning Process, A Political Analysis* (Ithaca, N.Y.: Cornell University Press, 1965).

[16]David C. Ranney, *Planning and Politics in the Metropolis* (Columbus, Ohio: Charles E. Merrill Publishing Company, 1969), pp. 147–50.

and recommendations on "professional" grounds; he rules out political feasibility and pressure. The confidential advisor works with a politician and seeks to advance the latter's political fortunes; his professional values give way to political expediency (or reality), and he lends his professional values to legitimate political ambition. The political activist makes decisions on the basis of professional criteria and then tries to build political support for his decisions. Of course, these roles may overlap, and no one of them can be categorically considered ideal for all planner-bureaucrats. In fact, any given planner is likely to play any of these roles at different times.

Traditional planning theory upheld the political agnostic role, and contemporary planning theory tends to support the political activist role. Ranney feels that the political agnostic has the least chance of getting his ideas translated into action. The confidential advisor has the best chance, but the planner's ideas may be watered down by political considerations. The political activist may or may not be successful, depending in part on the nature of his ideas, recommendations, and decisions. If his views are consistent with the interests of powerful community forces, he may be successful. However, if his views are strongly supported by only a single powerful community interest, and other powerful community interests exist and are hostile to these views, the planner's proposals may not only be defeated but his job may be in jeopardy should the "other" interests gain control of the planning bureaucracy. If a planner's views are *strongly* backed by a key local interest, another key interest will usually be in opposition. While the political activist role is somewhat risky, it may also be the most productive. Even though the political activist must deal with interest groups only this posture seems to protect professional values and foster their implementation.

The following hypothetical case will illustrate the difference between the political agnostic and the political activist. A planner-bureaucrat may decide that professional values dictate that development be clustered along radial corridors extending out from the city and that the areas between the corridors be retained in open space, park, and low density residential use. Let us assume that the planner-bureaucrat develops a plan incorporating these ideas. A political agnostic would then submit the plan to the planning board or the local governing body and let it decide on the merits of the plan; he did his job by deciding what was best for the community, and it is up to polititical decision makers to determine whether or not they want that plan. The political agnostic will answer questions about the plan, but he will not lobby for it.

On the other hand, the political activist will actively work for the plan's adoption and implementation. He is likely to receive support from citizens associations and, if they exist, from citizens planning associations; he will most likely also gain a sympathetic ear from public officials on the governing body and the planning board who are in agreement with the citizens groups or who owe their positions to such groups. Nevertheless, he is apt to encounter stiff opposition from developers groups, landowners in the "open space" areas, and the real estate community in general. Real estate interests, like citizens groups, are commonly powerful forces in the decision making process involved in community planning.

If the citizens associations have enough political strength, the plan may be approved and it may be implemented; if they do not, the plan may be defeated. Thus, success for the plan (and the accompanying professional principles) is not assured by taking on this administrative posture sympathetic to citizens groups; nevertheless, if this role does prove successful, it will not simply be because the professional values are "right" in the abstract but because an important interest wants the plan. The reasoning of the citizens group interest is less based on ideal conceptions of proper planning than on the practical consideration that the plan will limit development, keep new residents out of the community, keep taxes at present levels, and preserve the *status quo*. Citizens groups will favor such a plan for economic and social reasons, while developers and landowners will oppose it on economic grounds. To developers and landowners in the open space areas, such a plan means stymied growth, restricted development opportunities, lower land prices, and curtailed profits. General public presentations by both sets of interests tend to obscure these basic underlying differences. Planning administrators are usually made aware of such differences at an early stage in their careers, and this may affect the ultimate posture they choose.

Strategy is a narrower matter than an administrative posture or role. Strategy refers to the particular means and channels the planner-bureaucrat will use to achieve his ends, although it is not unrelated to the broader posture he may assume. Should the planner-bureaucrat limit his contacts to the planning agency, to professional planners, and to the planning board? Should he work with the local governing body, other bureaucracies, and other public officials in other than the routine manner? Should he develop contacts with private groups in the community, including citizens associations or developers' organizations—again, other than through formal, official meetings and functions? Should the planner-bureaucrat seek to blend into the community social fabric or remain aloof? All of these are important questions that cross the minds of many administrators, and they represent pressures on these administrators. It is natural that a planner will have many tasks and strategies determined for him by the formal structure and demands of the planning bureaucracy, but many additional choices remain. Because planners do not have operating programs, these choices are not made any easier; in fact, the desire to effect plans through programs over which planners have no basic control is a cause of much anxiety to many planner-bureaucrats.

Standard setting is another matter of considerable concern among professional planners. Some years ago, the planning profession seemed convinced that it had solutions to urban sprawl and urban blight, and that these solutions could be more or less uniformly enforced in city after city. However, no matter what may have been thought in the past, it is widely assumed today that no single set of operational principles or standards exist that should serve as guides to community planners. Standards such as "good planning" or "proper land use" are not operational and have little, if any, practical meaning. Consequently, the search continues.

In the meantime, the planner is asked to make recommendations, to give advice, and to render decisions. What standards are to be used? On rezoning recommendations, for example, should the planner adhere to the standard that land uses should not be mixed—that low-density residential should be kept separate from high-density residential, that commercial be kept separate from residential? On the other hand, should he be guided by the principle that land uses should be mixed, with residential, commercial, and other uses clustered in a single development? Are plans reserving wedges of open space between concentrated development in accordance with sound planning principles? If so, what are the principles? The planner has the responsibility for drawing up the community plan, and such questions are apt to arise.

Concerning administrative organization for planning: what standards should be drawn upon to determine whether this or that organizational structure is preferable? Is an independent planning commission needed? Should planning be put under the chief executive or under the city council? These are questions to which many planners will have to address themselves.

In the final analysis, it is unlikely that definitive standards or principles will ever be developed that will provide permanent answers to these and other planning questions. However, at any given time, there will be a prevailing sentiment which will provide at least temporary answers, and this sentiment will likely be construed as "principles" and "standards." For instance, the professional planning community presently seems to favor cluster development in residential areas, a concept that works toward concentrated development in certain portions of a residential subdivision and preserves large areas of open space for use in common (this is to be contrasted with the conventional layout pattern, with housing being spread out and with each lot having specified setback and yard requirements). Professional planners also lean toward mixed land uses, with high and low density residential uses integrated with commercial and public facility land uses. Such "principles" can serve to guide the planner-bureaucrat's zoning recommendations and his planning decisions. In addition, many professional planners appear to oppose the present administrative structure in planning. They favor an integration of the planning and the political process; again, this belief could be considered a "principle" that a planner bureaucrat might follow in working for organizational change in his own community.

PLANNING IN AN AGE OF CHANGE

Planning is not static and, given current pressures, it cannot be. Furthermore, planning is in a transitional state. Even though it is not as vigorously opposed by certain economic interests as it was in the past, it is not fully accepted today. One reason that its opponents are no longer active is that it has been often "turned around" by key community interests for their own purposes; thus, what appeared to many to be socialism has actually become merely an extension of capitalism, that is, an instrument of dominant economic interests. In the downtown areas, for example, planning has been "used" by big business interests to build the inner city economic base. In suburban areas, planning has been used by citizens associations to protect property values and to exclude unwanted economic and racial groups. In outlying metropolitan areas, planning has been used by the real estate community to foster development and to assure the provision and public financing of community services and facilities—in short, to underwrite the private market. Professional planners have often supported these groups; they usually have had no choice.

We have not seen much "real" planning in this country. Key changes in popular attitudes, government operations, and administrative structure will have to be made if planning is to make much headway. Planners need to be an accepted, and somewhat independent, force in the community decision-making processes. Planning decision-making processes need to be simplified, and planning organization needs to be streamlined. Planner-bureaucrats need to have the power to carry out plans, and they need a single ordinance, perhaps a combined zoning-subdivision code, which they administer and which will serve as the key implementation tool. They also need a strategic and influential position in the municipal bureaucracy. However, such changes cannot be superimposed by fiat. In all probability, the federal government can serve as the basic force to foster these ends.

SUMMARY

This chapter has focused on the administration of planning policy. It has explained the nature of planning policy, the administrative patterns in planning at the local, metropolitan, state, regional, rural, and national levels, the political forces involved in planning administration, and important practical management issues in planning. The chapter closed with a discussion of the dynamics of planning and the potential for planning in the United States.

Planning administration was found to be a political matter and to involve different values and interests. Any attempt to isolate planning, even planning administration, from the political processes will, by definition, fail. This attempt at isolation is just a way to assure dominance of a particular point of view or rule of a particular interest. The planning bureaucracy is immeshed in politics, and planning policy can normally be traced to a political base. The planning administrator cannot escape this reality.

4

ADMINISTRATION OF TRANSPORTATION POLICY

INTRODUCTION

The subject of this chapter is transportation policy, but its emphasis is on urban transportation and highways. We focus on the administrative aspects of policy in these areas. After beginning with an explanation of urban transportation and highway policy, the chapter studies administrative structures used to carry out this policy at the national, state, local, and metropolitan levels. The chapter then directs attention to the politics of transportation policy administration and, specifically, to the political ramifications of patterns of administrative organization in transportation.

Transportation administration can be viewed in both technical and political lights; we will consider both perspectives, but we will emphasize the latter. Politics should be interpreted in the broadest sense. The politics of transportation administration refers to the different forces and values that impinge on transportation bureaucracies and affect administrative operations and decision making. Transportation agencies at all levels in the political system also constitute political forces in themselves, and serve to shape public attitudes toward transportation and mold political processes and policy in transportation. In these and other respects, transportation bureaucracies can scarcely be pictured apart from a political framework. Ultimately, even the technical inputs in transportation administration, such as impartial studies of highway needs, can only be channeled into policy *via* politics—that is, they can be accepted as policy only if they are supported by key bureaucratic and political forces.

URBAN TRANSPORTATION AND HIGHWAY POLICY

We can best see transportation policy in terms of the degree and extent by which the American public and American business use the various transportation modes. The nature of the transportation used will in some manner reflect the emphases of public policy. The different governments in the United States significantly affect transportation activity, and this is done in both direct and indirect ways. Although there is no single transportation policy for the country as a whole, there is a considerable body of laws, administrative regulations, and expenditure policies that have a tremendous bearing on practical transportation activity; even though this body of laws, regulations, and policies is not administered by a single transportation agency or in a unified manner, it does have an enormous impact on transportation patterns.

The term "transportation policy" is a misnomer, for there is no transportation policy, only transportation policies. What is often referred to as transportation policy is nothing more than a number of different policies put into effect by a number of different governments that are broadly tied together by the word "transportation." The transportation policy processes in the United States are complex. All levels of government are involved in these processes, and although each level of government influences the others, they also act independently of each other in transportation.

Even within the same level of government, no single transportation policy exists, except perhaps in the loosest of senses. In Washington, for example, there is no single transportation act (as there is in housing), but separate acts for such transportation matters as highways, mass transit, and airports. Each of these transportation matters is handled by different substantive congressional committees, and each committee has its own internal power structure, its own transportation priorities, its separate connections to transportation bureaucracies, its independent ties to transportation interest groups, and its own interests to protect.

TABLE 4.1
Total Passengers Carried on Transit Lines of the United States
Distributed by Types of Service
At Five Year Intervals 1935–55 and Annually 1955–70

Calendar Year	Railway			Trolley Coach (Millions)	Motor Bus (Millions)	Grand Total (Millions)
	Surface (Millions)	Subway & Elevated (Millions)	Total (Millions)			
1935	7,276	2,236	9,512	96	2,618	12,226
1940	5,943	2,382	8,325	534	4,239	13,098
1945	9,426	2,698	12,124	1,244	9,886	23,254
1950	3,904	2,264	6,168	1,658	9,420	17,246
1955	1,207	1,870	3,077	1,202	7,250	11,529
1956	876	1,880	2,756	1,142	7,043	10,941
1957	679	1,843	2,522	993	6,874	10,389
1958	572	1,815	2,387	843	6,502	9,732
1959	521	1,828	2,349	749	6,459	9,557
1960	463	1,850	2,313	657	6,425	9,395
1961	434	1,855	2,289	601	5,993	8,883
1962	393	1,890	2,283	547	5,865	8,695
1963	329	1,836	2,165	413	5,822	8,400
1964	289	1,877	2,166	349	5,813	8,328
1965	276	1,858	2,134	305	5,814	8,253
1966	282	1,753	2,035	284	5,764	8,083
1967	263	1,938	2,201	248	5,723	8,172
1968	253	1,928	2,181	228	5,610	8,019
1969	249	1,980	2,229	199	5,375	7,803
*1970	235	1,881	2,116	182	5,034	7,332

*Preliminary.

SOURCE: *'70–'71 Transit Fact Book* (Washington, D.C.: American Transit Association, 1971), p. 6.

Even with the recent creation of a single Department of Transportation, this picture has not been substantially changed, and power over different transportation policies is still basically decentralized and fundamentally uncoordinated.

Urban transportation trends are clear, and these trends are a product of transportation policy. As shown in Table 4.1, the total number of passengers using public transit has declined from over 23 billion in 1945 to 7.3 billion in 1970. Declines are evident in all categories shown in the table, but they are particularly noticeable in the surface rail (streetcar) and trolley coach classes. Figures for subway and elevated rail systems and motor buses have leveled off somewhat in the 1960s, although neither category is gaining passengers. As a result, public transit companies have been showing operating deficits for each year since 1963, and these deficits are escalating with the passing of each year.[1] Public transit companies include bus and trolley coach firms and municipal operations and rail transit authorities.

By contrast, the popularity of the automobile continues, and the automobile industry is thriving. All told, there were some 90 million privately and publicly owned motor vehicles in 1970, and there has been a steady rise in automobile ownership over the years between 1945 and 1970. Automobiles are still the most popular means by which people travel to work. On a nationwide basis, 82 percent of commuters use the automobile, and most of these workers drive to their jobs by themselves; only 14 percent of commuting workers use public transportation.[2]

The preference for different transportation modes varies by occupation and income level. Higher income people have a greater preference for the automobile as a means of traveling to and from work, while lower income people are more likely to use public transportation. Compared to 64 percent of service workers and 75 percent of those in clerical and sales positions, nearly 90 percent of professionals and managers drive to work. No major occupational group is more likely to use public transportation in place of the automobile as a means of getting to work. It is also instructive to note that professionals and managers are considerably more likely than any other occupational group to drive to work alone (over two-thirds do). Although over two-thirds of central city commuters use the automobile, commuting by automobile is also more popular among suburbanites than central city residents.

Like automobile manufacturers, the trucking and airline industries are enjoying economic prosperity. On the other hand, railroads are not. Truck use has increased sharply since the early 1900s and, in 1970, there were approximately 17.8 million registered trucks in the United States, about a million more than in 1969.[3] As the years have passed, airlines have been carrying more passengers and cargo; the number of passenger miles jumped from 38.8 million in 1960 to 131.7 million in 1970, and freight business is also up over the same period. However, the number of plane passengers in 1970 dipped slightly from 1969. Although its net income declined dramatically in 1970, the airline industry is still profitable.[4] By contrast, the railroad passenger business is

[1] *'70–'71 Transit Fact Book* (Washington, D.C.: American Transit Association, 1971), p. 4.

[2] *1971 Automobile Facts and Figures* (Detroit, Michigan: Automobile Manufacturers Association, 1971).

[3] *American Trucking Trends 1970–71* (Washington, D.C.: American Trucking Associations, Inc., 1971).

[4] *Air Transport 1971* (Washington, D.C.: Air Transport Association of America, 1971).

down and running at a deficit; its overall revenues are up and the industry as a whole is turning a profit.[5]

National Highway Policy

Recent public policy in transportation has favored highways and, consequently, has served to underwrite the automobile and trucking industries. It has also been of substantial benefit to other businesses, those that serve automobiles and trucks, the most important of which are the rubber and petroleum industries. This public policy has worked against the economic interests of those in direct competition with the automobile and trucking forces; specifically, it has hurt public transit in cities and metropolitan areas, and it has had significantly unfavorable effects on railroads. Public transit is in competition with the automobile as a means of moving people, and the trucking and railroad industries are fierce competitors in the movement of freight and other cargo. Without the highway, automobiles and trucks could not move freely about the country, and highways are built and run by government. The motor vehicle and public transportation policy in highways are, to a great degree, responsible for the demise of the streetcar, the steady decline of public mass transportation in urban areas, the fiscal deterioration of the public transit industry, and the weakening of the railroads' economic position.

Until recently, transportation policy was a private matter between the different highway and the railroad interests. The highway group, led by the automotive, rubber, and oil interests, has supported massive public outlays for highways; the railroad lobby has opposed this. Obviously, with the help of organized motorists, the highway people have prevailed. In 1971, government revenues for highways reached an estimated $23.2 billion. The federal government alone provided over $5.5 billion of this figure, with the states contributing the bulk of it. In 1969, there were 3.7 million miles of roads and streets in the United States. Government assistance to other transport in no way approaches these dimensions.

The funding of the interstate system in 1956 was the key national transportation legislation. The 1956 highway measure established the federal Highway Trust Fund. The creation of the trust fund represented a significant victory for highway backers, because it meant that the money in the fund was earmarked for highways and could not be used for any other purpose during the life of the fund. Highway Trust Fund

[5]*Yearbook of Railroad Facts, 1971 Edition* (Washington, D.C.: Association of American Railroads, 1971).

proceeds come from taxes on motor fuel and automotive products; its chief source is the motor fuel tax. The protection afforded by the separate fund meant that highway bureaucracies and roads interests would not have to go back to Congress on a continuing basis for funding approvals; even if the trust fund revenue is not appropriated (an annual process), the money cannot be used for other government programs and is simply carried over to the next year.

The actual construction of highways rests with the states. Four categories of state roads are eligible for federal highway assistance: primary, interstate; primary, other than interstate; secondary; and urban extensions. The primary system encompasses approximately 270,000 miles of main highways and streets, including over 40,000 miles of interstate freeways; the secondary system includes farm-to-market and feeder roads, covering some 642,000 miles of state, county, and local highways; and urban extensions are the urban portions of the other two systems. The intrastate categories (usually called primary-secondary-urban) are known collectively as the ABC program, and they are to be distinguished from the interstate system. Federal highway money can be spent by the states only for construction, rebuilding, and improvement, but not for maintenance purposes.

The national government pays 90 percent of the construction costs of interstate highways, with the remaining 10 percent coming from the states or the states and localities. ABC program funds are made available to the states on a 50-50 matching basis. The 1970 federal highway legislation changed the ABC program ratio and, beginning in fiscal year 1974, the national government will provide 70 percent of the total cost. All federal highway revenues come from the Highway Trust Fund. The interstate system was planned for a 1972 completion date, and the Trust Fund was due to expire that year; however, in 1970, the interstate completion date was extended through fiscal year 1976 and the Highway Trust Fund was extended to October 1, 1977.

National Mass Transit Policy

National mass transit policy represents a much less ambitious effort. While the first federal highway legislation can be traced to 1916, the federal government did not get into urban mass transit until 1961, and then on a limited scale. The federal mass transit effort was broadened with the passage of the Urban Mass Transportation Act of 1964. The national government spent about $150 million for mass transportation grants in fiscal year 1970.

The U.S. Congress expanded the national transit program through the Urban Mass Transportation Assistance Act of 1970; this measure authorized $3.1 billion for mass transportation over a five-year period and set as a congressional aim the provision of $10 billion for transit over the next 12 years. Although this legislation represents a shift in federal urban mass transit policy, transit receives much less favorable federal treatment than highways. Federal highway policy represents a multibillion-dollar effort each year, while transit is dealing in millions of dollars each year. In addition, federal highway money is protected; transit money is not.

Urban mass transit is a responsibility of local government and private firms; federal urban mass transportation funds are made available to localities for a variety of purposes. Federal mass transit loans and grants can be used for: the advance acquisition of real property, including rights-of-way, station sites, terminals, parking lots, and access roads; capital improvements, including the acquisition of new transit system equipment and the modernization of facilities; demonstration, research, and development; technical studies; managerial training; and university transportation research.

It is important to note that urban mass transit policy does not apply only or even primarily to subway systems. Only five of the more than 200 metropolitan areas in the United States have subway systems (New York, Boston, Philadelphia, Cleveland, and Chicago), although several other subway systems are presently under way (San Francisco and Washington, D.C.) or in the planning stages. In 1970, for example, federal capital assistance grants aided more bus than rail transit systems. Federal transit funds come from general revenues and not, as with highways, from special taxes.

National Airport Policy

National airport policy can be traced to 1946 when congressional legislation authorized national airport assistance to local governments, the government bodies which have run most of the country's major metropolitan airports. Before 1970, the federal airport program did not amount to much financially; in fiscal year 1970, about $30 million was appropriated for local airports. However, national airport policy was substantially modified with the Airport and Airway Development and Revenue Act of 1970; this legislation obligated the federal government to spend over $5 billion for the next 10 years in order to expand, modernize, and improve aviation facilities. The measure authorized the spending of no less than $250,000,000 a year for ten years for the acquisition, establishment, and improvement of air navigational facilities —a total of $2.5 billion over a ten-year period for airport assistance.

To finance the expanded program, Congress increased the air passenger tax, levied a new tax on international travelers, imposed a new air freight tax, provided for taxing gasoline and jet fuel used in certain aircraft, and placed an annual registration fee on all air carriers and aircraft. In addition, Congress set up a separate trust fund, known as the Airport and Airway Trust Fund.

State and Local Transportation Policy

State and local transportation policy has been directed primarily toward highways. Municipalities have also put some emphasis on mass transit and airport development. Some states now assist localities in the funding and improvement of public transit, including subway construction. In general, highway policy is a product of national and state governments; mass transit and airport policy, of national and local governments.

TRANSPORTATION POLICY ADMINISTRATION

All levels of government in the American system have key transportation functions. Public power over transportation is a shared function, and no single level has exclusive jurisdiction over it. The administrative patterns in transportation vary by the level of government and sometimes within the same level of government. At the national and state levels, there has been a trend toward the administrative consolidation of the various transportation functions; a single department for transportation now exists in Washington, and a number of comprehensive transportation agencies have been formed in the states. This section concentrates on comprehensive transportation departments, highway agencies, mass transit authorities, and airport bureaucracies.

National Government

The Department of Transportation (DOT) administers basic transportation policy at the national level. The agency was created by the Department of Transportation Act of 1966, and it represents the newest of the present cabinet-level departments. The Department is headed by a Secretary, who is a member of the President's cabinet. He is assisted by an Under Secretary; a series of staff offices (public affairs, congressional relations, civil rights, executive secretariat, contract appeals board, and supersonic transport development); assistant secretaries for policy and international affairs, environment and urban systems, systems development and technology, safety and consumer affairs, and administration; and a general counsel (see Figure 4.1). It is important to note that the assistant secretaries do not have line authority but operate in a staff capacity. This has been a point of some contention in this newly created department.

The National Transportation Safety Board is an autonomous agency but works closely with the Department of Transportation. The Board investigates civil aviation and surface transportation accidents and makes recommendations to promote safety in transportation. The Board is composed of five members, who are appointed by the President, and is served by an administrative staff, including a general manager and hearing examiners.

The essential power in the Department of Transportation rests with the different administrations, especially the Federal Highway Administration. The Federal Highway Administration (FHWA) controls the federal roads program, including the interstate and the ABC systems. The Federal Highway Administration was formerly the Bureau of Public Roads (BPR), which was moved from the Department of Commerce to the new Department of Transportation. The BPR is a familiar name in highway circles and has considerable sentimental and historical meaning to highway administrators and highway backers.[6] For a time, the title of the "Bureau of Public Roads" was retained in the new department, and the bureau operated as part of the Federal Highway Administration. Recently, however, the Bureau of Public Roads designation was discarded by the department, and the federal roads program is carried out solely by the Highway Administration.

The power base of the Federal Highway Administration rests upon state highway bureaucracies, organized state highway officials, and private highway supporters. In addition, the Highway Administration controls over $5 billion within the Department of Transportation bureaucracy, and this makes it a major force in the hierarchy. Under both the Democratic and Republican regimes, there has been a certain degree of friction between the Highway Administration and the Secretary's office. In general, the Secretaries of Transportation have been more inclined to support urban mass transit than has the highway agency, and the Federal Highway Administration has feared that the Secretaries' advisers have plans to dip into the Highway Trust Fund for transit revenues. At times, the internal bureaucratic struggle between the Highway Administration and the office of the Secretary has been marked.

The state roads agencies are the Federal Highway Administration's

---

[6]See Christy Borth, *Mankind on the Move, The Story of Highways* (Washington, D.C.: Automotive Safety Foundation, 1969).

FIGURE 4.1: Department of Transportation

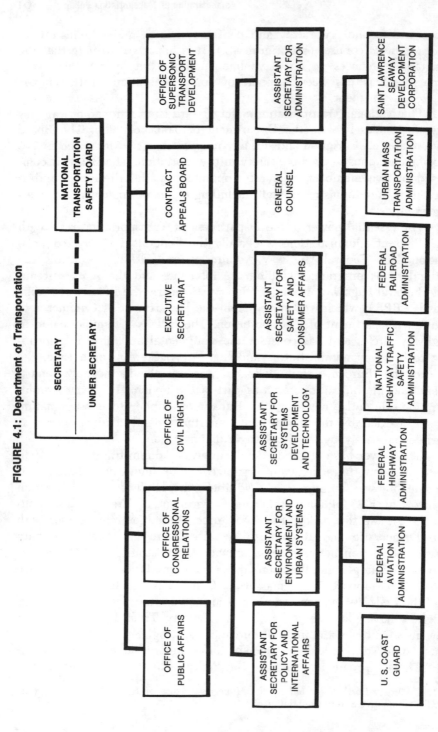

SOURCE: Adapted from *United States Government Organization Manual, 1971/72* (Washington, D.C.: Government Printing Office, 1971), p. 627.

key constituency. State roads departments are commonly headed by a commission and a director and typically enjoy considerable independence from the state governor. State highway bureaucracies are organized into a public interest group known as the American Association of State Highway Officials (AASHO), which serves as liaison between the Federal Highway Administration and state roads chiefs. All money spent by the Highway Administration on the nation's road systems must be funneled through state highway departments, even if this money is ultimately used by local highway agencies, and the states are held accountable for all federal highway expenditures. The Federal Highway Administration does not actually build or maintain highways; this is a responsibility of state and local highway agencies. Although federal highway funds account for about 40 percent of all new construction outlays, most highway money is raised and spent at the state and local levels.

The Federal Highway Administration also works closely with the congressional Public Works Committees which must authorize highway programs and expenditures; the Highway Research Board of the National Academy of Sciences, an organization financed by public and private sources but mostly by the state highway departments and the Federal Highway Administration; the Automotive Safety Foundation, financed mostly by the automotive, rubber, and oil industries and now connected loosely to the Highway Users Federation; the Highway Users Federation for Safety and Mobility, previously the National Highway Users Conference, a key group of highway backers; and other organizations and agencies that have an interest in highways.[7] A joint Federal Highway Administration–National League of Cities (NLC) committee exists to link the highway bureaucracy to municipalities; nevertheless, relations between the organized cities and the Highway Administration are cool, and the key federal highway clientele is the states, not the cities.

The Urban Mass Transportation Administration administers the national mass transit program. Unlike the Federal Highway Administration, its constituents are largely local governments, usually cities. In this light, it works with the city lobbying groups, especially the National League of Cities and the United States Conference of Mayors. Its clients also include members of the American Transit Association, which represents the nation's bus companies. The Urban Mass Transit Administration seems to have a close relationship to the office of the Secretary, and it gets its programs authorized through the House Banking and Currency Committee and the Senate's Committee on Banking, Housing, and Urban

---

[7]Helen Leavitt, *Superhighway—Superhoax* (Garden City, N.Y.: Doubleday & Co., 1970), p. 149.

Affairs. Along with the Secretary of Transportation, the Urban Mass Transportation Administration has played a leading role in securing enactment of the Urban Mass Transportation Assistance Act of 1970, a measure that served to boost the stock of the Mass Transportation Administration in the Transportation Department hierarchy.

The Federal Aviation Administration administers the national air navigational and airport assistance program. In the process, it works with local governments and airport authorities, and its ties in Congress are with the commerce committees, which provide the program and funding authorizations in the air navigational and airport field. Although, since the program's inception in 1946, the relationship in the airport assistance program has been between the national government and local airport agencies, over half of the states have enacted laws requiring federal airport aid to be channeled through the states. This represents a new pattern which has been opposed by key airport interests in Washington. With the passage of the Airport and Airway Development and Revenue Act of 1970, the Federal Aviation Administration can be expected to be an increasingly powerful force in the Department of Transportation.

Other agencies within the Department of Transportation include the National Highway Traffic Safety Administration, which seeks to coordinate and stimulate programs designed to improve traffic safety; the Federal Railroad Administration, which is concerned with rail transportation policy, development, and safety, and which runs the Alaska Railroad and sponsors high-speed ground transportation activities; the U.S. Coast Guard; and the Saint Lawrence Seaway Development Corporation.

Outside the Department of Transportation, other federal agencies with transportation responsibilities include the Interstate Commerce Commission, which regulates buses, trucks, railroads, pipelines, and other carriers; the Civil Aeronautics Board, which regulates the airlines' economic structure; and the Federal Maritime Commission, which controls waterborne shipping engaged in foreign and domestic offshore commerce.

The Department of Transportation is involved in the public policy processes in two basic ways: first, the Department helps shape transportation legislation and funding levels; and second, it makes policy in administering legislation. In its first role, DOT makes proposals for transportation legislation and program funding, coordinates its proposals with the federal Office of Management and Budget (the successor to the Bureau of the Budget) and the President's legislative program and budget, testifies before substantive and appropriations committees in the House and

Senate in support of its proposals, works with public and private interest groups in developing and gaining support for legislative and funding proposals, and actively lobbies for its legislative package.

Part of the Department's second role as the administrator of legislation is to make decisions on grant and loan programs, within congressional guidelines and stipulations. Congress normally permits considerable discretion in the administration of federal transportation activities (DOT may have drafted the legislation in the first place), and it is the responsibility of DOT to make administrative determinations that amount to policy. The Department must approve specific state and local government projects, and this represents one of the most important types of policy decision it has to make.

In practice, the Department carries on most of its policy functions through the particular administrations that have authority over highways, mass transit, and so on. The Secretary serves only as a general coordinator in this process, operating as a stimulator of the administrations and as an initiator of new ideas; the basic policy responsibility rests with the administrations. To some extent, the administrations may view the Secretary as an "outsider," and not part of the permanent administrative structure. The different administrations of the Department have important and, perhaps, independent power bases that make them formidable forces in the administrative hierarchy.

State Government

State transportation policy is administered by comprehensive departments of transportation, highway departments, public utility commissions, and aeronautics commissions. Some states may have other agencies that are engaged in transportation activities; for instance, all states have some form of highway safety program, including motor vehicle inspection, and this program may not be administered by one of the departments listed above.

The most recent administrative development in state transportation is the creation of state departments of transportation. As of October 1971, 15 states had such departments: California, Connecticut, Delaware, Florida, Hawaii, Illinois, Maine, Maryland, Massachusetts, New Jersey, New York, Oregon, Pennsylvania, Rhode Island, and Wisconsin. Fourteen additional states are considering establishing departments of transportation: Alaska, Colorado, Georgia, Iowa, Kansas, Michigan, Minnesota, Missouri, North Carolina, Ohio, South Dakota, Tennessee, Vermont, and Washington. The governors, in both their collective and individual capacities, have been the major political force behind the creation of these departments. The National Governors' Conference, the governors' public interest group, has backed the departments of transportation, as have individual governors; the governors' objective has been to bring highways under central control, thus adding to the power base of their office.

The formation of state departments of transportation is usually accomplished by the consolidation of different agencies found in various parts of the state administrative bureaucracy. In many cases, this process does not represent consolidation in the strictest sense; it merely represents a transfer of agencies from one department or from an independent administrative position to a department of transportation; in such cases, the new department serves as sort of an umbrella organization, housing different transportation units that may still operate somewhat independently.

State departments of transportation may include the following functions: highways, aviation, mass transit, harbor control, highway safety, motor vehicle license and inspection, certain public works, turnpike supervision, bridge development, airport operations, railroad transportation, highway patrol, and transportation planning. In its discussion of state transportation departments, the Council of State Governments argues that "the States have emerged as the most logical central place to coordinate and plan transportation."[8]

One of the—sometimes unstated—assumptions behind the move to a single transportation department in the states has been the hope that the independent power of the highway bureaucracy can be curtailed and that highway funds can, thereby, be siphoned off to mass transit and other nonhighway transportation needs. In 45 of the 50 states, road monies are found in what amounts to a state highway trust fund. In fact, over half of the states have adopted constitutional provisions barring the diversion of state gasoline and motor vehicle taxes, which are presently used for highways, for nonhighway purposes. The development of departments of transportation and the administrative subordination of the highway agency within these departments has not appreciably affected independent highway financing practices.

There is no magic in administrative reorganization. The transfer of the highway department to a new transportation agency does not necessarily mean a shift in power among the various forces in the state which are concerned with highways. Such a shift would be necessary before governors or heads of departments of transportation could dip into highway funds. These funds are considered sacred by highway

---

[8]James A. R. Johnson, "Transportation," in *The Book of the States 1970–71* (Lexington, Ky.: The Council of State Governments, 1970), p. 328.

backers; these forces include most state highway bureaucracies, state highway users conferences, roads contractors, and other highway interests.

Limited experience with state departments of transportation suggests that these agencies are very often little more than renamed highway departments. This is true in spite of the fact that most transportation secretaries have not previously been highway chiefs; still, in some cases, the highway director was appointed to head the new transportation department as a matter of political necessity, that is, to assure approval of the new department. Under the new departments of transportation, the highway bureaucracy still operates somewhat autonomously; this is due to its continued independent funding, its continued direct connections with powerful state legislators, its support in the Federal Highway Administration in Washington and among the key national and state public and private interest groups in highways, and its traditional recognition in the states as the custodian of a basic public function.

State highway departments are still predominantly independent, even in the administrative sense. Only a minority of the states have transportation departments, and all of these were created in recent years; Hawaii was the first (1960), and most states that have "little DOTs" created them after the national government did so in 1966. In a study done prior to the development of state DOTs, Robert Friedman found that most state highway operations were independent or partly independent of gubernatorial control. Only 13 states had highway departments that were termed "dependent" in relation to the governor. An independent highway department was defined as one governed by a board selected according to strict criteria (neutralizing partisanship and perhaps prescribing occupational and geographical representation) and chosen by legislative confirmation for specified terms (exceeding that of the governor). A dependent department was defined as one in which the highway director was selected directly by the governor, was appointed without restrictions, and served at the pleasure of the governor.[9]

9The independent state highway departments are found in Arizona, Arkansas, Colorado, Delaware, Florida, Georgia, Idaho, Indiana, Iowa, Maine, Massachusetts, Michigan, Mississippi, Missouri, Montana, New Hampshire, New Mexico, North Carolina, South Carolina, Texas, Utah, Washington, Wisconsin, and Wyoming. The dependent departments are found in Alabama, Alaska, Hawaii, Illinois, Kentucky, Nebraska, New Jersey, New York, North Dakota, Ohio, Pennsylvania, Rhode Island, and Tennessee. The partially dependent departments are found in California, Connecticut, Kansas, Louisiana, Maryland, Minnesota, Nevada, Oklahoma, Oregon, South Dakota, Vermont, Virginia, and West Virginia. From Robert S. Friedman, "State Politics and Highways," in Herbert Jacob and Kenneth N. Vines, eds., *Politics in the American States* (Boston: Little, Brown and Co., 1965), pp. 411–46.

State highway boards are common, and the powers of these boards vary according to state. In a number of states, board members must represent particular regions or areas within the state, a requirement which arises from political necessity and is justified on the grounds that local interests know their road needs better than do "statewide" interests. This appointment pattern tends to assure greater support for the state highway program and provides an important patronage source for local and county power structures. Highway boards often include representatives of key highway interests in the states, following a typical pattern of board composition in important functional areas in state and local government. The elimination of highway boards, incidentally, does not necessarily mean a depletion of influence by "highway interests," for the boards constitute only one means by which highway backers affect the course of highway policy.

Highway department funding provides an indication of their power. In 1971, of the predicted $20+ billion in total highway receipts, state highway bureaucracies controlled over $17 billion, at one point or another. This figure includes the sums the state highway departments spend directly, money received from the federal government (over $5 billion), and funds turned over to local governments. State highway budgets are likely to be exceeded only by state education expenditures, and highway outlays may constitute one-fifth or more of all state spending. This financial base of state highway agencies makes them formidable forces in state politics.

In addition, the state highway department may be an important source for job patronage. Although state roads agencies contract out construction work, they do maintain highways and perform a variety of administrative tasks. This means the employment of a large number of people. In some states, highway jobs constitute a chief source of patronage for political parties, especially county party units. Job patronage can serve to strengthen the political foundation of the highway effort and increase its support in the legislature and in local communities.

States also have public utility commissions. These commissions regulate intrastate transportation, including trucks, buses, street railways, interurban railroads, and aviation. State public utility commissions have multi-member boards and administrative staffs; the boards may be appointed by the governor (the predominant method), elected directly by the voters, or appointed by the state legislature. In two states, the public utility agency is headed by a director and not a board.

Nearly all states have aeronautics or aviation commissions or agencies. These agencies may regulate intrastate airlines, own and operate airports, channel federal airport money to localities, and plan airport and aviational development programs. The control of interstate aviation and other forms of interstate transportation is a federal, not a state, responsibility.

Local Government

Local governments administer three important transportation functions: highways, mass transit, and airports. In highways, local agencies tend to be overshadowed by the state and national governments, but they can be considered the dominant force in the federal system in some areas of mass transit and the airport.

American local governments have local highway and street construction responsibilities. In cities, this responsibility may be lodged administratively in a department of public works; in counties, townships, and towns, it may be assigned to a highway commissioner or a roads superintendent. As is common in the states, local highway departments may be headed by a board. It is estimated that nearly $3 billion was available in 1971 to local highway agencies for roads purposes. It should be noted that there is a tendency for local highway agencies to shift the roads burden upward in the administrative hierarchy: townships seek to unload their roads on counties, and counties attempt to pass off theirs on the states. Furthermore, the states tend to push roads into categories that qualify for federal assistance.

Local government agencies run all of the subway and rail rapid transit systems in the country; also, a number of local governments own bus systems, especially in the larger cities. Local governments may also regulate privately owned bus transit systems (in the United States, most such bus systems are privately owned), a function shared with state regulatory agencies.

Organizationally, subway and rail rapid transit systems are operated by special districts, usually known as authorities. This is a form of local government organization. The following agencies run the rail systems for their respective cities: in Boston, the Massachusetts Bay Transportation Authority; in New York City, the Metropolitan Transportation Authority in conjunction with the New York City Transit Authority; in Chicago, the Chicago Transit Authority; in Philadelphia, the Southeastern Pennsylvania Transportation Authority; and in Cleveland, the Cleveland Transit Board. Only in Cleveland can the transit agency be considered a part of the general-purpose city government; also, the Metropolitan Transportation Authority is technically part of the New York state government, of course a general-purpose unit. The two urban subway-rail systems currently under construction are both controlled by special districts, including one created by interstate compact; these are the Bay Area Rapid Transit District (San Francisco) and the Washington (D.C.) Metropolitan Area Transit Authority. The latter agency was formed by interstate compact, representing an agreement among the states of Maryland and Virginia and the District of Columbia, and approved by the U. S. Congress.

The Bay Area Rapid Transit District, called BART, represents an important breakthrough in public administration. The BART experience constitutes a fine example of intergovernmental cooperation, political responsibility, and political-administrative unity. BART was established by the San Francisco Bay Area Rapid Transit District Act, a special act of the California state legislature. The legislation created a five-county district: the counties of Alameda, Contra Costa, Marin, San Francisco (city and county), and San Mateo. Marin and San Mateo counties withdrew in 1962, and this was permitted by the original legislation. Counties, furthermore, may be added to the district. The agency held its organization meeting in November of 1957.

BART is run by a board, composed of 12 members, and a staff, headed by a general manager. Board members are appointed by the county supervisors and "city selection committees" composed of mayors of incorporated communities; this method follows the "constituent unit" principle, considered by experts to be the most effective way of running special districts (it promotes political responsibility to general-purpose local governments, especially elected officials in these governments). The board membership is comprised of four appointees each from the counties of Alameda and Contra Costa and four appointees from the city of San Francisco.

The general manager and other major administrative officers are appointed by and serve at the pleasure of the board. Although final policy determinations are made by the board, the board and the administrative staff work together in developing the transit system. The board has the power to tax, issue bonds, and fix rates and charges in order to finance the system. BART receives grants from the federal government; the main role of the state has been to authorize taxing and other financing powers for the agency. The ultimate control rests with the community.

The estimated cost of the basic system to be built by BART is slightly over $1 billion; the system will cover 75 miles, nearly all of which is either completed or under construction.

Nearly all of the nation's major airports are run by local agencies. These include most of the big metropolitan airports in the country; a few are operated by the federal government or private enterprise. Some states also own airports, but these are not considered major ones by the Airport Operators Council International, the municipal airport public interest group. The administrative responsibility for airport facilities may rest with a department of city government (for example, the Department of Airports in Los Angeles) or a special district (the Massachusetts Port Authority in Boston).

Metropolitan Transportation Planning Organizations

The Federal Aid Highway Act of 1962 required, in effect, that all metropolitan areas have transportation planning processes no later than mid-1965; the alternative was the loss of federal highway funds. As a result, all metropolitan areas now have such a process. Its purpose is threefold: to stimulate general transportation planning (not just highway planning); to link transportation planning to comprehensive land-use planning; and to bring local governments and community interests into highway planning and development.

The transportation planning process is to be carried on by the states and metropolitan area local governments. The basic inputs come from the state highway bureaucracy and local general-purpose governments. Antihighway forces initially saw this legislation as a means of corralling the free-wheeling state highway commissions; some saw it as a means of freeing blacks, minorities, and others from the threat of the highway bulldozer. Although no one can say for sure, it may have had some of these effects. At present, portions of the interstate system are being held up in 11 cities: Baltimore, Boston, Charleston (W. Va.), Cleveland, Detroit, Hartford, New York (a 27-mile segment), Philadelphia, Pittsburgh, Providence, and the District of Columbia (a 24-mile segment).

The transportation planning process may be carried on administratively by one of the following organizations: a metropolitan planning commission; a metropolitan council of governments; an organization especially created for transportation planning; or a pre-existing organization, other than a planning commission or council of governments, that was assigned the new function. In the larger metropolitan areas, the metropolitan planning commission or the council of governments organizational form seems to prevail as the agency responsible for the transportation planning process. However, within these two organizational forms, the particular administrative structure and arrangements vary by area.

In Philadelphia, the transportation planning process is under the

Delaware Valley Regional Planning Commission. The key forces in the Philadelphia area transportation planning process are the Pennsylvania Department of Transportation, which runs the state's highways, and the metropolitan area local governments. A similar situation exists in Pittsburgh, where the transportation planning process function is assigned to the Southwestern Pennsylvania Regional Planning Commission. In the nation's capital, the process is handled by the Metropolitan Washington Council of Governments, and specifically by its transportation planning board.

The metropolitan transportation planning process agencies have tended to avoid controversial issues, namely contested freeways; this may be reflective of bureaucratic behavior generally. Still, some patterns are emerging. The planning process has not substantially affected the power of highway bureaucracies, including their power to locate freeways in cities. Most metropolitan area freeway projects are proceeding; where such projects are being challenged, it is unclear whether the reason lies in the transportation planning process. For example, the Delaware Valley Regional Planning Commission has ducked the controversial Crosstown Expressway issue; if pressed for a vote, at least the suburban and the highway representatives could be expected to favor this or an alternative freeway. In another metropolitan area, where a vote was actually taken on a controversial city freeway, the transportation planning process agency voted for it; the vote represented a victory for the suburbs and the highway bureaucracy (which had been pressing for the freeway for years); only the city delegates voted against it. In this case, the disputed highway was to run from the suburbs into the city, through a relatively low-income area. It should be noted that the combined suburban and highway department strength on the transportation planning process agency is likely to outweigh that of the central city. Still, in most areas, cooperation, not conflict, has been the rule.[10]

THE POLITICS OF TRANSPORTATION POLICY ADMINISTRATION

The previous section has covered the politics of transportation administration to some extent. The purpose of this section is to present systematically the different interests and groups directly concerned with basic administrative and policy decisions in transportation agencies. In the next section, the stress is on the political and public policy ramifica-

[10]See the following study of transportation planning processes in over a dozen metropolitan areas: David E. Boyce et al., *Metropolitan Plan Evaluation Methodology* (Philadelphia: University of Pennsylvania Institute for Environmental Studies, 1969). The study was prepared for the Federal Highway Administration.

tions of alternative administrative organizations in transportation. The present section deals only with highways and mass transit.

Highway Policy Interests

Those groups with the greatest interest in highway policy administration are:

1. the highway bureaucracies at all levels in the political system;
2. the automotive industry;
3. the rubber industry;
4. the petroleum industry;
5. highway users;
6. motorists;
7. road contractors;
8. the trucking industry;
9. the railroad industry; and
10. legislators on legislative roads committees.

All of these groups except legislators on roads committees are organized into interest groups; legislators are organized into an interest group (the National Legislative Conference), but this group includes more than the members of roads committees. All of the organized groups have lobby organizations in Washington, and the majority of them have state or local (perhaps both) outlets; all work with administrative and legislative interests with highway responsibilities.

The highway bureaucracies include state and local highway departments and the Federal Highway Administration in the Department of Transportation. State highway officials possibly have the greatest collective power of any organized interest in highways; their chief resources are the state highway bureaucracies and technical expertise. State highway administrators are organized through the American Association of State Highway Officials, a public interest group. It should be noted that the organization of state highway officials does not work closely with other state public interest groups, namely the Council of State Governments, a broad-based state public interest group, and the National Governors' Conference. The relations between the state highway officials and the Council of State Governments are cool, and there is some hostility between the highway officials and the governors' interest group. The reason is disagreement over the use of highway trust fund money.

Automobile makers are organized into the Automobile Manufacturers Association; the rubber industry into the Rubber Manufacturers Association; and the petroleum industry into the American Petroleum Institute. These are all private interest groups, and they represent the "big three" backers of highway policy. They supported the 1956 federal highway legislation, the landmark measure that financed the interstate system and set up the Highway Trust Fund; the big three also provide considerable chunks of money to promote the highway cause.

Highway users are organized into the Highway Users Federation, an umbrella organization that receives most of its funds from the big three industries but which has a wide ranging membership. The Highway Users Federation is the highway interests' public relations and public education arm; it is an interest group, with state and local outlets called highway users conferences, which is a basic force in highways. The main motorists' interest group is the American Automobile Association (AAA), an active participant in public highway councils. The Triple A boasts that it was instrumental in gaining enactment of the first national highway act (1916) and that it played a key role in the passage of the 1956 interstate funding legislation. It has local clubs and branches.

Road contractors are organized into the American Road Builders' Association, an important ally of the highway interests; truckers are represented by the American Trucking Associations, Inc., a federation of state trucking groups and a key highway interest group; and the railroads are organized into the Association of American Railroads.

The railroads are the only group of the 10 that does not generally support highway policy, ambitious highway financing programs, and the separate highway trust fund. The 1956 highway bill dealt the railroads a major blow, as they were the only important interest to work against its enactment; some cynics suspect them of stirring antifreeway forces since then. The railroad lobby opposes the current Highway Trust Fund and feels the fund's proceeds should be used for rail and other nonhighway transportation purposes. Organized railroads argue that automobiles are chief polluters of the air and that highways disrupt the environment, destroy low-income housing, hurt minorities, and lead to congestion. Furthermore, the railroads believe they can make a substantial contribution to the alleviation of these problems, more so if a single transportation trust fund were established.[11] Organized truckers and organized railroads, incidentally, are key antagonists over transportation policy in state capitals and in Washington.[12]

---

[11]America's Sound Transportation Review Organization, *The American Railroad Industry: A Prospectus* (Washington, D.C.: Association of American Railroads, 1970), pp. 24–5. (This is called the ASTRO report; it has been endorsed by the Association of American Railroads; its support of a transportation trust fund has been labeled "deceptive" by the American Trucking Associations.)

[12]Andrew Hacker, "Pressure Politics in Pennsylvania: The Truckers vs. The Railroads," in Alan F. Westin, ed., *The Uses of Power* (New York: Harcourt, Brace & World, 1962), pp. 323–76.

The most important legislators in highway policy and administration are on roads committees in national and state legislatures. They include key members of both substantive and appropriations committees and subcommittees in both houses of national and state legislative assemblies. In some instances, legislators seek out roads committee assignments because of their ties with highway interests or because of investments they have that are affected by highways. Such legislators represent basic forces in the roads policy and administrative processes; for example, they may be active in opposing comprehensive transportation departments. Significantly, the National Legislative Conference does not endorse a single trust fund, as does its sister group, the National Governors' Conference; this may be because of the influence of the highway backers in state legislatures.[13]

A number of citizens', conservation, and environmental groups now oppose highway policy, particular aspects of it, or specific highway projects. Such policy or projects may come from legislative or administrative determinations, or both. Some of these groups have been formed recently, and many are organized at the local level, where they have come out against specific highway proposals. Neighborhood citizens' associations have been especially active in opposing particular freeways.

The Sierra Club, the National Wildlife Federation, and the Citizens Committee on Natural Resources are among the groups that have been cool to highways and wary of the Highway Trust Fund. The Emergency Committee on the Transportation Crisis has been organized specifically to fight highway bureaucracies; it has been most active in Washington, D.C.

It would appear that the power of the various citizens', conservation, and environmental groups is growing, at least in certain respects. Such interests, however, are not likely to have much voice in highway administration, for roads administrators are seldom anxious to meet with them. The power of these groups is more apt to be exercised as a veto over certain types of action rather than through initiatory action; it is also mainly *ad hoc* power since it is usually related to particular projects, decisions, and issues. The influence of antihighway forces does not rival the more "positive," continuing, and broad-ranging administrative and legislative strength of the major groups generally supportive of highway policy.

---

[13]See National Legislative Conference (Intergovernmental Relations Committee), *Policy Positions and Final Report* (Washington, D.C.: Council of State Governments, 1971); and *Policy Positions of the National Governors' Conference, 1971–72* (Washington, D.C.: Council of State Governments, 1971), pp. 49–50.

Mass Transit Interests

In mass transit administration, the major interests are:
1. urban mass transportation bureaucracies;
2. bus companies;
3. city governments;
4. mayors;
5. manufacturers of railway equipment; and
6. legislators on committees with mass transit duties.

The most powerful of the urban mass transportation bureaucracies are at the local level; these include the transportation authorities that run the subways and urban rail systems, such as BART and the Metropolitan Transportation Authority in New York. Urban mass transit authorities are organized into the Institute for Rapid Transit, a Washington-based interest group. The Urban Mass Transportation Administration of the Department of Transportation is also an important mass transit bureaucracy, although its power in urban transportation is less awesome than the Federal Highway Administration's is in highways. Some states have urban mass transportation divisions, usually in state departments of transportation; at present, these agencies wield little influence.

Bus companies and municipal transportation bureaucracies are organized into the American Transit Association, a Washington lobby. There is keen competition between the American Transit Association and the Institute for Rapid Transit for the allegiance of municipal transportation interests. The American Transit Association played a leading role in the enactment of the national urban mass transit program in 1970; its members of course will receive substantial subsidies under this measure.

City governments are represented by the National League of Cities; their mayors by the United States Conference of Mayors. Both are public interest groups, and both work closely with the federal Department of Transportation, especially with DOT's mass transit supporters. The cities' lobby wants highway funds released for use in cities and has sought to develop an administrative base in DOT toward this end; it was a key force behind the Urban Mass Transportation Assistance Act of 1970.

Manufacturers of railway equipment are organized into the Railway Progress Institute; the group includes companies that make transit cars. The Railway Progress Institute backed the 1970 urban mass transportation measure.

The final participants in the mass transit administrative and policy processes are national legislators and, to some extent, state legislators on legislative committees that consider urban transportation bills and funding levels. These legislators can be expected to be more powerful as added public funds are pumped into the mass transit industry.

POLITICAL AND POLICY EFFECTS OF ADMINISTRATIVE ORGANIZATION IN TRANSPORTATION

The most visible organizational issue in transportation administration today is the location of the highway department in the bureaucracy. For years, highway departments operated with virtual independence at the state level and, to a considerable extent, in Washington. Recently, the picture has changed somewhat, or so it appears. The federal government has shifted the highway bureaucracy into a comprehensive department which has been assigned many transportation tasks; 30 percent of the states have done the same, and a host of others are considering similar moves. Prior to the development of DOTs, some had urged the states to put the powerful highway agencies more directly under the control of the chief executive, and some states sought to do this.

Several reasons account for recent trends. First, the development of a single department of transportation or the positioning of the highway function under the governor is designed to promote executive accountability. The chief executive is held politically responsible by the voters and the legislature for the administration of the executive branch; increasing central control over highways would help make this political responsibility a reality. Second, centralization should improve prospects for coordination. A single executive would control highways and perhaps other transportation activities; highway boards, with many executives, would go. Third, unity of command would result. Fourth, under a comprehensive department of transportation, the chief executive's span of control would be more reasonable, more realistic. Fifth, under a comprehensive department, general transportation planning would be possible; highway planning, previously carried out separately, would be coordinated with other transportation planning. This reasoning is consistent with the early principles of public administration (see Chapter 8).

Two issues have arisen which affect the politics of reorganization. First, urban mass transit supporters believe administrative reorganization will help their cause. They favor a balanced transportation system, and they are convinced that reorganization will advance that end. Second, in some states, a power struggle is going on between the highway bureaucracy and the governor. A single department of transportation, the elimination of the roads commission as highway policy-maker, the substitution for the commission of a secretary appointed by the governor, and the lowering of the administrative level of the highway agency would represent a political victory for the governor. Highways would be "put in their place," and the governor could assume command of the highway function. The politics of administrative reorganization in highways is particularly important in the light of the amount of money at stake and the administrative isolation of highway funds. This is true at both the national and state levels.

Key interests back highways; key interests back mass transit. The disagreement between highway and mass transit supporters is not so much one among individuals as it is among organized groups; individuals on both sides tend to reflect group positions. Essentially, highway bureaucracies and supporting interests want to be "left alone"; as they see it, they have a job to do, and they want to be free to use "their" money to do it. Mass transit forces and governors reject this reasoning. They want the power of highway interests brought in tow and subordinated to broader ends; most important, they want the billions of dollars made available to highway bureaucracies each year to be used for mass transit and other nonhighway transportation, as well as for highways. Administrative reorganization is their vehicle. Only time will tell whether they will be successful. In the meantime, highway bureaucracies remain strong.

The creation of a comprehensive department of transportation does not mean the emasculation of the highway function. At least three alternative outcomes are conceivable. First, the highway bureaucracy could operate as a coequal with other transportation bureaucracies inside the transportation department. Second, highway bureaucracies could operate independently of other transportation agencies in the comprehensive department. Third, highway bureaucracies could dominate the new department. In the latter two cases, the reorganization would represent little change from the previous situation. Furthermore, in practice, the latter two possibilities are at least as likely a development as the first.

Bureaucracies represent power. Power has economic and many other bases. A change in organization does not necessarily represent a change in the distribution of power. The transfer of highway bureaucracies to transportation departments has not normally been accompanied by a shift in funding; specifically, it has not been coupled with a freeing of highway funds for nonhighway transportation purposes. As long as highway agencies have independent funding, they will operate with some degree of administrative independence, whether in or outside a department of transportation. In a department of transportation, often the most a secretary or mass transit interests can do is "bargain" with the highway people; the new administrative structure may give them new tools by which to bargain, but it does not mean that the secretary (or the governor, or the President) can "tell" the highway bureaucracy what to do. The principle of this matter was a central point in Richard Neustadt's *Presidential Power*.[14] If this principle were not true, the

---

[14]Richard Neustadt, *Presidential Power* (New York: John Wiley & Sons, Inc., 1960).

highway bureaucracies of the nation would have most likely waged a fierce battle against departments of transportation; actually, they have not.

Outside of the transportation department movement, the organization and administration of the highway agency in states has been an issue for years. A number of political skirmishes have surrounded this matter.[15] Many actors in transportation politics assume that this or that administrative structure will produce this or that result, policy, or power distribution pattern. What do the studies show? Thomas Dye finds that states that organize the highway function independently of the governor spend more for roads; public outlays for highways in states with independent highway organizations run $64 per capita, while states in which the governor controls highways spend only $56 per capita.[16] On the other hand, Robert Friedman found no relationship between the formal administrative organization of highway activities and comparative spending patterns in states.[17] Thus, it would seem that it is unclear whether highway spending policy can be attributed in any way to variances in administrative organization.

It should be noted that, among highway administrators, the amount of money allocated to roads is important; perhaps equally important is control. Highway bureaucracies support ambitious funding for roads, but they also want control of roads funds. Above a minimum funding level, it is likely that highway departments would value control more than added funding. Full control over a smaller amount of money may be preferable to limited discretion over larger sums. In this light, the independent organization of highways is not merely a strategy of wringing more money out of the public; it may be more of a means of maintaining control of whatever money is available.

SUMMARY

This chapter has discussed the administration of transportation policy. It started by examining the substance of urban transportation and highway policy and the practical effects of this policy. It then studied the administrative patterns in transportation in national, state, and local governments and in metropolitan transportation planning organizations.

---

[15]For a case study of highway department politics in Vermont, see R. Joseph Novogrod, Marshall Edward Dimock, and Gladys Ogden Dimock, *Casebook in Public Administration* (New York: Holt, Rinehart and Winston, 1969), pp. 33–40.

[16]Thomas R. Dye, *Politics, Economics, and the Public: Policy Outcomes in the American States* (Chicago: Rand McNally & Co., 1966), p. 163.

[17]Robert S. Friedman, "State Politics and Highways," in *Politics in the American States*, p. 440.

This was followed by a review of the major forces influencing the highway and mass transportation administrative processes. The chapter closed with an analysis of the political and public policy ramifications of alternative administrative organizations in transportation.

Transportation administration is usefully viewed in a political context. A number of internal and external forces affect the administration of the transportation function, and public transportation agencies help shape the broader political processes within which they operate. This represents the dynamics of transportation policy administration.

5

ENVIRONMENTAL POLICY ADMINISTRATION

INTRODUCTION

One of the leading contemporary issues is that of the environment. Increasing attention is being focused on air and water pollution and the means of curtailing it. In America, the basic task of reducing and eliminating pollution has been assigned to government. Government determines what constitutes pollution, sets standards by which pollution levels should be judged and controlled, develops plans for fighting pollution, and enforces pollution control measures. Government formulates pollution control policy, and government administers pollution control programs.

Pollution control is primarily an administrative activity. Legislation in the field can provide general directions and broad guidelines, but most specific determinations and much policy-making activity are in the hands of administrators. Thus, the legislative role is somewhat restricted, although by no means unimportant.

Part of the reason for this is that government only recently moved decisively into the field, and there is considerable emphasis on experimentation and administrative judgment. In addition, technical expertise plays a greater part in pollution control than in many other policy fields, and this dictates a substantial administrative input.

Pollution control policy is an intergovernmental matter. All levels of government have pollution control powers. The national government has been assuming increasing responsibility for various aspects of pollution control, but the role of state and local government has also expanded rapidly in recent years. Basic pollution control policy is determined at the national level, although the bulk of the administrative activity is at the state and local levels.

The most notable trend in pollution control policy administration has been the administrative reorganization of pollution control activities at different levels in the political system. The goal has been greater coordination, and the means has been administrative unification and consolidation. The philosophy has been that the attack on air and water pollution and associated environmental problems should take on a singleness of purpose. The creation of a lone agency on the environment is viewed as a basic step in this battle. Until recently, the various pollution control programs were uniformly dispersed administratively in both national and subnational governments. Now, the national and some state and local governments have a single environmental agency with powers over most or all pollution control matters.

This chapter begins with an examination of the general problem of environmental pollution, including the present extent of pollution and the costs of pollution control. It then reviews: pollution control policy, concentrating on basic legislation in the field; administrative organization patterns at the national, state, and local levels; and the experience in, and the prospects for, the coordination of pollution control programs with the activities of other administrative agencies in the federal system. This chapter closes with a general discussion of the problems encountered so far in the development and administration of pollution control activities.

POLLUTION: THE PROBLEM AND ITS CONTROL

Pollution can come from a variety of sources, and it is measured in a variety of ways. It can come from automobiles, for example, or from the disposal of industrial or municipal wastes. Pollution can be measured by its effect on air—or water—quality. It is safe to say that the term "environment" has taken on a broader meaning in recent years, and this has had its effects on what is considered pollution. Government is being asked to deal with an ever-increasing number of environmental problems, including population and land-use control, in addition to the conventional air and water pollution control activities.

The key sources of air pollution are: transportation, primarily the automobile; fuel combustion in stationary sources; industrial processes; solid waste disposal; and miscellaneous. Transportation sources contribute over 144 million tons of air pollutants a year (1969), stationary fuel combustion sources 44 million tons, industrial processes nearly 40 million tons, solid waste disposal sources about 12 million tons, and miscellaneous sources 41 million tons.

A general increase in the degree of air pollution occurred from 1968 to 1969, and the largest jump was registered in the miscellaneous category, primarily because of forest fires. The greatest single polluter of the air is the automobile, and transportation contributes more to air pollution than all of the other categories combined; yet, pollution from transportation sources declined slightly from 1968 to 1969. Fuel combustion refers to coal and oil burning; industrial processes include pollution by factories, mills, refineries, and power plants; and solid waste disposal includes open burning at municipal dumps.

The causes of water pollution are several. On a national scale, industrial wastes are the major contributor, and these are followed by municipal and agricultural wastes. However, in some regions of the country, municipal wastes are the biggest source of water pollution; in others, agricultural wastes. The national government has estimated that only 10 percent of the nation's watersheds are unpolluted or only slightly polluted. About a quarter of the watersheds were found to be "predominantly" polluted (watersheds in which 50 percent or more of the stream miles are polluted); another 50 percent were "extensively" polluted (20–49.9 percent of stream miles polluted), and another 18 percent were "locally" polluted (10–19.9 percent polluted). Wastes may or may not be treated before being discharged into waterways. The number of fish killed by water pollution is on the rise, as is the number of oil spills into U.S. waters.

The following are also part of the environmental pollution picture: radiation exposure, stemming from natural "background" sources (cosmic rays and radioactive material found naturally in the soil, water, air, and human body) and medical applications; the effects of pesticides, including DDT; and the effects of toxic substances, including metals such as mercury, lead, copper, and manganese. Environmental agencies have increasingly been concerned with wildlife protection, focusing especially on the effects of habitat changes, the loss of wetlands, the urbanization of open space, and agricultural practices on wildlife populations.

The economic costs of continued pollution range into the billions of dollars each year; noneconomic costs, including esthetic costs, are also enormous. The costs of pollution control are equally high. In three pollution categories alone, the estimated cost of pollution control between 1970 and 1975 is $105 billion; 23 percent of this sum is needed for air pollution control (exclusive of solid waste management), 36 percent for water pollution control, and 41 percent for solid waste management. The bulk of this money is tagged for the development of sewage treatment and collection and for solid waste disposal systems; only a small percentage of the total is destined to air and water pollution regulation and standard setting. These figures include both public and private costs.

POLLUTION CONTROL POLICY

Because most general government and police powers under our system have been assigned to subnational governments, pollution control has traditionally been a state and local responsibility. However, for years, the pollution control policy of subnational units has primarily amounted to spending funds for sewage treatment and waste disposal facilities, essentially a function of local governments in urban areas. Little regulation of polluters by state and local governments could be cited in the early years, and it was not until the national government began to move decisively in environmental control that state and local policy began to change.

Basic federal legislation in water pollution can be traced to the Water Pollution Control Act of 1948. This measure gave the national government some power over pollution in interstate waters and authorized loans for local sewage treatment plant construction. The Water Pollution Control Act Amendments of 1956 extended federal authority over the pollution of interstate waterways and made it easier to gain compliance with abatement standards; in addition, this legislation established a grant program for local sewage treatment systems. The sewage treatment grant program survived a political assault by Eisenhower administration forces (they wanted the program returned to the states), has prospered ever since, and for years represented the primary federal water pollution control effort.[1]

[1] The Joint Federal-State Action Committee urged that the sewage treatment grant program be scrapped; Congress rejected this recommendation. See Thomas R. Dye, *Politics in States and Communities* (Englewood Cliffs, N.J.: Prentice-Hall, 1969), pp. 63–4.

In 1961 legislation expanded the federal role in water pollution control and enlarged sewage treatment plant authorizations. The Water Quality Act of 1965, which authorized the establishment and enforcement of water quality standards, represents the keystone of national water quality policy. Under the 1965 legislation, the basic responsibility for standard setting and enforcement rests with the states. Still, the national government provides a substantial input into both the standard setting and enforcement processes and may take unilateral action under certain circumstances.

Although Congress authorized money for air pollution research and other purposes in 1955, the first major federal air pollution control legislation came with the enactment of the Clean Air Act of 1963. This legislation provided for the regulation of interstate air pollution and authorized a stepped up state and local government air pollution control grant program. In the Motor Vehicle Air Pollution Control Act of 1965, Congress authorized the establishment of standards for the emission of substances from new motor vehicles. The air pollution control amendments of 1965 included assistance for certain solid waste disposal program purposes. The Air Quality Act of 1967 provided for federally designated air quality regions and assistance to states to set and implement air pollution control standards. Under the 1967 measure, standards were to be established by the states and to be approved by the national government.

In 1970, the federal role in air quality was strengthened. The Clean Air Amendments of 1970 called for the federal establishment of national air quality standards, stringent standards for major new pollution sources (new automobiles), and emission standards for facilities producing hazardous substances. The 1970 measure also established a framework for states to set standards for air pollution stemming from existing sources. At present, the national government appears to have the primary responsibility for air pollution control, and the states the primary role in water pollution control. However, both levels have key duties in each area.

Recent federal policy has stressed the need for proper sewage treatment and solid waste disposal facilities and practices. In fiscal year 1971, the national government appropriated $1 billion for sewage treatment facilities; this money goes primarily to municipalities for the construction of sewage treatment plants. The Resource Recovery Act of 1970 advanced federal funds for recycling system demonstration purposes and expanded the federal solid waste treatment program. Sewage treatment facilities are used for liquid sewage, and solid waste disposal facilities are used for discarded containers, bottles, paper, and other solid wastes. While the regulation of air and water pollution is primarily a federal-state effort, the sewage and solid waste programs are essentially a federal-local matter.

Basic federal legislation in the pollution control field has not been contained in a single act covering all aspects of environmental quality. Separate enactments are found in air pollution control, water pollution control, and other environmental quality areas. There is not in this sense a single environmental policy. However, in 1969, Congress passed the National Environmental Policy Act, which established a Council on Environmental Quality and required "environmental impact" statements on proposed federal legislation and projects. The Council on Environmental Quality is composed of three members appointed by the President; it assists the President in the preparation of the annual Environmental Quality Report (required by this legislation), gathers information on environmental quality, reviews and appraises various federal pollution control programs and activities, and performs other functions.

The National Environmental Policy Act also directed all federal agencies to include in all proposals for new legislation or new actions significantly affecting the environment a written assessment of the following: the environmental impact of the proposal; any adverse environmental effects which cannot be avoided with the proposal's implementation; alternatives to the proposal; the relationship between short- and long-term environmental effects of the proposal; and any irreversible and irretrievable commitments of environmental resources needed for the proposal's implementation.

State and local air and water pollution regulation policy has tended to follow the federal lead, and its sewage treatment and solid waste disposal activity has been stimulated by federal assistance and guidance. All states now have legislative authority for air pollution control, and all states have developed and had approved standards for the regulation of pollution in interstate waterways.

ADMINISTRATIVE PATTERNS IN POLLUTION CONTROL

At the national level, pollution control policy is now administered in the Environmental Protection Agency (EPA). The Environmental Protection Agency was created in December of 1970; it is headed by an Administrator, who is appointed by the President but does not serve in the President's cabinet. EPA assumed responsibility for different environmental quality programs previously found in several federal departments. Among the key federal responsibilities transferred to EPA were the air pollution control program of the Department of Health,

Education, and Welfare and the water pollution control program of the Department of the Interior.

The Environmental Protection Agency organization chart is pictured in Figure 5.1. The basic line functions of EPA are assigned to assistant administrators: planning and management, enforcement (including the general counsel), media programs, categorical programs, and research and monitoring. The substantive programs of EPA are administered by the assistant administrator for media programs (air and water programs) and the assistant administrator for categorical programs (pesticides, radiation, and solid waste management). EPA has staff offices in the Offices of Congressional Affairs, Equal Opportunity, International Affairs, and Public Affairs. The agency works through ten regional offices.

EPA's budget for the fiscal year 1971 was approximately $1.3 billion, most of which was for sewage treatment facility construction grants; during this year, it had a staff of 7,192. The agency requested a budget for the fiscal year 1972 of $2.45 billion, a 90 percent jump over 1971 funding levels; it also requested a manpower hike of over 1,600. Two billion dollars of the 1972 request would represent grants for sewage treatment facility construction.

EPA estimated in 1971 that an additional $12 billion would be needed for municipal sewage treatment works over the next three years, and it requested $2 billion for each of these three years to meet the federal share of this amount. The agency has found that only about 40 percent of the nation's sewage treatment systems are adequate. Many sewage treatment plants are overloaded or in need of substantial upgrading, and some sewage systems provide no treatment of wastes prior to discharge.

In pollution regulation, EPA has made the greatest strides in water pollution control. EPA has approved the water quality standards of all the states, although some states' standards have been approved with exceptions. Under present law, these standards are for interstate or navigable waters, but EPA has encouraged the states to develop standards for intrastate waters as well, and a number of states have done so. As defined by EPA, water quality standards include both the criteria that set water quality or purity levels and plans for implementing these criteria. Although the standards may be adopted and enforced by EPA, EPA assumes that the standards will be enforced by the states, toward the end of abating water pollution. Implementation of water quality standards may be effected through joint federal-state conferences, during which representatives of EPA and the states seek to work out an acceptable pollution abatement program with industrial or municipal polluters.

FIGURE 5.1: Environmental Protection Agency

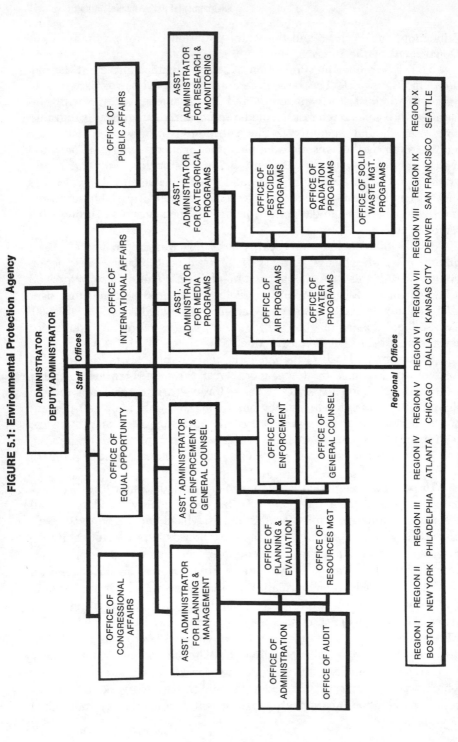

SOURCE: *United States Government Organization Manual 1971/72* (Washington, D.C.: Government Printing Office, 1971), p. 632.

With EPA backing, some states have moved with considerable force against polluters (Illinois and Pennsylvania are examples). EPA has also acted unilaterally in initiating enforcement proceedings under the new water quality standards, and these include actions taken against an industrial polluter in violation of the standards set for Spring River in Kansas and Oklahoma, and against industrial and municipal polluters in violation of Lake Erie's standards. Generally, EPA has found the enforcement conference to be an effective mechanism for handling complex and deepseated pollution problems.

The procedure for the adoption and implementation of air quality standards is shown in Figure 5.2. EPA designates air quality control regions, prepares air quality criteria, and publishes reports on control techniques. EPA expects the states to indicate their intent to set air quality standards within 90 days; the states have 180 days to set these standards, during which time public hearings are to be held, and another 180 days to adopt a plan for implementing the standards. The state standards and plans are to be submitted to EPA for review; after EPA approval, the states are expected to implement them.

FIGURE 5.2

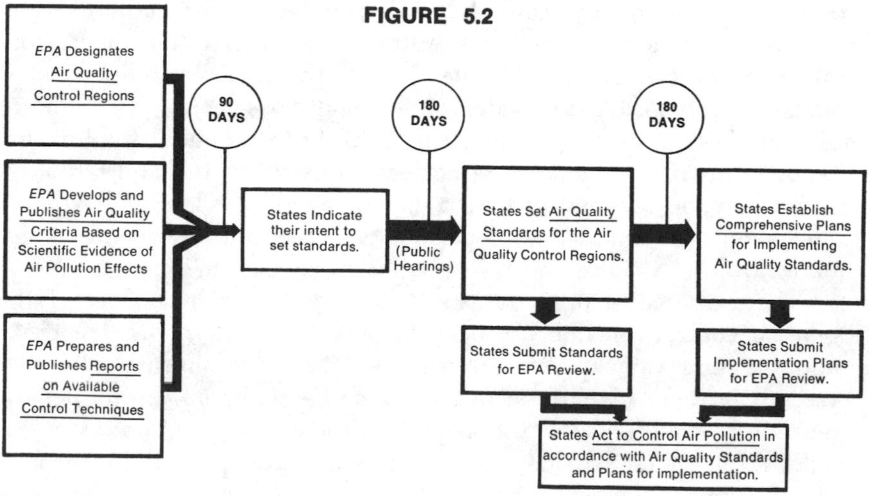

As of March 31, 1971, EPA had designated 235 air quality control regions and all states had at least one region. In a report issued in May of 1971, EPA noted that nearly all the states had signified their intention of adopting air quality standards for the designated regions; the adoption of standards and the formulation of implementation plans were to follow. Progress under this process has been slow and, to date, the EPA has not approved comprehensive air quality standards and an implementation plan for any state. It appears that EPA questions the ability of the states to prepare acceptable implementation plans.[2]

At this point, it is unclear what effect the air pollution control amendments of 1970 will have on the states' role in air quality standard setting and enforcement. Under this legislation, air pollution control is likely to become more of a federal matter, and the part that EPA plays in the process will be expanded. In fact, under previous federal legislation, the national government had certain enforcement authority, and this authority was strengthened in the 1970 measure. EPA has exercised this enforcement power and has used the conference procedure in the process; in one EPA action, the Union Carbide Corporation plant in Marietta, Ohio, agreed to cut its pollution emissions by 70 percent in a stipulated time period.

In the states, a number of agencies, departments, boards, and commissions typically have the pollution control power. Within a given state, the pollution control power may be divided between two or more agencies. In nearly half the states, a board or department of health has the air and water pollution control responsibilities.[3] Air quality control duties may otherwise be assigned to a state air pollution, air resources, or air quality control board, commission, or authority; and water quality to a water resources, water pollution, or water quality control board or commission. A state department of natural resources is sometimes responsible for water or air pollution control, or both. In addition, the state pesticides program is likely to be under the jurisdiction of a department or board of agriculture; solid wastes and radiology control may be administered by a health agency. All told, boards or commissions (as opposed to departments) have power over air pollution control in 12 states and water pollution control in 16.

The most recent organizational trend in state management of the pollution control function has been the creation of a single agency to handle air and water quality and perhaps other environmental activities. Presently, at least 12 states have given a single pollution control department the responsibility for the major environmental programs. This excludes those states that have placed air and water pollution control in a single nonenvironmental agency such as a department or board of health.

It is instructive to note that the states started to reorganize their

---

[2]*Progress in the Prevention and Control of Air Pollution: Annual Report of the Administrator of the Environmental Protection Agency to the Congress of the United States* (Washington, D.C.: U.S. Government Printing Office, 1971), p. 7.

[3]Information on state pollution control agencies is taken from *State Administrative Officials, Supplement II, The Book of the States, 1971* (Lexington, Ky.: Council of State Governments, 1971), pp. 69–71.

pollution control activity prior to the formation of the Environmental Protection Agency at the national level; furthermore, to date, only one state has adopted the federal agency title. This is unlike the situation in transportation in which the states generally formed state transportation departments after the federal government did; and the states usually adopted the same title, the department of transportation.

Comprehensive pollution control agencies in states go by different names. In New Jersey, it is the Department of Environmental Protection; in Minnesota, the Pollution Control Agency; in Alaska, the Department of Environmental Conservation; in North Carolina, the Department of Water and Air Resources; and in Washington (state), the Department of Ecology. In all cases, the new departments include air pollution and water pollution control programs; in some states, other programs including solid waste management, pesticides, natural resources, and land-use planning were transferred to the new agency.[4]

Two somewhat different reorganization patterns are evident. They are reflected in the experiences of New York and Washington. On Earth Day 1970, the State of New York passed legislation creating the Department of Environmental Conservation (DEC). The new department was handed not only the air and water pollution control functions but other environmental, several natural resources, and land-use planning programs as well. The other environmental programs included pesticides control, noise pollution control, and solid waste disposal regulation. The natural resources programs given to the agency were lands and forest, fish and wildlife, marine and coastal resources, mineral resources, and resource management. The agency also has several staff divisions (administration, communications and education, planning and research, and legal affairs), and works in cooperation with the Environmental Facilities Corporation, the State Natural and Historic Preserve Trust, and the Natural Heritage Trust. The department has nine environmental conservation regions, located throughout the state, is headed by a single commissioner, and is served by a State Environmental Board. The agency's chief line divisions are environmental quality (air and water pollution regulation) and environmental management (natural resources). DEC's organization chart is pictured in Figure 5.3.

The new agency in New York departs slightly from the organizational model that would be consistent with traditional public administration principles (see Chapter 8). It has a board that is more than advisory. The creation of this board, however, represents some advance

---

[4]For a discussion of state environmental planning and its link to land-use matters, see Elizabeth Haskell, "New Directions in State Environmental Planning," *Journal of the American Institute of Planners* vol. XXXVII, no. 4 (July 1971), pp. 253–8.

FIGURE 5.3: New York State Department of Environmental Conservation

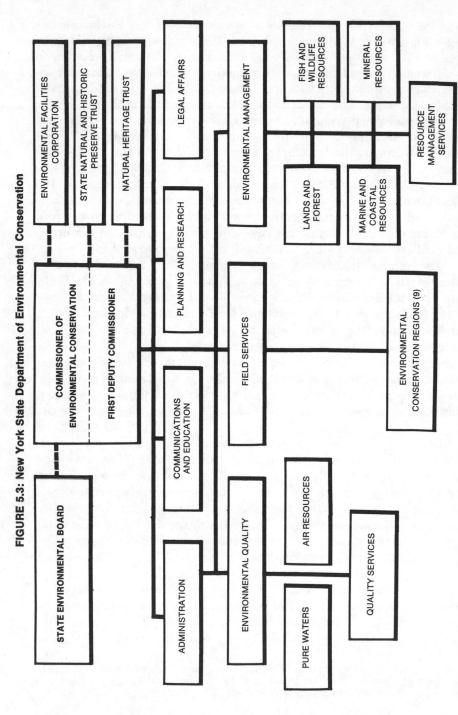

SOURCE: Elizabeth H. Haskell, Victoria Price, and others, *Managing the Environment; Nine States Look for New Answers* (Washington, D.C.: Elizabeth H. Haskell, 1971), p. 271.

over earlier practice in that it replaces three independent commissions in air resources, pesticides control, and water resources. The State Environmental Board advises the Department of Environmental Conservation and has the veto authority over departmental environmental standards, criteria, rules, and regulations. This veto authority could interfere with central, coordinated direction of the agency by either the governor of the state or the commissioner of the department. The board is justified on professional grounds, but it may have been included in the new agency's structure as a matter of political necessity.

A somewhat less ambitious reorganization has been effected in the State of Washington. Washington's Department of Ecology (DOE) was also created in 1970. The department's establishment was part of a general reorganization of the state executive branch. DOE has authority over water and air pollution control, solid waste management, and water resources. It does not have the wide ranging environmental, natural resources, and land-use planning powers of New York's DEC; nor does it have responsibility, for example, for pesticides control (which remained in the state's agriculture department) or most of the natural resources functions.

As in New York, Washington's DOE has a board which is known as the Ecological Commission. This is a seven member board that has both advisory and veto power. It advises the department and has veto authority over all substantive (nonprocedural) rules and regulations of the department, including water and air quality standards. An extra special majority vote of the board is required to override departmental proposals.

DOE's organizational structure is shown in Figure 5.4. DOE is headed by a director, who is responsible to the governor. Line assistants to the director are the deputy director and the assistant director. Staff offices are organized around governmental relationships, legal services, program reviews, legislative relationships, public affairs, and planning affairs. Significantly, the department is not organized according to substantive programs (air pollution control, for example) but administrative functions. The two line divisions are the administration and planning branch and the public services branch; each is headed by an executive assistant director. Administration and planning and public services represent functions that are performed for all the major programs administered by the department.

Not pictured on DOE's organizational chart is the Pollution Control Hearings Board, which is composed of three members, serves in a quasi-judicial capacity, and hears appeals concerning DOE and local air pollution control authority decisions. The Board represents a step between the environmental quality administrative agency and the courts, a procedure not characteristic of all states' pollution control mechanism.

The states have increasingly moved into the sewage treatment and solid waste disposal business, both of which have traditionally been local functions. In 1970, for instance, Maryland created the Maryland Environmental Service (MES), a state agency. MES has responsibility for liquid and solid waste disposal management and is authorized to construct and operate sewage and solid waste disposal systems; it may also contract with local governments or private parties to provide these services. The agency may provide these services when a local government or private firm fails to meet pollution standards, and then pass the cost along to the violator. Ohio's Water Development Authority and New York's Environmental Facilities Corporation also have certain

FIGURE 5.4: Washington Department of Ecology

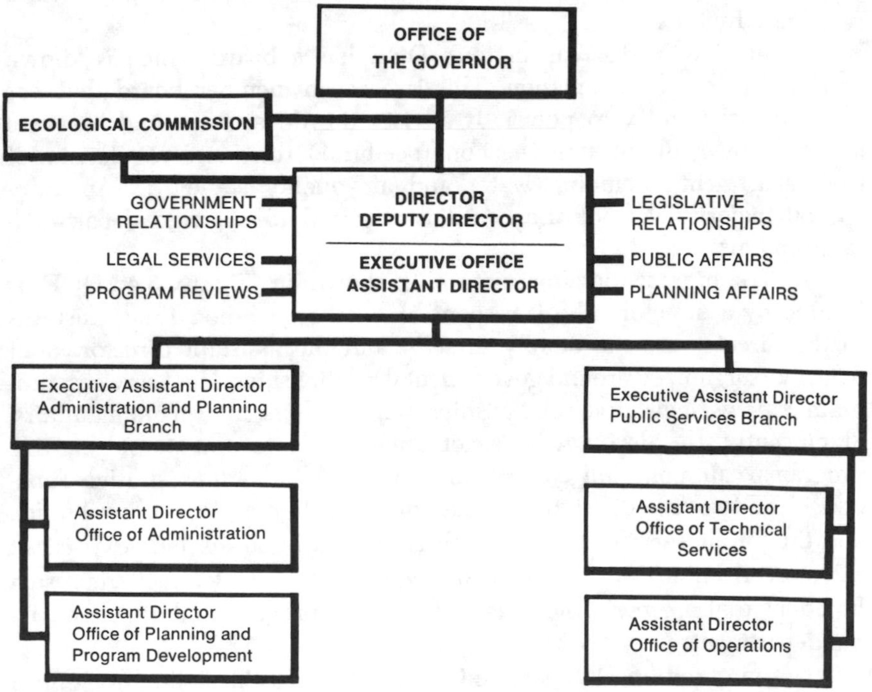

SOURCE: Elizabeth H. Haskell, Victoria Price, and others, *Managing the Environment: Nine States Look for New Answers* (Washington, D.C.: Elizabeth H. Haskell, 1971), p. 185.

waste management functions. The Maryland, Ohio, and New York agencies began operations within the last three years.

Progress made by the states in the development of water quality program elements, air quality program elements, and solid waste management planning is shown in Figure 5.5, Table 5.1, and Figure 5.6. Figure 5.5 shows which states have developed different water quality program elements. Interstate waterway standards are required for each state; Figure 5.5 indicates which states have had their standards fully or partially approved by the Environmental Protection Agency. Intrastate waterway standards are not required by Washington, but EPA has urged each state to develop them and all but seven states have done so.

Planning based on water quality standards is somewhat lagging. Most states have permit systems under which permits may be issued for municipal and industrial discharges into waterways. Some states have the authority to provide assistance to localities for municipal sewage treatment plant construction; in addition, a federal "bonus" may be given for the provision of state sewer grants. Most states routinely inspect local sewage treatment plant facilities and have state water quality monitoring systems.

TABLE 5.1
State Air Quality Program Elements, January 1971[1]

Legislative Authority	States with authority	States without authority
Adopt emission standards and promulgate other regulations	54	0
Require information on processes and potential emissions from sources of air pollution	39	15
Issue permits for construction of new sources of air pollution	38	16
Inspect facilities causing pollution	52	2
Require emission information from polluters and make it available to public	20	34
Require monitoring of emissions by polluters	13	41
Issue and enforce compliance orders	51	3
Enjoin standards violators	52	2
Take special, prompt action in case of air pollution emergencies	44	10
Regulate land use and transportation to meet air quality standards	5	49
Inspect automotive pollution control devices	16	38

[1] Includes District of Columbia, Guam, Puerto Rico, and U.S. Virgin Islands. In some cases, figures are approximations based on best available data.
SOURCE: *Environmental Quality: the Second Annual Report of the Council on Environmental Quality* (Washington, D.C.: Government Printing Office, 1971), p. 46. The Council received this information from the Environmental Protection Agency.

FIGURE 5.5
State Water Quality Program Elements, May 1971

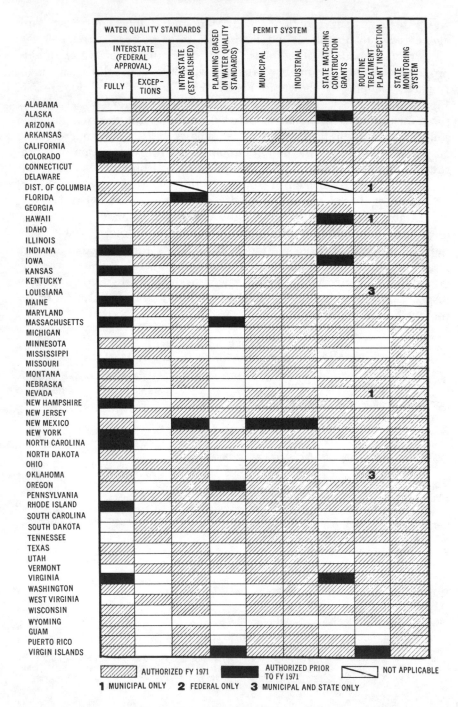

SOURCE: *Environmental Quality: the Second Annual Report of the Council on Environmental Quality* (Washington, D.C.: Government Printing Office, 1971), p. 45. The Council received this information from the Environmental Protection Agency.

FIGURE 5.6
Progress in State Solid Waste Management Plans, June 30, 1971

SOURCE: *Environmental Quality: the Second Annual Report of the Council on Environmental Quality* (Washington, D.C.: Government Printing Office, 1971), p. 48. The Council received this information from the Environmental Protection Agency.

Table 5.1 indicates the existence of state legislative authority for the different elements required by EPA in state air quality implementation plans. It can be seen that few states have the power to regulate land-use and transportation to meet air quality standards; to the extent that it exists, this is a local government matter. Figure 5.6 shows that all states have started the solid waste management planning process, although only 17 have completed their plans.

The states are stepping actively into the pollution control and waste management fields. In these areas, state administrative agencies are conducting both operating and planning programs. In the past, some of these activities have not been seen as belonging in the states; for example, waste management has normally been a local matter. Nevertheless, EPA seems convinced that the states are more apt to bring a broader, regional perspective to pollution control and related programs.[5] Recent federal policy has thrust states more prominently into waste management and other related areas, such as land-use planning.

Local governments may engage in a variety of pollution control activities. As in other areas, the states grant communities their power over the environment. Local air and water pollution control functions are most frequently found in city or county health departments. Air quality may be assigned to a local or regional air pollution control authority, the power to construct and operate sewage treatment facilities to a local or metropolitan sewer district or sanitation authority, and solid waste disposal services to a municipal sanitary engineering or public works department.

Pollution control functions are still administratively decentralized in local governments. Different environmental programs may well be under different governments, even in the same geographical area. Environmental reorganization is likely to be more difficult under these conditions than at the state level. One difficulty is that each government is apt to have its own constituency base, and this is almost a political necessity in view of its independent status.

COORDINATION WITH OTHER AGENCIES

Policy makers at all levels have sought to develop coordination mechanisms designed to bring various programs and agencies together and to facilitate unified action. The organization of administrative programs by policy field is one way of approaching this matter. As we

---

[5]See *The Costs of Clean Water, Volume II, Annual Report of the Administrator of the Environmental Protection Agency to the Congress of the United States* (Washington, D.C.: Government Printing Office, 1971), pp. 104–20.

have seen, in Washington and an increasing number of states, this has been done in the pollution control field.

The coordination of environmental quality programs with other policy fields is also an objective. This is not accomplished by administrative consolidation but by other means. At the national level, it is done to some extent by the Council on Environmental Quality. In states, it has been done in some cases by the state planning agency or governor's office. In localities, it may be accomplished by a local planning commission, the mayor or county executive, a metropolitan planning commission, or a council of governments. At the subnational levels, comprehensive program planning has been encouraged by the Intergovernmental Cooperation Act of 1968 and Office of Management and Budget Circular A-95 (see Chapter 6). This planning encompasses pollution control programs.

However, it is not at all clear that the mere establishment of coordinating mechanisms will achieve the desired end. Throughout our system, operating programs are assigned to specific agencies. These agencies are not easily "coordinated"—with the pollution control unit or any other, for that matter. Those most likely to have programs that have an impact on the environment include highway bureaucracies; natural resources agencies (forest, parks, fish, wildlife, water resources, open space); sewer authorities; housing authorities; urban renewal agencies; mass transit districts; public utility commissions at the state and national level; public works departments; port authorities; local planning departments; and river and harbor agencies.[6]

Coordinating organizations normally lack program authority. Their role is essentially advisory. To the extent that agencies with operating programs have the legal authority and, as important, the political power, they are apt to ignore central coordinating bodies. Our system is largely directed by the wishes of the operating agencies and their constituencies, not by central officers or planners.

ORGANIZATIONAL AND ADMINISTRATIVE PROBLEMS

Pollution control agencies do not as yet have a powerful constituency base. Certainly, whatever base they do have is not as influential as that undergirding a number of other bureaucracies. Although they may not have permanent "opponents," pollution control agencies do have at least *ad hoc* ones—those adversely affected by agency decisions.

---

[6]William O. Douglas, "The Corps of Engineers: The Public Be Damned," in Walt Anderson, ed., *Politics and Environment* (Pacific Palisades, Calif.: Goodyear Publishing Co., 1970), pp. 268–84.

Those interests which are most greatly concerned with pollution control policy are: conservation interest groups, such as the National Wildlife Federation, the Sierra Club, the Izaak Walton League, the Citizens Committee on Natural Resources, and Friends of the Earth; public interest groups, such as the National Association of Counties (NACO); and industries affected by pollution control regulations.[7]

The conservation groups are most likely to emerge as the political base for the antipollution agencies. The Sierra Club claims 95,000 members and the National Wildlife Federation 2.2 million members. Local conservation and citizens groups are apt to provide support to decisions made by state and local environmental quality agencies. The public interest groups represent both polluters (municipalities and counties) and pollution control agencies. State pollution control bureaucracies now have their own public interest group, the Association of State and Interstate Water Pollution Control Administrators, which provides somewhat of a support base for EPA in Washington.

No industrial or business interest group opposes pollution control programs across the board. Nevertheless, industrial interests obviously try to influence pollution control policy and agencies. Although little behavioral research can be cited on this point, it is generally believed that industries seeking more lenient pollution control regulations are more effective at the state and local levels. Nader's Raiders found considerable evidence of corporate influence on air pollution control policy and administrative practices at the federal level.[8] Presumably, no level of government is immune.

To be successful, pollution control bureaucracies will have to have some kind of a political base. Their present powers have come largely as a result of heightened public awareness; however healthy it may be, this foundation will not sustain administrative agency operations over a long period of time. Every evidence suggests that pollution control bureaucracies are floundering; they are searching for power and for a meaningful role. So far, they have not been completely successful.

About the only type of antipollution agency that presently has a permanent and influential support base is the local sewer bureaucracy. Local sewer authorities account (ultimately) for the overwhelming bulk of pollution control spending. These agencies demonstrated their political strength when the Eisenhower administration sought to scuttle the federal sewage treatment grant program; their representatives pressed Congress until the proposal was dropped. Such authorities

---

[7]J. Clarence Davies III, *The Politics of Pollution* (New York: Pegasus, 1970), p. 85.
[8]John C. Esposito, *Vanishing Air* (New York: Grossman Publishers, 1970), especially Chapters 11 and 12.

remain strong today; they are well organized for political action, and they are frequently backed in the community by important builder and developer interests who need sewer facilities to service their subdivisions.[9]

Some pollution control administrators argue that local governments are too small to handle key antipollution programs. As noted, local governments normally control sewage and solid waste treatment programs; local governments may also regulate polluters. The argument is that administrative determinations at the local level are more likely to be based on political considerations than at the regional, state, or federal levels.

It has been suggested that local governments are more interested in their own survival as distinct entities than in implementing such goals as economy, efficiency, and problem-solving. From this point of view, it has been argued that pollution control powers should be shifted upward in the political system, that pollution control programs should be administered at least on a metropolitan, regional, or state-wide basis.[10]

Administrative reorganization in pollution control by no means assures effective operations. Power centers exist in larger organizations and in comprehensive regionwide and statewide pollution control agencies, and these power centers may be as responsive to special or local interests as more formally decentralized bureaucracies. Furthermore, administrative agencies and particular governments do not relinquish powers readily. Such political considerations are likely to play a role in any effort to reorganize a pollution control program.

Other problems in the administration of a pollution control program include the following: the lack of trained pollution technicians and professional personnel, especially at the state and local level; the absence of a pollution control implementation strategy (only specific decisions); inadequate funding for community waste treatment facilities; and insufficient aggressiveness in antipollution agency enforcement of existing laws.[11]

---

[9]National Commission on Urban Problems, *Building the American City* (Washington, D.C.: Government Printing Office, 1968), p. 232.

[10]For a relevant case study of this matter, see John M. Richardson, Jr., and Howard Maier, "Incongruent Goals, Politics and the Pollution of Lake Erie," a paper delivered to the Fourth Annual Midwest Student Seminar on Urban and Regional Research, Northwestern University, April 24–25, 1970.

[11]*Administration of the Construction Grant Program for Abating, Controlling, and Preventing Water Pollution, Report of the Comptroller General of the United States to the Subcommittee on Air and Water Pollution of the Committee on Public Works, United States Senate* (Washington, D.C.: Government Printing Office, 1969).

SUMMARY

This chapter has examined the nature of environment pollution, anticipated costs of pollution control, environmental quality policy, administrative patterns in the pollution control area, the coordination of pollution control with other relevant government programs, and some of the problems in the administration of environmental quality agencies.

The chapter has emphasized that pollution control agencies were part of the political process and are beginning to carve out a broader role for themselves. Pollution control bureaucracies will need support to carry out their most important duties, and this support may well be forthcoming at present. In the past, pollution control meant essentially the construction of sewage treatment plants; in the future, it is likely to mean much more.

6

COORDINATION OF
POLICY
ADMINISTRATION

Morton Grodzins has described the structure of American government as chaotic: it "flaunts virtually all tenets of . . . administrative effectiveness."[1] Yet, as he notes, the system works. One reason that it does function to the extent it does is the degree of cooperation found in it. And this cooperation carries over into the administrative sphere.

There are over 80,000 units of government in the United States. This does not refer to departments, agencies, or bureaucracies but to full-fledged governments. Included are municipalities, special districts, school districts, and others. The most important functions of these governments are shared, and no one level of government, no single government, has exclusive power over any major function.

[1]Grodzins is referring to the entire federal system. See Morton Grodzins, *The American System* (Chicago: Rand McNally, 1966), p. 7.

THE PROBLEM

The problem is one of coordination, and coordination in administration is part of the problem. Although functions are shared, powers in American democracy are divided. It was planned this way because the nation's founders were fearful of concentrated power. They insisted that government powers be widely distributed.

The constitutions of the early states set the precedent: power was placed in each of three branches; it was further subdivided in the legislature; and each branch was given checks on the other two. The founding fathers' greatest concern was executive tyranny, and, consequently, administrative powers were severely curtailed. Although the federal Constitution later gave the national executive more power, it also established three separate branches, each of which had certain prerogatives. From the beginning, powers were also divided between national and subnational governments.

The picture of present-day American governments is a complex one. Several theories can be cited. Some suggest that competition characterizes the federal system; others find that cooperation is the rule.[2] Some hold that the basic power rests in the states, or in the states and the communities; others argue that it resides in Washington. Nearly all are agreed, however, that authority is broadly distributed throughout the political system, both by the level of government and within any given level. In this discussion, authority refers to legal designations, not necessarily to practice. Yet, any realistic assessment of American politics is likely to lead to the conclusion that the actual exercise of power is widely distributed as well.

If we examine the American system legally, we will find two levels: the national and the state. The U.S. Constitution provides for these levels, delegates specific powers to the national government, and reserves (initially by implication, later by specific language) powers to the states. Local governments are not mentioned in the Constitution, and for legal purposes they are part of state government. Local governments have no inherent authority but only what is given them by states. This line of reasoning has been upheld by the U.S. Supreme Court.

In practice, however, note that American politics is comprised of three levels: national, state, and local. This is so because, although local governments are legally subordinate to the states, local governments do operate with a certain degree of autonomy from state rule. Part of the reason for this is that states have little inclination to control localities,

---

[2]For a discussion of these theories, see Richard H. Leach, *American Federalism* (New York: W. W. Norton & Co., 1970), pp. 10–17.

at least in the immediate sense. Another reason for local autonomy lies in the power base local governments have built, a process fostered to some extent by direct federal-local ties in key grant program areas. Although they are under the authority of the state, local governments raise their own money, and their diverse sources of funding provide localities with a somewhat independent financial base.

However, this is not the entire story. There are also "levels" that fall outside this trichotomy of federal, state, and local. In view of recent developments it is now reasonable to also talk in terms of a "metropolitan" level as distinct from the "local" one. In the past 15 years, a variety of metropolitan-wide institutions have emerged, and these institutions perform different public functions. They may or may not be subject to local or state government control, although they usually have legal ties. In a number of instances, they tend to operate with some degree of independence. Metropolitan institutions are found in all of the more than 200 metropolitan areas of the nation, and they include governmental units with both a planning and an operating program authority. A metropolitan institution operates across an entire metropolitan area (central city and suburbs) or a substantial portion of it. Some metropolitan organizations are metropolitan planning commissions, metropolitan councils of governments, and metropolitan transit districts.

We may now also speak of the regional "level." A region will normally cover more than a single state, and may include several metropolitan as well as rural areas. A number of regional units have been created to handle governmental matters that transcend state and metropolitan boundaries but do not extend to the nation as a whole. The most dramatic development in this respect has been the formation of the various regional economic development commissions for the Appalachian, Ozarks, Upper Great Lakes, Four Corners, New England, and Coastal Plains regions of the nation. The Ozarks Regional Commission, for example, has jurisdiction over the areas of four states; the Appalachian Regional Commission serves all or portions of a 13-state area. Regional water resources development commissions also characterize the regional pattern. An example is the Delaware River Basin Commission, organized in 1961 to plan, develop, and manage the water resources of a four-state area. Regional agencies are at least ultimately responsible to one or more of the traditional three levels of government, but, like metropolitan units, they may operate with some autonomy.

Metropolitan and regional agencies that are special districts are counted as independent governments by the U.S. Bureau of the Census, and they are lumped into the "local government" category.[3] The Census Bureau's determination of what is and is not a government is as accurate as any listing available. Other metropolitan or regional agencies are arms of the state, local, or national governments. In any event, these units are legally accountable to local, state, or national governments, and this tends to weaken the argument that they form separate levels in the political system; nevertheless, local governments are also legally accountable to state governments. As local governments have managed to develop their own political foundations somewhat outside the legal framework, so have many metropolitan and regional units. It is in this sense that it is possible to expand the number of levels in the federal system to five: national, regional, state, metropolitan, and local. The national, state, and local levels are certainly the most basic ones; yet, the other two levels cannot be overlooked. They may also represent semi-independent forces in the political system.

Within each level of government, a wide distribution of formal authority and actual power exists. At the national level are the traditional three branches, and, within each branch, different power centers are present. The legislature, for example, is split into two chambers, and each chamber contains a number of committees and subcommittees which exercise the basic congressional power. The executive branch is organized into 11 cabinet-level departments and dozens of other agencies, including the independent regulatory commissions.

To an extent, each branch is independent of the others, and this legal independence helps form a collective power base in each; thus, Congress as a whole has a separate identity which will help shape the behavior of congressmen as congressmen, and the same is true of the executive branch. Power centers within Congress and the executive branch are of equal or greater influence. Congress, for instance, rarely acts on policy in its entirety, only on particular policy matters. Consequently, power centers tend to form around each key policy area; these power centers include representatives of the legislative branch and administrative agencies, as well as nongovernmental interests. These power centers, numerous as they are, form the backbone of national politics. Housing policy is not made by the Congress, the executive branch, or the national government as a whole (except in a purely formal sense), but by the "housing policy power center." The housing policy power center will at least include federal housing administrators, key congressmen (or their representatives), and housing interest groups (see Chapter 2).

---

[3]U.S. Bureau of the Census, *Census of Governments, 1967: Vol. 1, Governmental Organization* (Washington, D.C.: Government Printing Office, 1968).

We find a similar situation at the state level. Authority is divided among the legislative, executive, and judicial branches, and further subdivided in each. All state legislatures but one (Nebraska) are bicameral. State legislatures contain committees, although their relative influence in the state legislative process appears to be less than that of legislative committees in congressional politics. The executive branch authority in states is typically more dispersed than it is at the national level because state administrations are commonly characterized by independently elected officers for different administrative or policy fields, a score or more of independent boards and commissions responsible for administrative activities, and a chief executive with restricted formal power.

At the local level, one finds thousands of governments, many of which act independently of each other and of other levels of government (at least, in many respects). Local governments include city governments, county governments, New England town governments, township governments, special districts, and school governments. Special and school districts are the most numerous, and there are presently over 20,000 of each. Special district governments include natural resources units, housing authorities, mass transit districts, sewer authorities, and a variety of others.[4]

In addition, power may be divided within each local government. In cities and counties, for instance, it is divided between the executive and legislative branches (the judicial function is not technically in the hands of local government in America). Mayors and city councils serve as checks on each other, have different legal responsibilities, and may have different constituency bases. The same is true of city managers and municipal legislative bodies, county executives and county legislative boards, and town and township administrators and their governing bodies. In school and special district governments, power is split between the governing board and the administrative bureaucracy, although legally the board has the final say. Governing boards of cities, counties, towns, and townships are elected, and those of school and special districts may be appointed or elected. Chief executives in cities, counties, towns, and townships may be elected or appointed. School and special district boards typically appoint their chief administrative officers.

In metropolitan and regional governmental units, the formal power is nearly always in boards or commissions, whose members are selected by officials in national, state, or local governments or who serve by

---

[4]For an assessment of the decentralization effects of special districts, see Advisory Commission on Intergovernmental Relations, *The Problem of Special Districts in American Government* (Washington, D.C.: Government Printing Office, 1964).

virtue of a position they hold in some other government. The administrative operations in such units are not given separate "branch" status, although the administrative staff may constitute a power in and of itself.

The processes of government outside the national and state governments are essentially administrative in nature; even in national and state governments, it is the administrative branch that seems to set the basic tone of the policy processes. However, even within the administrative sphere, power is likely to be divided and decentralized.

In general, it seems that two basic forces contribute to decentralization in power assignments in the federal system and within particular levels of government: legal and formal stipulations; and power drives. By law and formal practice, authority is divided and decentralized. National and state constitutions often prescribe power deconcentration, as do statutes of national, state, and local governments and other formal authorizations (administrative regulations, for instance). "Power drives" refer to the maintenance and enhancement concerns of different government branches and agencies and their supporting interests. Governments and particular government agencies seek to survive, and also most seek to grow and expand. They may be supported in this process by interests that stand to gain material or symbolic returns from their operations.

At the same time, some forces serve to centralize or concentrate power. These include: chief executives; interest groups; and political parties. We are not suggesting that these forces must, by definition, serve this end, only that they are prominent among the forces that may work toward centralization; the latter two in particular may also have the opposite effect.

Chief executives at all levels in the political system appear to be the basic force behind efforts to centralize power. Chief executives often serve as the most important impetus behind legislative actions, and they have sought to reorganize their administrative branches to provide for the more concentrated exercise of power. Of course, they usually seek to centralize this power in a particular manner: they want it in the hands of the chief executive.

Interest groups may work in a similar direction. Interest groups tend to bring the different levels and branches of government together, at least in the policy areas that concern them. For example, public interest groups represent cities and counties in state and national capitals, and they represent states in Washington. The public interest groups encourage the different levels of government to work together in order to advance a common end. The interest groups push through certain legislative measures that bring the levels of government into contact with one another. In the states, public interest groups include associations of cities and counties; in Washington, the National League of Cities and the United States Conference of Mayors. Private interest groups may have the same effect, to the extent that they back intergovernmental programs.

Interest groups may also produce closer ties among different branches of government. This closer cooperation results in a concentration of power over particular policy areas and involves both public and private interest groups. For example, the National Association of Housing and Redevelopment Officials (NAHRO), a public interest group composed of local housing and urban renewal bureaucracies, and the National Association of Home Builders (NAHB), a private interest group composed of building contractors, both favor an ambitious housing program. Neither is concerned particularly with the legislative or executive branch; both want certain actions taken by government (in this case the national government). Both work closely with legislative and administrative officials in Washington, and, together with these officials, they constitute a "power center." The effect of this relationship is a blending of legislative and administrative powers and the concentration of power in a particular policy area (regardless of legal assignments). Ultimately, because of this relationship, the affected legislative and administrative officials are perhaps less likely to view themselves in terms of their formal (and differing) government roles than as "housing people" or "housing decision-makers."[5]

Political parties are essentially coalitions of interest groups. Although particular interest groups (representing specific industries and government bureaucracies) tend to shift their party allegiances as political reality dictates, business forms the base of the Republican party, and labor forms that of the Democrats. Political parties technically control the executive and legislative branches at the national and state levels and in some local governments; furthermore, the same two political parties are found at all levels in the political system. Allegiance to a party is likely to have some effect on officials, regardless of the branch or level of government they represent; thus, when the same party is in power in both branches or in more than one level of government, chances for cross-branch or cross-level cooperation may be better.[6]

However, in this context, there is a difference between political parties and interest groups. Interest groups are numerous and permanent; there are hundreds of them, and each represents a single interest.

---

[5]See Harold Wolman, *Politics of Federal Housing* (New York: Dodd, Mead & Co., 1971).

[6]This is an important point made by V. O. Key, Jr. See his *American State Politics* (New York: Alfred A. Knopf, 1956).

Interest groups are internally united and not characterized by internal conflict; also, they are not ousted in elections.[7] Furthermore, interest groups are concerned with particular policy and administrative matters rather than with the whole of policy and administration. Finally, different interest groups of a similar kind do not compete with each other in the same policy area.

Political parties, on the other hand, represent "moving" interests, and there are only two major parties. Parties represent such broad interests that they are internally divided along congressional (and intra-congressional), executive, state, county, and city, as well as philosophical and sectional, lines. Either party can be ousted from one or both branches or from any level of government. Also, parties are concerned with all, or a broad range of, policies, and they compete with each other.

In this light, interest groups may constitute a more permanent centralization force than parties. The parties have the greater potential for effecting wider centralization, but practical facts—their internal structure, their basic divisions, and the fact that there are two of them—work against their realizing this potential. In the meantime, interest groups effect centralization in their own way.

No discernible force is working toward a truly broad-based centralization in the entire political system. The forces of centralization described above may have their effects in particular governments or levels, particular policy areas, or even across levels; however, none of them will promote centralization in all of these governments, policy areas, and levels simultaneously. To the contrary, the stimulation of centralization in any one of these ways may well have the opposite effect overall; it may also have no effect overall. In this sense, our political system will remain decentralized even if particular aspects of it are centralized. If some force could achieve overall centralization, it is doubtful if this centralization could be sustained over the long run; the roots of decentralization in American politics run deep.[8]

Administration is fruitfully viewed as part of the broader political processes. The problems and characteristics of these processes affect administrative agencies. By the same token, the problems and characteristics of administration are related to and have some effect on the political processes (the evidence in Chapters 2 through 5 points in this direction). In fact, particular problems or matters of concern in specific administrative agencies may be of greater interest to certain legislators

---

[7]Seymour Martin Lipset, *Political Man* (Garden City, N.Y.: Doubleday & Co., 1960), pp. 21–2.

[8]See Morton Grodzins, "Why Decentralization by Order Won't Work," in Edward C. Banfield, ed., *Urban Government: A Reader in Politics and Administration* (New York: Free Press, 1961), pp. 122–31.

or interest groups than to others in the executive branch, including the chief executive. The administrative branch does not represent a monolith any more than the legislative branch does; each is related to the other in important ways, and both interact with other forces in the political system. In fact, power centers found in particular policy areas may represent the most basic dimension through which we can identify and understand administrative operations; it may be that the fundamental political and administrative decisions are made in these power centers.

Yet, there is more than one power center in government. There are many, and they may be in conflict with one another, especially when resources are limited. Furthermore, some political participants may draw their strength from several power centers and develop their own base outside these centers; in this case, they may be able to challenge any particular power center at a given time. Formal authority assignments outside of particular policy areas, or encompassing all policy areas, may encourage or promote such additional "external" power centers. In this light, no single power center which is formed around a policy area has complete freedom to do entirely as it pleases; there are constraints, both political and formal, on what an agency or congeries of institutions can do.

ADMINISTRATIVE REORGANIZATION

The administrative system is a microcosm of the political system, as well as part of it. Power decentralization in administrative systems is as common as it is in the broader political system, and decentralization in the political system generally spells decentralization in the administrative system. Administrative reorganization has as its prime objective the centralization of power and authority. Nevertheless, centralization of power is not necessarily an end in and of itself; it is desirable as a means of promoting the prospects of coordinated rule, of a unified administration. Administrative reorganization may take place across the board in the executive branch, or in particular policy areas. Administrative reorganization is apt to have effects outside the executive branch and, perhaps, outside the affected government; nonexecutive branch and private interests, as well as administrative officials, are likely to play an important role in any reorganization effort.

The President of the United States is currently seeking to revamp the executive branch of the national government. He has proposed a sweeping reorganization program to Congress, and this program is presently under consideration. A number of states have recently undertaken to reorganize their executive departments, some in wide-ranging fashion. This section examines the President's and one state's reorganization plans.

Federal Reorganization Proposal

On March 25, 1971, the President sent a reorganization package to Congress. The package included a general reorganization plan and several reorganization bills. The plan is based on the premises that government is operating ineffectively at present and that current administrative mechanisms are inadequate. In his reorganization message, the President noted that federal administrative power is "exceedingly fragmented" and "broadly scattered" throughout the national bureaucracy.

The consequences of the present pattern of power distribution are:

1. the absence of a coordinated attack on complex problems;
2. the piecemeal analysis of public needs;
3. the rule of special interests and the representation of parochial viewpoints in the bureaucracy;
4. the lack of a comprehensive strategy for promoting the public interest;
5. the failure to consider key problems;
6. duplication and overlap in agency assignments and operations;
7. conflict in agency missions and programs;
8. the proliferation of interagency committees;
9. ineffectiveness in state and local governments; and
10. the weakening of elected leadership.

The following paragraphs represent the administration's reasoning. At present, diffused responsibility and authority make it difficult to launch a coordinated attack on basic problems. Different agencies are operating independently of each other. The existing federal departments are often not now organized to analyze effects and impacts, only the portion of problem areas within their sometimes limited purview. Under present arrangements, special interests, parochial positions, and narrow constituencies tend to rule.

Current structure inhibits the development of a comprehensive strategy to meet public needs; each agency has its own strategy, and it may be based on narrow ends. Since particular departments may have highly specialized assignments, some problems are overlooked. And since these assignments have not been made rationally, on the basis of a single coherent policy goal, duplication and overlap in agency activities have been detected. For example, nine federal departments and 20 independent agencies have education functions; seven departments and eight independent agencies have public health duties.

Furthermore, some agencies are working against others, although not necessarily at a conscious level; one department's watershed project, for instance, may impede the flow of water to another department's reclamation project. After reorganization, such a situation would be rectified; watershed projects, now under the Department of Agriculture, and reclamation projects, now in the Department of the Interior, would be transferred to a single department.

Because of present confusion in assignments, functions, authority, and responsibilities, some 850 interagency committees have been created, and these committees have now become a source of confusion themselves. State and local government administrators must now work with several different federal agencies and departments, perhaps even in the same general program area; this situation may necessitate these governments to hire specialists to handle grant programs alone, and such a diffusion of effort consumes valuable time and resources. Reorganization could lift this burden from the shoulders of subnational units.

Finally, the executive branch must be made more responsive to popular wishes and the will of the people. Democracy rests on the assumption that bureaucracies will act in a politically responsible manner. The President and the Congress are elected. Administrative operations can be made compatible with the aims of elected officials only if executive agencies are properly organized. Reorganization will promote responsible government.

The President's plan proposes organizing around goals and purposes, rather than the present model of methods, subjects, and narrow constituencies. The President urges a broadening of horizons to take account of ends; at present, departments are frequently organized according to means. An example of an "end" would be community development. The "means" to community development might include sound housing and better transportation. Currently, housing and transportation constitute the base of separate cabinet-level departments. Under the administration's proposal, this would be changed; housing and key transportation functions would be placed under a department of community development.

The administration has asked for a reduction in the number of executive departments to eight. These would include four new departments and four existing departments. The new ones would be the Department of Natural Resources, the Department of Human Resources, the Department of Economic Affairs, and the Department of Community Development; the carry-overs are the Department of State, the Department of the Treasury, the Department of Defense, and the Department of Justice. The four new departments would replace seven existing executive departments and several other agencies. All eight departments would report directly to the President. The proposed administrative structure is pictured in Figure 6.1. There are presently eleven executive departments, and they are shown in Figure 6.2.

The President has also stressed the importance of proper organization within the new departments. Each of the new departments is to be headed by a secretary, and the secretaries would be given broader managerial discretion and wider appointment authority than they presently enjoy. Furthermore, each department would be subdivided into major program areas, each of which would be directed by a high-level administrator. In addition, each department's field structure would be composed of regional offices headed by regional directors who would have responsibility for all departmental activities outside of Washington; regional directors would represent the "secretarial presence" in the field. In the past, different agencies and bureaus in the same department have

FIGURE 6.1: Proposed Departments and Major Functions

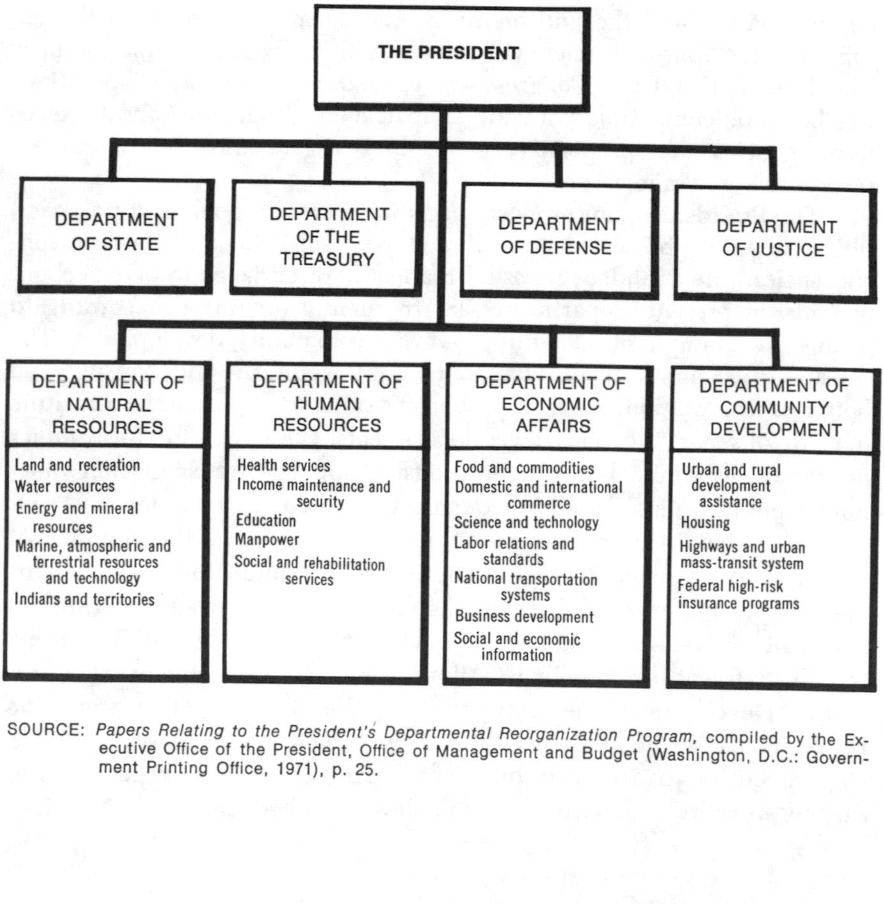

THE PRESIDENT

| DEPARTMENT OF STATE | DEPARTMENT OF THE TREASURY | DEPARTMENT OF DEFENSE | DEPARTMENT OF JUSTICE |

DEPARTMENT OF NATURAL RESOURCES	DEPARTMENT OF HUMAN RESOURCES	DEPARTMENT OF ECONOMIC AFFAIRS	DEPARTMENT OF COMMUNITY DEVELOPMENT
Land and recreation Water resources Energy and mineral resources Marine, atmospheric and terrestrial resources and technology Indians and territories	Health services Income maintenance and security Education Manpower Social and rehabilitation services	Food and commodities Domestic and international commerce Science and technology Labor relations and standards National transportation systems Business development Social and economic information	Urban and rural development assistance Housing Highways and urban mass-transit system Federal high-risk insurance programs

SOURCE: *Papers Relating to the President's Departmental Reorganization Program*, compiled by the Executive Office of the President, Office of Management and Budget (Washington, D.C.: Government Printing Office, 1971), p. 25.

FIGURE 6.2: Executive Department of the National Government 1971

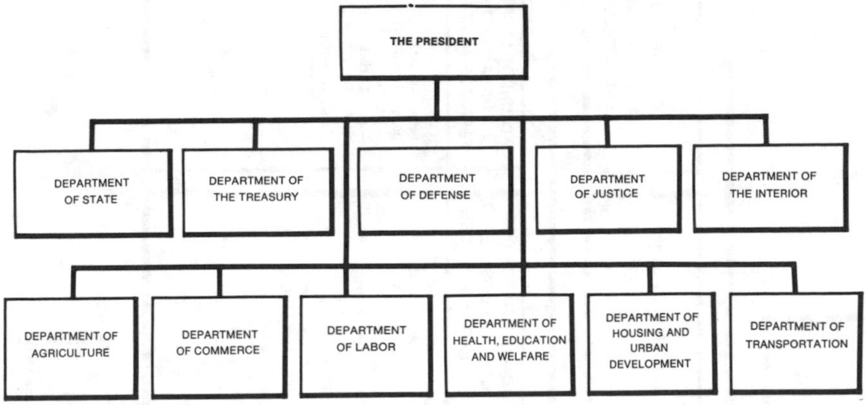

SOURCE: *United States Government Organization Manual 1971/72* (Washington, D.C.: Government Printing Office, 1971), p. 610.

sometimes had their own separate field structure; no single field administrator had authority over all departmental activities in a given region or area. The present administration has already reorganized some departments' field operations around this new principle.

Let us turn to an examination of two of the four proposed "new" departments: natural resources and community development. The organization charts for these two departments are shown in Figures 6.3 and 6.4.

The functions of the Department of Natural Resources would include: conservation, management, and utilization of natural resources; maintenance of ecological balance; exploration of the earth, atmosphere, and oceans; scientific research in natural resources; development of various energy sources; management of federal lands, including parks, forests, wildlife refuges, and fish hatcheries; assistance in the provision of outdoor recreational opportunities; facilitation of the development of commercial fisheries; protection of the health and safety of miners; promotion of oil and gas pipeline safety; and assistance to Indians, Alaskan natives, and other territorial peoples.

The Department of Natural Resources would assume responsibility for a variety of natural resources functions presently administered in several different departments and agencies. The bulk of its activities would come from the present Department of the Interior, and it is built basically around this Department's programs. Key duties of the present Department of Agriculture and the U.S. Army's Corps of Engineers would also be shifted to the new department.

FIGURE 6.3: *Proposed Department of Natural Resources*

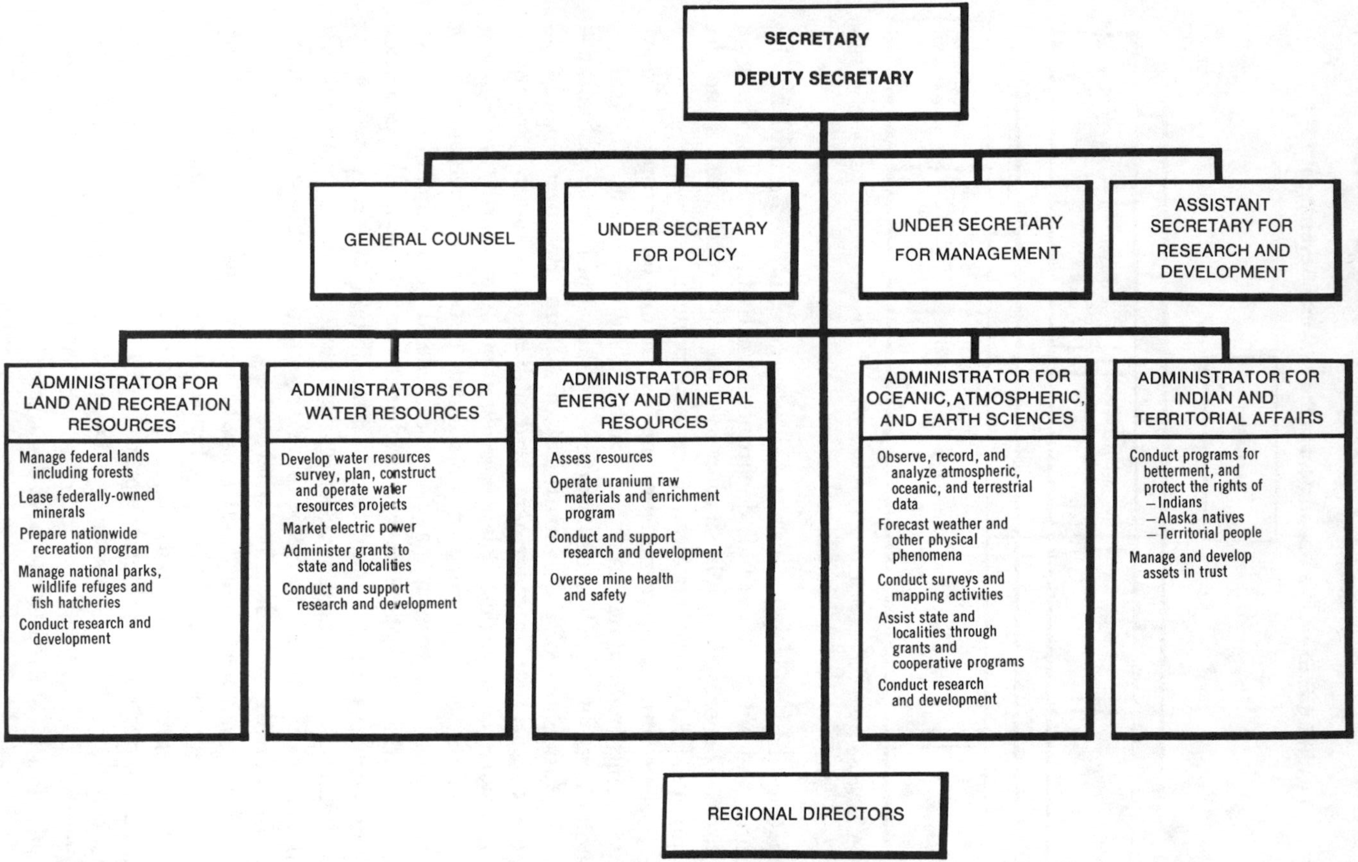

```
                    SECRETARY
                 DEPUTY SECRETARY
```

GENERAL COUNSEL

UNDER SECRETARY FOR POLICY

UNDER SECRETARY FOR MANAGEMENT

ASSISTANT SECRETARY FOR RESEARCH AND DEVELOPMENT

ADMINISTRATOR FOR LAND AND RECREATION RESOURCES

Manage federal lands including forests

Lease federally-owned minerals

Prepare nationwide recreation program

Manage national parks, wildlife refuges and fish hatcheries

Conduct research and development

ADMINISTRATORS FOR WATER RESOURCES

Develop water resources survey, plan, construct and operate water resources projects

Market electric power

Administer grants to state and localities

Conduct and support research and development

ADMINISTRATOR FOR ENERGY AND MINERAL RESOURCES

Assess resources

Operate uranium raw materials and enrichment program

Conduct and support research and development

Oversee mine health and safety

ADMINISTRATOR FOR OCEANIC, ATMOSPHERIC, AND EARTH SCIENCES

Observe, record, and analyze atmospheric, oceanic, and terrestrial data

Forecast weather and other physical phenomena

Conduct surveys and mapping activities

Assist state and localities through grants and cooperative programs

Conduct research and development

ADMINISTRATOR FOR INDIAN AND TERRITORIAL AFFAIRS

Conduct programs for betterment, and protect the rights of
— Indians
— Alaska natives
— Territorial people

Manage and develop assets in trust

REGIONAL DIRECTORS

SOURCE: *Papers Relating to the President's Departmental Reorganization Program*, compiled by the Executive Office of the President, Office of Management and Budget (Washington, D.C.: Government Printing Office, 1971), p. 164.

FIGURE 6.4: *Proposed Department of Community Development*

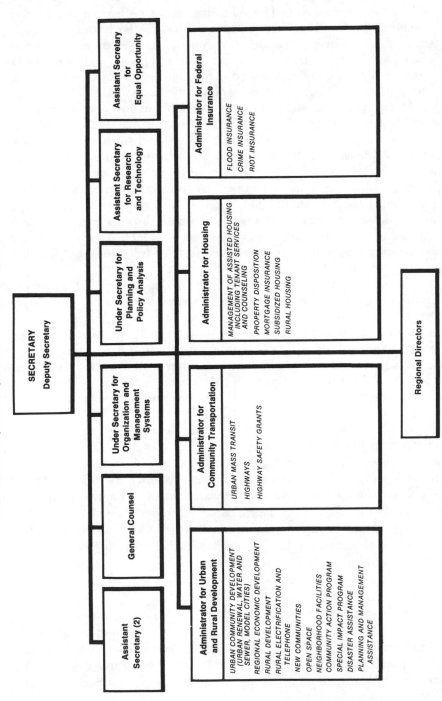

SOURCE: *Papers Relating to the President's Departmental Reorganization Program,* compiled by the Executive Office of the President, Office of Management and Budget (Washington, D.C.: Government Printing Office, 1971), p. 53.

The new department's line functions would be carried out by five "administrations": land and recreation resources; water resources; energy and mineral resources; oceanic, atmospheric, and earth sciences; and Indian and territorial affairs. The secretary would be assisted by a deputy secretary, two under secretaries (one for policy, one for management), a general counsel (legal matters), and an assistant secretary.

Among the most important responsibilities of the new department would be management of the national forests and parks; this would involve the transfer of the Forest Service of the Department of Agriculture and the National Park Service of the Department of the Interior. The new department would also handle the civil functions of the Corps of Engineers. Although the department is given ecological and environmental missions, it would not administer air and water pollution control, sewage treatment plant assistance, solid waste disposal assistance, and other basic environmental quality programs; in fact, none of the new departments would have responsibility for the full range of pollution control activities.

The new Department of Community Development would essentially be formed around the present Department of Housing and Urban Development (HUD). Its functions would basically be the provision of assistance to local and state governments and private parties at the community level. Unlike HUD, which works mostly in urban areas, the new department would stress community development in urban and rural areas alike. Thus, in addition to HUD programs, the new Department of Community Development would take over certain activities of the present Department of Agriculture.

The new department is based on the assumption that key community activities of the national government should be brought into a single agency. As an example, transportation can be divided into "community" and "national" components. The "community" transportation components should be placed in a department of community affairs. In this light, the present Department of Transportation's "community" programs are to be transferred to the Department of Community Development; these include the highway and urban mass transit assistance activities of DOT. (DOT's "national" transportation programs, including aviation and railroads, would be moved to the new Department of Economic Affairs.)

The new Department of Community Development would be administered by a secretary, who would be assisted by a deputy secretary, two under secretaries, four assistant secretaries, and a general counsel. Four administrations would be created: urban and rural development; community transportation; housing; and federal insurance. Key programs of the proposed department would include urban renewal assistance; public housing subsidies; highway grants; urban mass transit assistance; comprehensive planning assistance; and the community action program (presently in the Office of Economic Opportunity). For the first time, under the reorganization, a single agency would control both urban and rural federal housing assistance and both urban and rural public facilities assistance (however, not all categories of public facilities assistance would be in the new department).

The President's reorganization plan is presently being studied by Congress. At this writing, no action had been taken. The plan is based in large part on the recommendations of the President's Advisory Council on Executive Organization, known as the Ash Council. The Ash Council made its findings known to the President in 1970, and the Council's report was released in February, 1971.

State Administrative Reorganization

Comprehensive executive branch reorganization has been effected recently in such states as Massachusetts and Florida. In a number of states, reorganization in specific policy areas such as transportation, pollution control, natural resources, health and welfare, law enforcement, and manpower is on the upswing. In addition, reorganization study commissions presently exist in about 30 states.[9] In most states, reorganization can be accomplished only by legislation; in eight states, however, the governor has this authority, subject usually to the veto of one or both houses of the state legislature. This veto must be exercised within a specified time period, such as 60 days.

The State of Delaware's reorganization proposal is a good example of a comprehensive state administrative restructuring plan. In this state, the Governor's Task Force on Reorganization of the Executive Branch of Government found over 140 administrative departments, agencies, boards, and commissions. It proposed the creation of a new administrative structure, to be composed of 10 major departments plus an executive office of the governor. The proposed organization is shown in Figure 6.5.

The Delaware Task Force discovered that power was widely dispersed throughout the executive branch. In the natural resources policy area, for example, 23 independent agencies existed, including the Delaware Water and Air Resources Commission, the Delaware Apple Com-

---

[9]George A. Bell, "State Administrative Organization Activities, 1968–1969," in *The Book of the States 1970–1971* (Lexington, Ky.: Council of State Governments, 1970), pp. 135–38.

FIGURE 6.5

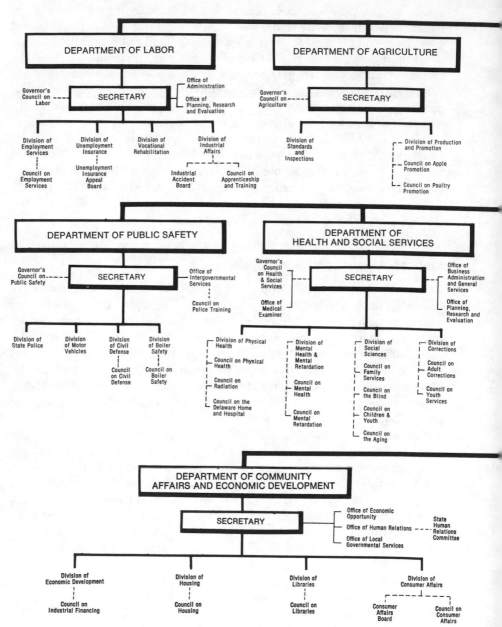

SOURCE: Governor's Task Force on Reorganization of the Executive Branch of Government, State of Delaware, *Final Report on Cabinet Departments* (Dover, Delaware: Governor's Task Force on Reorganization of the Executive Branch of Government, 1970), p. 65.

DEPARTMENT OF STATE

SECRETARY

Division of
Corporations

Division of
Archives and
Cultural Affairs

Council on
Archives and
Cultural Affairs

DEPARTMENT OF FINANCE

SECRETARY

Division of
Accounting

Division of
Revenue

Tax Appeal
Board

Division of
the Treasury

Board of
Pension
Trustees

DEPARTMENT OF HIGHWAYS AND TRANSPORTATION

SECRETARY

Office of
Business
Administration

Office of
Planning
Research and
Evaluation

Division of
Highways

Council on
Highways

Division of
Transportation

DEPARTMENT OF ADMINISTRATIVE SERVICES

SECRETARY

Division of
State Buildings

Council on
State
Buildings

Wilmington
Civic Center
Office
Building
Commission

Division of
Purchasing

Division of
Central Data
Processing

Division of
Business and
Occupational
Regulation

Delaware Harness Racing Commission — Public Service Commission
Delaware Racing Commission — Delaware Alcoholic Beverage Control Commission
State Board of Electrical Examiners — Delaware Real Estate Commission
Board of Pilot Commissioners — Bingo Control Commission
State Board of Accountancy — State Athletic Commission
Board of Trustees of the Delaware — State Board of Registration for
Standardbred Development Fund — Professional Engineers and Land Surveyors
State Bank Commissioner — Board of Examiners and Registration of Architects

Council on
Banking

DEPARTMENT OF NATURAL RESOURCES AND ENVIRONMENT CONTROL

Governor's
Council on Natural
Resources and
Environmental Control

SECRETARY

Division of Fish
and Wildlife

Council on Game
and Fish

Council on Shell
Fisheries

Division of Parks,
Recreation and
Forestry

Council on Parks

Recreation Advisory
Council

Council on Forestry

Division of Soil
and Water
Conservation

Council on Soil
and Water
Conservation

Division of
Environmental
Control

Water and Air
Resources
Commission

EXECUTIVE OFFICE OF THE GOVERNOR

Executive Staff

Office of the Budget

Budget Commission

State Planning Office

Council on State Planning

Office of Personnel

Personnel Commission

mission, the State Forestry Commission, the State Park Commission, a mosquito control district, and a Board of Ditch Commissioners. As pictured in Figure 6.5, the proposed Department of Natural Resources and Environmental Control is composed of only four major divisions: fish and wildlife; parks, recreation, and forestry; soil and water conservation; and environmental control. This represents a substantial consolidation and a significant regrouping along lines of a single policy area.

The Delaware reorganization panel also urged the transformation of administrative and policy-making boards and commissions in the executive branch into advisory councils. It argued that plural executives were not well suited to administrative and policy tasks and that the present procedure of assigning these multimember bodies substantive powers interfered with the development of an effective cabinet system. Policy-making belonged in the hands of the governor and his cabinet departments, not independent administrative boards.

Under the reorganization plan, departmental secretaries were to be appointed by the governor, with the advice and consent of the state senate; the secretaries were to serve at his pleasure. Division directors were to be selected by the secretaries of the departments, with the written approval of the governor. All other administrative personnel were to be covered by the state merit system.

The proposed reorganization in Delaware is based, to some extent, on the creation of departments by major policy areas and, to some extent, by clientele or constituency group. The proposed Department of National Resources and Environmental Control represents the first pattern; the Departments of Labor and Agriculture the second. Of course, a given departmental pattern, once in effect, is likely to structure policy fields and interest group representation along departmental lines.

COORDINATION OF PROGRAM ADMINISTRATION IN THE FEDERAL SYSTEM

The enactment of the Intergovernmental Cooperation Act of 1968 represents the boldest step so far in the coordination of domestic programs in the entire federal system. Although the legislation applies directly only to national government activities, its effects have been felt throughout the federal system. State and local governments are significantly dependent on federal assistance, and federal assistance programs fall under the act's jurisdiction.

The Intergovernmental Cooperation Act states that the "President shall . . . establish rules and regulations governing the formulation, evaluation, and review of Federal programs and projects having a significant impact on area and community development." The coordination of certain proposed federal assistance activities in metropolitan areas was also required under the Demonstration Cities and Metropolitan Development Act of 1966. Pursuant to these two measures, the Office of Management and Budget prepared Circular No. A–95. Since the circular was originally written, Congress passed the National Environmental Policy Act of 1969, which required environmental impact statements for certain federal and federally assisted projects. All three acts now form the base of Circular A–95.

Office of Management and Budget Circular A–95

1. encourages the establishment of a project notification and review system at the state and local level to promote intergovernmental planning for certain federal assistance programs;
2. provides for the means of coordinating direct federal development programs and projects with state and local planning bodies; and
3. provides for the means of securing the comments of appropriate state and local government agencies on the environmental impact of certain federal or federally assisted projects.[10]

In accordance with this circular, "clearinghouses" are to be designated in states and communities. These clearinghouses would at least have planning authority. Clearinghouses are of three types:

1. state clearinghouses—state-level agencies, to be designated by the governor or state law;
2. metropolitan clearinghouses—or metropolitan area-wide planning agencies, which are recognized by the federal Office of Management and Budget; and
3. regional clearinghouses—or nonmetropolitan planning agencies, to be designated by the governor of the state or by state law.

These clearinghouses are to comment on proposed direct federal projects (new buildings, planned public works) and proposed federal assistance programs (grants and loans to state and local government and others); they are to review the environmental impact of such projects and programs. The clearinghouses are to ascertain the consistency of proposed federal action with state and community plans, development, and programming. The clearinghouses do not have veto power, but they may make recommendations.

Not all federal activities are covered under the clearinghouse process, but many are. Examples are urban renewal projects (administered by the Department of Housing and Urban Development), outdoor recreation assistance (under the Department of the Interior), watershed projects (under the Department of Agriculture), highway assistance

---

[10]This circular was originally released on July 24, 1969. (The Office of Management and Budget is a federal agency; it is located in the Executive Office of the President.)

(in the Department of Transportation), and community action programs (in the Office of Economic Opportunity).

In practice, state clearinghouses include state planning agencies and the governor's office; metropolitan clearinghouses include metropolitan planning commissions and councils of governments; and regional clearinghouses include economic development districts and rural planning boards operating under the state government.

It is too early to assess the effects of these clearinghouses' operation. Problems detected so far include: the absence of state and local plans and development policies; the failure of some local, state, and federal agencies to comply with Circular A–95; confusion as to the standards that should be used to judge proposed federal activities; and insufficient public official interest in the process.[11]

Every indication is though that the process contains the potential for promoting coordination in the administration of public policy throughout the federal system. It may initially have the effect of stimulating comprehensive planning at the state and local level. At a later point, the benefits should be far-reaching.

Revenue Sharing

Some feel that comprehensive coordination of administrative activities cannot be achieved without revenue sharing. Under revenue sharing, the national government would advance lump sums, based on some formula, for the general use of state and local governments. Revenue sharing differs from the present federal aid procedure in that money would be provided by Washington on an open-ended basis; under present federal assistance programs, funds are made available only to particular programs.[12] Present funding practices may undermine central direction at the state and local level, encouraging vertical relationships in the federal system. Some revenue sharing proposals make a restructuring of state and local governments a condition in order for them to receive federal revenues.

Midway through his first term, President Nixon submitted a revenue sharing package to Congress. Action on it was delayed for some time for the following reasons: the lack of support by powerful bureaucracies; the absence of sufficient backing by key interest groups; partisan

---

[11]These conclusions are based in part on a recent analysis of the clearinghouse process; see Council of State Governments, *The Intergovernmental Cooperation Act of 1968: Federal and State Implementation* (Washington, D.C.: Council of State Governments, 1971).

[12]Deil S. Wright, *Federal Grants-in-Aid: Perspectives and Alternatives* (Washington, D.C.: American Enterprise Institute for Public Policy Research, 1968).

politics (GOP executive, Democratic Congress); and disagreement among state and local public interest groups on particulars. Revenue sharing has the greatest chance of passing if it does not disturb existing federal grant programs (that is, if it is "new money"). Only such a proposal would be likely to get the strong backing of important federal bureaucracies. However, such a measure may compromise the goal of administrative centralization. In fact, late in 1972, a revenue sharing bill following this pattern was approved. Others are still under consideration.

SUMMARY

This chapter has examined the American administrative system, and the effect of the political system on it. Although some forces of centralization are at work, decentralization is often a key trait of administrative and political systems. This decentralization should not be understood in ideological terms; it has to do with the administration and execution of public policy. We looked at proposals to centralize the administrative process, including the President's reorganization plan, a state reorganization effort, a new federal program review system, and revenue sharing.

The prospects of administrative centralization are not particularly bright. Yet, they are not bleak either. Change is in the wind, and administrative structures may be affected.

7

EARLY FOUNDATIONS OF ADMINISTRATIVE THEORY

INTRODUCTION

This chapter begins with an examination of the contributions of the classics in political philosophy to administrative thought. It then turns to early thought on administration and organizational behavior. In the following chapter, we complete our study of administrative theory by focusing on developments in the last 40 to 50 years, including the orthodox principles growing out of the depression era and more recent trends.

It has not been until relatively recently that administration has been viewed as an area deserving special treatment and independent study. In political science, public administration did not emerge as a clearly distinguishable aspect of the study of politics until the latter part of the nineteenth century and the early part of this century. For centuries, political theory served as the sole base for both public administration and other processes of government, and there was no separate administrative theory. Now, there is.

ROOTS OF ADMINISTRATIVE THOUGHT

Political science is the parent discipline of public administration, and, in the West, political science can be traced to the thought of the ancient Greek philosophers. Most scholars today hold that political theory forms the frame for public administration, and, up until the time that public administration became a recognized field of study, political theory was really the only theory that had applicability to governmental administrative institutions and processes. What Plato had to say about politics in general had relevance to administration; what Machiavelli had to say on states had application to administration.

Although public administration now has its own set of axioms, principles, and theories, public administration is still part of political science even though it has theories that have special meaning for administrative institutions. Political theorists may still address themselves to administrative matters, but public administration presently operates from separately identifiable concepts.

Public administration also has another set of roots. Prior to the time that public administration was singled out for special consideration in political science, much attention was being devoted to management in the private sector. In fact, this is where the study of uniquely administrative processes got its real start. In the late 1800s and the early 1900s, several scholars began work in the private management area, concentrating on industrial and profit-making enterprises; studies were conducted, ideas about management and industrial operations were advanced, and administrative thought developed. These investigations and the thought surrounding them had a bearing on the later development of thought in public administration. Thus, public administration owes much to those concerned with the workings of private businesses, and some of its premises and thought were originally drawn from this field. As time went on, the study of administrative techniques, strategies, and operations in private business became known as business administration; in the same way as public administration traces its origins to political science, business administration locates its early roots in economics.

Public administration builds on other fields as well. For example, sociology has contributed much to reducing organizations of all kinds to their fundamental dimensions; to the extent that public administrative institutions can be considered "organizations," what sociologists have to say about organizations has some meaning in public administration. Psychology has also helped to shape administrative thought and has had its effect in the field of public administration.[1]

In the light of the interdisciplinary roots of public administration and in view of the somewhat independent operational styles and modes fashioned by public agencies, it has been suggested that public administration is now in reality a discipline of its own; it is no longer dependent on its previous "parent," political science, and some even contend that it is an independent area of study and no longer a part of political science. Public administration has its own professional association, the American Society for Public Administration (ASPA), and this organization is separate from the American Political Science Association, the organization of professional political scientists. Unlike the American Political Science Association, ASPA is composed of both academics and practitioners in public administration.

Some also argue that, if public administration is to occupy a part of a broader field, it should be linked to the methodologies of administrative science or organizational behavior, not political science; in such a case, administration in public (governmental) institutions would be tied to general administration which covers both public and private institutions. The contention here is that the principles of public administration are really the principles of administration, and thought about public institutions is really part of thought about institutions in general; thus, the study of public administration is just an illustration of the study of a particular (governmental) administrative process, which is to be related to the study of administrative processes elsewhere. Whatever merit these arguments may have and no matter what level of academic support they may enjoy, public administration remains a part of political science; it has not been cut loose, nor has it merged with any other field.

THEORY OF ADMINISTRATION

The theory of administration simply refers to the process of conceptualizing administrative operations. We are, of course, concerned with the theory of public administration, or the theory of administrative operations in government. The administrative operations of government in modern western societies can be somewhat readily isolated for academic study, for administration can be separated from other processes of government, and government can be distinguished from other institutions; in contemporary developing nations and in many societies (probably a

---

[1]See Robert Presthus, *The Organizational Society* (New York: Vintage Books, 1962). Presthus points out how psychological theories have molded contemporary organizational thought. These theories also have relevance to public administration.

majority) in the past, such separations and distinctions are less easily made or are impossible to make.

Conceptualizing about administrative operations covers a vast number of particulars. For instance, such conceptualizing may be normative. We might argue that administration works best when power is concentrated in a single office, that government can be more efficiently run when the basic administrative authority is in the hands of a top manager. We might suggest that all administrative power be placed in a collective body, representing different societal interests, or we might be convinced that the best way to operate a state is to appoint a group of experts to administer policy. We generally consider this type of theory as normative theory. It is theory that represents certain norms or values that we hold, and, on the basis of these norms or values, we believe that this or that should be done, that this or that is best. This is only one kind of theory.

Another theory is that which is concerned with administrative practice in the scientific sense. This theory is directed toward conceptualizing about actual administrative activities, about the development of ideas and principles that reflect practical administrative operations. This theory attempts to lay aside values and norms and to substitute objective inquiry. This theory does not tell you what is good or what is best; it tells you what is. It is, nevertheless, one kind of theory. Behavioralists (see Chapter 9) use this sort of theory to explain administrative patterns, although others in public administration use this theory as well. We may consider this kind of theory a scientific theory.

It is not always easy to distinguish between scientific and normative theory. The two are often blended in practice. Norms seem to play a role in scientific theory, and science may not be completely excluded from normative theory. Put another way, few, if any, persons are exclusively normative or scientific in their approach to public administration. It might be better to describe normative and scientific theory as tendencies in administrative thought which are not totally separate.

Theories also have different uses. Theories of politics or administration may be developed for different reasons. One gets the impression, for example, that the goal of the philosopher Plato was to advance a conception of the ideal state, including the proper assignment of administrative authority; whether Plato's state would (or could) ever be used was of less concern than his desire to philosophize about the ideal political order. Nevertheless, others may develop theory for less abstract purposes. They may wish to point out how existing administrative structures should be rearranged for maximum advantage, or they may formulate theory for the purpose of shifting power away from one group and to another. It is difficult to determine what the purpose of particular theory might really be. In any event, we should not overlook the point that theory may well serve practical ends; theory may not merely be someone's abstract views about politics and administration. Furthermore, the ultimate use of a theory may have little to do with its intended purpose.

The previous comments about theory seem to have particular relevance to America, and to public administration in America. We have commonly viewed theory as an abstract matter and equated it with idealism. This leads to the notion: it sounds nice in theory, but it does not work in practice. In America, this notion has less application than elsewhere because American political theory has not been divorced from practice; in a variety of ways, it has built on practice. By the same token, American public administration and administrative thought have an essentially practical base.

An example of this practical base is the two contrasting theories of administration which were advanced in the early days of the American republic. One held that administrative power should be exercised by a collegial body, a body composed of representatives of both the legislative and executive branches of government. This pattern had the advantages of encouraging publicly responsive administration and of checking the abuse of administrative power through its concentration in a single man or office. This was the theory of the democrats, the more liberal of the political forces active in the original structuring of our administrative institutions; this theory prevailed in the formation of the early state governments and the government under the Articles of Confederation.[2] In the early states, the governors were typically surrounded by a council that shared administrative power with the chief executive; under the Articles of Confederation, all power rested with the legislature, which performed both administrative and legislative duties.

The other theory was that administrative power should be placed in the hands of a single executive official. The administrative and legislative functions should be separated and the chief executive be given a free reign within certain broad limitations. This was the theory of the more conservative interests at the time; it was particularly representative of the administrative thought of Alexander Hamilton and the Federalists.[3] To Hamilton, administrative power should be concentrated, and the executive should be independent of other branches; also, the executive must be strong, for "a feeble execution is but another phrase for a

[2]The democratic forces were considered "radicals" at that point. See Merrill Jensen, *The Articles of Confederation* (Madison: University of Wisconsin Press, 1940).

[3]Leonard D. White, *The Federalists: A Study in Administrative History* (New York: Free Press, 1948).

bad execution."[4] Hamilton was not happy with "plural execution," either in the early states or in other countries in the past; he opposed the "republican maxim" that administrative power was safer in the hands of many than one. The Federalist theory prevailed in the new national government.

We have two theories, and they are in conflict with one another. Both theories are drawn from practice. The democrats had enough of concentrated administrative power under British rule; they found that power to be used in tyrannical fashion, and they wanted no part of it. The Federalists, on the other hand, concluded that a far greater danger ensued from the dispersal of administrative authority; they had a chance to observe conditions in the early states and the experience under the Articles. Neither theory can be isolated from practice, and neither can be divorced from the practical considerations of the distribution of power and public policy. Both drew on practical reality; both were sensitive to the effects of one administrative pattern on power distribution and on public policy. The Federalists felt that their power would likely be greater in the executive branch and that their conception of good public policy would receive more favorable treatment in the executive than the legislative chamber; the democrats leaned to a theory that supported the legislative branch, the branch where they would likely be strongest, and they wanted executive power curtailed. Of course, neither the democrats nor the Federalists developed their administrative theories to mask power drives or policy ends; both felt their views to be in the best interests of the people and of the country as a whole.

CONTRIBUTIONS OF POLITICAL THEORY

The ancient Greek philosophers and historians had much to say about government and administrative matters. However, in ancient Greece, sharp distinctions between government and the private sphere and between the administrative and other processes of government were not made; perhaps they could not have been made because they did not exist. Also, in ancient Greece, the conception of the proper role of the state differed from the one currently prevailing in the west. The purpose of law, for example, was not to guarantee personal freedom and individual liberties but to assure that all would be assigned to their proper place in the economic and social structure. Different orders of men were an accepted part of the way of life in both authoritarian and democratic

---

[4]Alexander Hamilton, James Madison, and John Jay, *The Federalist Papers* (New York: The New American Library, 1961), p. 423.

regimes, and the state seemed to have a more positive and a broader role than is the case in most western democracies.

Thucydides contributed to the realist tradition in political science and public administration. To Thucydides, politics was a struggle for power, dominance, and material advantage. He did not view politics as he might have wanted it to be but as, he believed, it was. Of particular relevance, in his study of the Peloponnesian War (431–404 B.C.), Thucydides describes different patterns of decision-making. In Athens, decisions were made in democratic fashion; in Sparta, in an authoritarian manner. Athens prided itself on democratic institutions and popular participation in public decision-making, while Sparta was ruled by an oligarchy, a relatively small class of landowners and aristocrats.

Thucydides had much praise for the democratic Athens, for its spirit and for its dashing qualities. However, while he found that Athenian democracy had satisfied the aspirations of a wide segment of the public, he noted that Athenian power was exhausted over the long pull, subject to the excesses of the democratic spirit, to rash judgments, to internal strife and jealousies, and to intemperate passions.

Plato's political science was much more idealistic. To Plato, the ideal political and administrative order can be known only through rigorous thought and disciplined inquiry; nothing was to be left to chance, no stone left unturned in the quest for the good state. Plato rejected the notion that politics is a struggle for power and called for a union of knowledge and power. To be legitimate, power must be based on knowledge and virtue. Other foundations, such as private interests, have no place in his thinking.

Plato also stressed the importance of a properly structured educational system as a means of providing the political and administrative talent needed to run the state. He proposed an extensive training program, which included formal preservice work up to the age of 35 and inservice training up to the age of 50. Only after this background and experience would individuals be prepared to assume significant responsibilities at the top of the political hierarchy.

Although upward mobility was permitted, Plato's ideal order was strictly structured. In the top class were the guardians, the philosopher-kings, the rulers; in this class, he concentrated all powers, including basic decision-making and broad administrative direction. The second class was comprised of soldiers, and key administrative authority is lodged in this group; however, the class is to exercise no independent administrative power because it is subject to the general guidance of the guardians. The third class was to be the workers, the operatives, the producers; they were to be ruled, and they did not participate in the decision-making process. Plato was no democrat, and he scoffed at notions of majority rule.

Presumably, administration would not amount to much in Plato's state. Because he taught that the public should be educated on proper values and expected behavior, it would not seem necessary to him that there would be much need for the enforcement of the guardians' decisions; these decisions would be followed automatically. In addition, Plato seemed to be suggesting that policy making and policy execution could be somewhat divided. This would appear to be the reason for separating the top from the second class; both would have certain powers, but the division would tend to be along the lines of decision-making and decision execution, that is, to the extent that the latter would be needed. Plato referred to the soldiers as auxiliaries; they serve to carry out the decisions of the guardians. However, in view of the way Plato distributed various qualities to his classes, it is likely that the rulers would not have the skills that a contemporary bureaucracy would, for this is a task that is left to those spirited but unphilosophical souls in the auxiliary category.

Aristotle was Plato's student, and he built on his mentor's basic philosophy. Yet, Aristotle was more practical, and he conducted scientific analyses and studies of actual states and constitutions. Aristotle contributed to political science and political philosophy and to public administration and administrative theory. Aristotle sought to link political ideas and political practice. His contribution to administrative theory is contained in the concept of balance in political systems, his identification of different processes in government, and his classification of decision-making into different categories.

To Aristotle, government represented balance among social classes. He recognized that different classes exist in society and that these classes are apt to see government and public policy in different lights. He did not equate the public interest with the views of any particular class, arguing that it transcended class interests; however, he saw certain practical advantages in mixed government, a government representing different social classes. This view was important in the later development of separation of powers in government, a separation that had both social and political implications; also, as finally translated into practice, it formed the rationale for the separation of the executive (administrative) from the legislative function.

Aristotle also identified the key processes of government: the deliberative, magisterial, and judicial; these processes correspond to the legislative, executive, and court systems in modern states and suggest the analytic separation of the administrative from other processes of government. Depending on the character of the government, these elements are found in different degrees and operate differently.

Aristotle also advanced a sixfold classification of political systems and decision-making:

Monarchy	Tyranny
Aristocracy	Oligarchy
Polity	Democracy

The three classes on the left represent desirable forms of government; the three on the right are their undesirable (perverted) counterparts. Aristotle defined monarchy as the rule of one, aristocracy as the rule of a few, and polity as mixed rule. These forms represented his conception of proper, legitimate, and acceptable rule; they represented rule in the general interest.

Tyranny was the rule of one, oligarchy of the few, and democracy of the many. They were different from the above forms because they did not rule in the general interest; they represented rule in the interests of some part of the public, not the entire public, and this included the majority ruling in its own interests. Aristotle's distinction is important to students of public administration for it shows different patterns of public decision-making, which apply in administrative institutions, and advances a standard or norm by which legitimacy can be judged. To Aristotle, like Plato, politics and administration should not represent the interests of the stronger, the interests of a single class; broader rule is required.

Polybius, a Greek historian-statesman who was taken prisoner by the Romans and wrote between 200 and 100 B.C., presented a more refined conception of the different processes of government. Polybius detected in the Roman constitution a division and balance of power among different forces, namely the consuls, the senate, and the popular assemblies. The Roman consuls exercised the basic executive power and had key administrative authority, including jurisdiction over the military and the geographical area outside Rome (the city); the consuls represented the monarchical element in the Roman state. The senate had certain checks over the consuls (for example, the provision of supplies for the army), represented the interests of the wealthy, and constituted the aristocratic power. The popular assemblies served to set the general limits to the senate's power and represented the democratic authority of the state.

Polybius did not find that this distribution was planned, only that the government operated this way. Also, he found that it worked to the advantage of the Romans. Polybius' theory of a mixture of government power bases contributed to the later consciously planned separation of powers in government, including the assignment of the administrative authority of the state to a separate branch. After Polybius discovered that balance and distribution of powers was a basic ingredient in the strength of the Roman state, serving to keep different political interests within safe bounds, the next logical step would be a planned division which could work to check political power and, in addition, protect the liberties of the people and the rights of different groups in society.

Polybius may have been the first to point to the merit of a purely political division of power (Aristotle's balance was social and economic), although economic interests were involved even in Rome. However, Polybius' powers, are not to be confused with the more familiar executive-legislative-judicial arrangement; for example, the consuls were not the only administrative authority and the senate performed some executive functions. It is simply the principle of essentially a political balance that is important here. Polybius was read by some of the founders of the American government, and he is cited specifically by John Adams, whose work had much to do with keeping the administrative power independent of the legislature in American politics.

Polybius also presented a theory of the development and degeneration of political systems. This theory is important to public administration in view of the role that administrative institutions play in molding political behavior and in setting the tone for societal and political trends. Polybius, building on Aristotelian analysis, suggested that political forms follow a predictable cycle. Political development begins with monarchy; this degenerates into tyranny; aristocracy follows tyranny; and this, in turn, degenerates into oligarchy; democracy is the next stage and ultimately degenerates into mob rule pure and simple; then, the cycle starts again, going through the same stages in the same order. Polybius' concept of political degeneration seems to have been borne out in practice, although the specifics appear to vary with the situation; certainly this was true with the Romans. In fact, government to the Romans seemed to be essentially a matter of administration, and the Romans built one of the most effective public works bureaucracies that the world has ever known. We do not fully know to what extent the administrative patterns in the Roman government contributed to the decline of the Roman state.

Among the early Christian thinkers, the one who has had the most lasting impact is St. Augustine. St. Augustine wrote at a time when Christianity had been established as the legal religion of Rome and after Roman power reached its peak. His *City of God* was written to refute the charge that Christianity was responsible for Rome's political decay. St. Augustine taught that one should not confuse the city of God with the city of man, the heavenly city with the earthly city. In the empirical city, evil and corruption are apt to reign, and, even if holy and wise men are put in government positions, they are subject to the forces of practical reality, a reality characterized by fluctuation, conflict, strife, ambition, defeat, and victory.

To Augustine, those participating in politics and administration cannot achieve the morally good life; the most that they can expect is material well-being. Politics and government are directed to such matters as appetites, lust, self-interest, personal aspirations, state glorification, and raw power—not ethics. The administrator who seeks to lift the lives of the people spiritually is naive, for he misunderstands the essence of politics. St. Augustine called the charge that Christianity caused the decline of Rome "nonsense." Particular governments and administrations come and go, and Rome is no exception. Augustine had his own views as to why Rome had weakened, but the specifics did not matter.

Augustine carries forth the realist tradition in political science and public administration, and he represents one thread of thought in Christianity. St. Thomas Aquinas, prominent medieval scholar and church philosopher, represents another, a more optimistic and moralistic one.

The next key period in western history was the feudal period. Feudal institutions were operating in a rudimentary manner in the fifth century, and they had blossomed fully by the eleventh and twelfth centuries. Feudalism continued as the basic political form in the West up until at least the sixteenth century, at which time it was challenged by new systems of politics. In the feudal pattern, political organization and governmental administration were highly decentralized. The basic power was at the local level, and higher-level forces were conditioned and constrained by this pattern of authority. As with Rome, though, government during this period seemed to be basically a matter of administration.

Although feudal institutions were localized, they were, nevertheless, highly structured; class and hierarchical levels were characteristic of the feudalistic political and administrative order. Representation, debate, and constituent assemblies were not yet important political elements. Rule seemed to be a somewhat private matter, with public power in the hands of lords, barons, kings, the clergy, and others with important economic or political interests. In other words, public and private authority were fused, and both became administration.

Although there are few theorists who proclaim the virtues of feudalism, this period represents one pattern of administration. It had the advantage of being based on local conceptions of public need, and seemed suited to a simple, basically agrarian, society. However, it could not realize the opportunities afforded by operations of scale, including administrative efficiency, and it tended to overlook broader conceptions of the public interest; it may also have served to inhibit some of the more common tendencies in politics and economics toward coalitions, mobility, and a widening of the marketplace.

Even under feudalism, new patterns began to emerge. Demands were made in politics and inside the church for a sharing of the policy-making and administrative authority. Representative assemblies and parliaments were formed, serving as constraints on monarchical power; in the church, some sought to curb the power of the pope through the device of representation. What this eventually meant was that the leadership's administrative authority was institutionally restrained, and this was the first step toward modern democracy. Democracy has its roots much more in historical necessity than political theory; representative institutions arose because key interests felt they were not adequately represented in politics. As long as all interests were satisfied, direct representation was presumably not required, and politics was essentially administration. The development of representative bodies challenged this pattern and made government something else, something more.

Machiavelli ushered in the modern period of political history, and what he had to say is of great relevance to public administration. Author of the *Prince* and *Discourses on the First Ten Books of Titus Livius*, Machiavelli presents the first wholly rationalist approach in political science, advancing thereby the realist tradition. He warned that morality and politics should not be confused. Political theory is not moral theory, and the two should be separated. Machiavelli never denied the existence of morality and ethics; he never suggested that they were purely imaginatory, only that they had no relevance to politics. The state had its own set of values and principles, and morality was not one of them.

To Machiavelli, politics and administration were basically strategy making; this was his standard, his "morality." The good politician or the effective administrator was a strategy-maker and, the better he was at strategy-making, the more efficient he was at ruling. Machiavelli's conception of politics was a technical one. This orientation caused him to focus on power, for it was power that moved men and states. Machiavelli found political man to be motivated by glory, power, and material well-being. He did not propose curbs on these. Nature did it for him. The quest for these ends was virtually insatiable, but the quantity of each was limited. This imbalance of supply and demand caused perpetual dissatisfaction, animosity, and conflict, and these terms pretty much describe political activity.

Nevertheless, the strategy minded political or administrative leader is no more disturbed by this than Machiavelli was; he simply takes these factors into account. The effective leader will employ political resources in a manner that allows him to get the most from them. His every move is calculated; each action must build his political base or, at least, not serve to deplete his power resources. No strategy, no move, is automatically ruled out; however, restraint must be used in such a way as to avoid needless offence, unnecessary cruelty, the appearance of deception, and the flouting of conventional belief. No power is to be used to excess, thereby working to the disadvantage of the ruler; all powers must be used rationally.

It was important to Machiavelli that power seem to be exercised in the public interest, for the benefit of all; his point is that the ruler should never be deceived by such talk, only his subjects. Machiavelli's ideal government official is not one that appears as cruel, evil, and self-serving; he is one who seems to be moral, just, honest, one who appears to be concerned only with the interests of the people, the good of the nation. Machiavelli's model politician is apt to be known as a crusader for justice, as a defender of the rights of the people, as a selfless foe of corruption and special interest rule. In other words, the best Machiavellian is unlikely to be so identified.

Applied to contemporary administration, Neustadt's *Presidential Power* represents a good example of the use of Machiavellian-directed analysis.[5] Neustadt observes that the formal authority of the presidency is sufficient to allow the incumbent considerable latitude and freedom of operation. Whether the full complement of presidential power will be tapped is another matter, and this depends primarily on the temperament of the occupant.

Writing before the regimes of Kennedy and Johnson, Neustadt finds that, of those studied, Franklin Roosevelt best understood power and how to use it. Roosevelt successfully mastered the art of administration, as shown, for instance, in his ability to gather information from subordinates, to create self-imposed deadlines, and to put pressure on himself. Roosevelt's skills in arranging forces in and outside government to the advantage of the White House and its programs were unexcelled. Neustadt suggests that whoever is chief executive is by no means automatically powerful; the President is surrounded by a constellation of interests, including Congress, administrative departments and bureaucracies, the chief executive's own staff, and departmental clientele, and he must bargain with each to achieve his ends.

Thomas Hobbes presented the case for authoritarian rule and con-

---

[5]Richard E. Neustadt, *Presidential Power* (New York: John Wiley & Sons, 1960).

centrated power. He also presented the case for strategic reasoning, and his position has important implications for politics and administration. Hobbes rejected the moralistic interpretation of politics and of human nature. His view of mankind is mechanistic, and this view molds his entire philosophy, his entire outlook on politics. Man is a collection of sensations, matter in motion. Man's greatest desire is self-preservation; man fears death most of all. Out of this human condition comes a search for power. Power includes such matters as domination, wealth, security, friends, prestige, honor, and knowledge. The search for power represents a kind of rationality, a rationality that recognizes only instrumental relationships.

Man's reasoning ability allows him to manipulate the world around him to his advantage. It permits him to determine how things relate to each other. One learns of relationships through experience, feelings, observation, and schooling. Man's job is to refine his understanding of these relationships, to develop sharper analyses of them, in order to gain a clearer insight into reality. All other reasoning, including a morally based rationality, is unacceptable; it is "false" and to be studiously avoided.

Hobbes would insist that the effective practitioner in politics and administration is one who looks at matters only as they exist, who decides how to get where he wants to go and what he wants to get done, and who spends his time on strategies and ordering events to suit him. He doesn't worry about "why" things are the way they are; he is unconcerned with whether or not they could be "better"; he concentrates only on advancing his own power base and that of the organization or interests he represents.

Hobbes is more commonly associated with the idea that power be concentrated in the hands of a single leader. Hobbes came to this conclusion because he was convinced that it is the only way to preserve peace, to avoid conflict. The sovereign is absolute. He is above the law; he is the maker of the law, and he cannot be constrained by it. With rare exceptions, man must obey this law, and, in return, the state offers protection, security, and stability.

Yet, the wider lesson from Hobbes is that organizations cannot operate unless there is a final authority, an ultimate judge, a single basic source of power. This would apply to administrative organizations in government as well as to the society at large. Hobbes' theory does not require totalitarian rule, only that a single power source be established. Not all matters have to be subject to the will of this power, and many decisions can be left to the discretion of the individual or of particular interests.

Another English theorist of note is James Harrington, author of *The Commonwealth of Oceana* (1656). Harrington located the foundation of government in sociological forces, not in law or ethics. He pointed out that both internal and external factors affect government; the internal factors are wisdom, courage, and "officiality"; the external are economic. The first constitute the "authority," and the second comprise the "power" of the state. Both sets of forces help shape governmental operations and mold the character of government, but only the latter is important over the long-run. Economic forces represent the decisive influence in the state. Administrators and politicians must work within the economically directed power base of the state, or they will not be effective. Government must be built on an economic base lest disorder and chaos result.

What Harrington is saying is that government must be compatible with its foundation. If wealth is widely distributed, the authority in government should be dispersed; if wealth is concentrated, then so should government authority. Government cannot act for long outside its interest base; the most important interests in a society will determine how government is structured, how it is to be organized, how it is to be administered, and what public policy will be. No feasible alternative exists. Governments must be directed by key interests. The administrator must recognize this and act accordingly. Of course, what action is consistent with the basic interests is subject to differing interpretations, and the administrator will have an opportunity to roam the field searching for suitable practices.

The political theory of *The Federalist Papers* was directed specifically to administrative power. In *Federalist,* Numbers 67–77, Alexander Hamilton discusses the executive power. To Hamilton it was administration, not other processes or functions, that counts: ". . . we may safely pronounce that the true test of a good government is its aptitude and tendency to produce a good administration."[6] Hamilton had no use for abstract philosophies and held that a government that was not properly executed was a bad government no matter what it may be ideally. Hamilton was unalterably opposed to a plural executive, to collegial administration. He described the ingredients that constitute "energy in the executive" as:

1. unity—or power in a single person;
2. duration—or a specified and reasonably long term;
3. adequate provision for support; and
4. competent powers.

Once in power, the Federalist party had an opportunity to run the

---

[6]Alexander Hamilton, James Madison, and John Jay, *The Federalist Papers*, p. 414.

executive branch. The Federalist theory of public administration called for a strong executive and an administration somewhat independent of the legislative branch. In addition, this theory was founded on the doctrine of rule by gentlemen—antimonarchical, to be sure, but not entirely democratic. It was not until Jackson that a new theory was advanced. While the Jacksonians did not oppose strength in the executive, they did seek to turn the administration of government over to the common man by introducing rewards into the appointment process.[7]

EARLY ADMINISTRATIVE THOUGHT

The origin of modern administrative thought can be traced to Frederick W. Taylor, who also marked the beginning of the modern efficiency movement. Before Taylor, operations in organizations were not subject to much intensive and scientific examination. One reason for this had to do with the changing economic structure. It was not until the 1800s that the Industrial Revolution took hold in the west; at this point large scale economic operations were introduced for the first time, and it was not long after that large scale governmental operations became common. The scientific study of industrial and governmental organization and activities coincided generally with the development of scale in industrial and governmental operations.

Taylor wrote *The Principles of Scientific Management* (1911).[8] Taylor held jobs in industrial plants; in 1880, he began as a foreman in the Midvale Steel Works in Philadelphia. He disapproved of the notion that intuition, hunch, and traditional wisdom could provide proper standards for industrial operations. He insisted on scientific testing and examination. For example, he called for the scientific study of all elements in a work situation; the proper movements and shortest time for each movement should be known and reduced to rules and mathematical formula. Furthermore, tools should be standardized, and the same size and weight tools should be used for a given task. Workmen should be scientifically selected and trained. Taylor found that scientific techniques were not used, and scientific practices not followed.

Taylor is also known for his "functional foremanship" idea. He argued for the elimination of a single foreman who served in a both technical and managerial capacity, providing workers both substantive information and administrative leadership. He urged that work be divided functionally and supervised accordingly. It was not necessary to

---

[7]Leonard D. White, *The Jacksonians: A Study in Administrative History* (New York: Free Press, 1954).

[8]Frederick Taylor, *Scientific Management* (New York: Harper & Row, 1947).

follow the traditional military practice of each subordinate having only a single superior. Instead, there would be several bosses, one for each major aspect of the work.

Taylor saw no reason for conflict between labor and management; both should be guided by scientific principles. Taylor felt that science should determine a fair day's work, the proper level of production under given circumstances. Guess and whim commonly served as the basis of decision-making, and this led to conflict; replace this with science and conflict can be curtailed. It was the absence of scientifically determined standards, not human nature, that caused friction.

Taylor's scientific management was not limited to industrial organizations and factory operations. There was no reason why it could not apply elsewhere, including government. Taylor Societies sprung up, and disciples spread the gospel. Scientific management had become a movement. Its effects were felt both in the United States and abroad. Even Lenin and the Communists embraced it.

Nevertheless, Taylor's ideas were not accepted by all, at least initially. Management was wary of this new science and found that it infringed on traditional managerial prerogatives; no longer could the "personal" aspect of administration be considered; science determined all. To the extent that scientific management helped to increase the production of labor, executives were happy. So long as it strengthened the hand of management vis-à-vis labor, executives were pleased. When it interfered with management though, the executives resisted it. Labor was particularly resentful of Taylorism in the early years. Labor did not want to be clocked and timed, and labor did not want to give up its skills and knowledge to a management chart and formula. The unions lobbied against the use of certain scientific management practices in army arsenals.

Taylor's scientific management had much bearing on public administration. Early public administration scholars, such as Leonard White and Luther Gulick, adhered to the basic scientific management doctrine. Scientific management could not be lifted in its entirety and applied to government organizations and public administration, but the general idea of scientific operations had relevance. After all, management in government was not too different from management in industry. In the early years, students of public administration generally agreed with Taylor's doctrine: there was "one best way," the scientific means, and it should be discovered and followed. It was not until later that critics claimed that Taylor overlooked the "human" element.

A second early contributor to modern administrative thought was Henri Fayol, a Frenchman, who wrote *General and Industrial Manage-*

ment (1916). As Fayol was a manager, his vantage point differed from Taylor's. This may have provided him a broader view of organizational operations, allowing his ideas to complement those of Taylor, who viewed matters from a different angle.

Fayol broke down the elements of the administrative process into: forecast and plan; organize; command; coordinate; and control. He based his work on the doctrine that a "body corporate" exists and characterizes the entire organization; accordingly any particular part of the organization must fit into this broader scheme.

He also called for unity of command, finding that successful administration required a single superior. He, therefore, rejected Taylor's "functional foremanship" notion and collegial administration generally. He additionally believed that management needed staff assistance for planning and management improvement. The staff should be free of operational—or line—responsibilities, serving as an adjunct to the administrator.

Max Weber

Max Weber represents an intellectual tradition in and of himself. In a sense, he does not fit neatly into our study of contributors to administrative thought, for his objective was different from that of others; his goal was to describe, and to do so in the most academically precise manner. A German sociologist, Weber (1864–1920) had wide-ranging interests, and his impact on the social sciences has been enormous. Some of his work was directed toward administrative processes. Max Weber's thought was a forerunner of modern behavioralism, and much of the behavioral doctrine can be traced to his ideas and analysis.

Max Weber's approach to administration was not the same as that of Taylor or Fayol; nor is it the same as many others who followed him. The following are the key characteristics of his thoughts on administration:

1. Weber was interested in the "is" and not the "ought." Weber did not explain what organizations "should" be like or what practices they "should" follow. He separated his own values from scientific inquiry and concentrated on analyzing what exists.

2. Weber's approach to administration was descriptive, not prescriptive. He attempted to describe what he saw; he did not prescribe.

3. His approach was scientific and value-free. Weber's method represented scientific analysis, detached observation, and value-free inquiry. At least, he strove toward these ends. His science was not used to "improve" operations but to understand them, in the most scholarly of senses.

4. He was interested in all aspects of organizations, not just the administrative processes narrowly defined. In this sense, his approach was sociological.

5. His approach was academic and precise. Weber sought not to cloud his observations with matters that had no academic value; he attempted to develop a language that described what was found in reality. He insisted on precision in analysis and the elimination of generalities that have different meaning to different persons.

6. His approach was abstract. Weber advanced models of authority, models that could not be perfectly replicated in the real world, although they were drawn from it. He developed abstractions so that reality could be better understood, so that scientific descriptions would be possible.

Weber examined authority in society, and the authority patterns he found have a bearing on the study of administration because authority patterns set the general frame within which administration operates. Weber was concerned with societies at large, and with authority in the broader society; yet, what he had to say can be applied to specific organizations as well.

Weber advanced three pure or ideal types of legitimate authority: traditional authority; charismatic authority; and rational bureaucratic authority. His authority types are not pure or ideal in the moral sense; nor do they represent what he would like to see. Each is internally consistent and is drawn from certain tendencies Weber found in different societies; there is no necessary counterpart of any, in its entirety, in the real world.

Under traditional authority, obedience is to the rulers and not to rules; authority is constrained by a tradition defined by precedents; the person exercising control is the "chief" not the "superior"; and status of rulers takes precedence over tradition if the two are in conflict. Impersonal rules, a rational ordering of relationships in the administrative hierarchy, scientific training, and a routine system of appointment and promotion are absent. Although authority is generally exercised within the framework of tradition, this framework leaves much room for the conferring of personal grace and favors.

Under charismatic authority, one finds loyalty to a special leader, a hero, a devotion to edicts issued or ordained by the leader, a personally based network of commands and authority, and the rejection of routine. Under this model, there are no "officials," only followers, agents, disciples; no formal rules, no impersonal legal principles, and no established or permanent spheres of authority. The administrative staff is chosen on the basis of a "call" of the leader, not examinations, social privilege, or wealth.

Charisma, however, cannot remain stable for long, and the society may become traditionalized, rationalized, or a combination of the two. Charisma becomes routinized because of pressures from the administrative staff, who wish to make their own status legitimate; a prerequisite for the routinization of charisma is the growth of the administrative staff and the development of some form of fiscal organization.

Under rational bureaucratic authority, there is obedience to rules not rulers; authority is founded on formal legal principles and practices, and status is given to the impersonal and abstract legal order. The legal-rational type of authority is pure only if it contains a bureaucratic administrative staff, which is characterized by: a continuous organization of official functions bound by rules; specified and established spheres of competence and divisions of labor; the hierarchical principle; offices where officials work (they do not operate out of their homes); officials who hold office by virtue of appointment (not "appropriation," such as election); and the existence of rules that govern activity. Weber finds that the single-executive idea is most consistent with this model (it is superior in precision, stability, and reliability), although he does not exclude collegial bodies. The bureaucratic model seems to be most characteristic of modern western states and it is linked with a capitalist economic system. Weber assumed that bureaucracies would become powerful forces in such societies and that the more fully developed the bureaucracy is the more influential it would become; it is doubtful if any force ultimately can stand up to it.

Weber has been both praised and criticized for his work. He has been praised for the contribution he made to the social sciences, especially in terms of his refinement of methods of social research. He has been criticized mostly for the concepts in his last model. It has been suggested that Weber was overly influenced by the experiences of German-Prussian bureaucracies and in other societies in the past that had highly structured authority patterns and advanced civil service systems (ancient Rome, for example). Additionally, some have claimed that Weber overlooked psychological and political factors that must, to some extent, shape any administrative operation; he has been sharply criticized for not considering the human element as a key administrative force. It has also been noted that Weber's models were developed prior to the emergence of the modern communist and fascist states and that his authority patterns therefore do not take into account these kinds of systems.

Most likely, Weber would not agree with these criticisms. In the first place, he advanced three types of authority, not one (as the first criticism would suggest); the other two types of authority contain other kinds of patterns. He might also have responded that he did not set out to study psychological or political factors—and that his models were of the "ideal" variety, not those found in the real world. He was simply trying to develop the models logically; they do not reflect any particular situations anyplace, at least not in their entirety. Furthermore, he would probably find that the new political forms would be accommodated by one of his three types. Russian communism under Stalin and German fascism under Hitler may well come within the scope of the charismatic model. Russia under Khrushchev may represent the routinization of charisma, and the present Soviet regime may approximate the legal-rational model with a bureaucratic staff. Chinese communism seems to have a charismatic base, as does Cuban communism.

8

PRINCIPLES OF MODERN PUBLIC ADMINISTRATION

THE HIGH NOON OF ORTHODOXY

It was not until the 1920s or 1930s that public administration was really recognized as an independent field or, at least, a separate subfield in political science. In 1929, Leonard White published the first edition of his *Introduction to the Study of Public Administration*. In the 1930s, the cause of public administration was promoted by the *Papers on the Science of Administration* (1937), edited by Luther Gulick and Lyndall Urwick; and the *Report of the President's Committee on Administrative Management* (1937).

The President's Committee on Administrative Management was known as the Brownlow Committee, after Louis Brownlow who, along with Gulick and Charles Merriam, comprised the panel's membership. The *Papers on the Science of Administration* represented a project that was initiated by Gulick while he was serving on the President's Committee. Gulick felt the group needed a broader work to guide its deliberations. It is the *Papers* and the *Report* that constitute much of the base for this section of the chapter.

The concepts of 1920s and 1930s are:

1. Planning is paramount. Organizations must plan to attain their ends, and planning takes into account both objectives and the means of achieving objectives.

2. Goals must be established. Administration is not conducted in a vacuum. Goals are necessary to guide administrative activity. Goals are to be set, and efforts structured to achieve them.

3. Structures are to be developed to achieve objectives. This would include administrative institutions and organizations. Proper organization is a must.

4. Personnel must be found to man structures. This is not to be a haphazard process. Individuals must be recruited to attain corporate ends; they must fit the organizational pattern. Not just anyone will do; care must be taken to secure the right skills and appropriate backgrounds.

5. All efforts must be coordinated. This will require a single executive to head the entire organization. Plural executives—boards and commissions—will not do. Administrative units throughout government are to be led by a single administrator; only in this way can cooperation with other agencies and a united effort be effected.

6. There must be unity of command in administrative organizations. Lest confusion result, all subordinates are to have only one superior. This is consistent with the teaching of Fayol, but contrary to that of Taylor.

7. The number of subordinates per supervisor must be limited. This is known as the span of control principle. Effective direction requires that only a few subordinates report to a superior; efficiency is impaired if a supervisor has more than six individuals under him.

8. The organization is to be hierarchically structured and formed around executives. Executives play the key role in organizations, and the organization must be subject to their will and discipline.

9. Executives should have general and special staff assistance. Executives cannot be expected to perform all functions in an organization. They need two kinds of staff assistance. The general staff assists the executive in matters of command and direction; it relieves the executive of detail, issues orders and directives within the framework of the superior's explicit authority, permits the executive to have a broader span of control, and serves in a line capacity for the executive. The special staff serves in a purely auxiliary relationship to the executive, performing as finance, personnel, or management improvement ad-

visers to executives. Unlike the general staff, the special staff has no line authority. (Line activities generally refer to those authority patterns directly related to the accomplishment of the organizational mission.)

10. The number of levels in the organization should be kept to a *minimum.* This is to keep the organization as simple and manageable as possible.

11. Control and reporting techniques must be instituted. Executives must have knowledge of what is happening in their organizations; this requires the establishment of procedures designed to provide information for the top leadership. There must be records, formal communications channels, and effective fiscal control. The executive budget was seen as a key control technique.

12. Politics and administration were to be separate. This is known as the politics-administration dichotomy. The administrative sphere was assumed to be independent of politics, to have its own values and principles. Administration was to be neutral and impartial; it was to be based on expertise. Politics and policy-making were appropriate concerns of the political branches of the government.

13. In government, a career civil service was to be developed; the career service was to be founded on merit and operate according to the dictates of rationality.

14. Efficiency was to pervade administrative operations. This principle was taken from scientific management. The goal was the accomplishment of objectives with the least expenditure of resources and manpower.

THE POLITICAL PHILOSOPHY OF EARLY PUBLIC ADMINISTRATION

Without saying it directly, the early students of public administration were advancing a political philosophy of sorts. Early public administration scholars included Gulick, Urwick, White, and others (such as Frank Goodnow, author of *Politics and Administration,* 1900; and W. F. Willoughby, author of *Principles of Public Administration,* 1927).

Dwight Waldo has described some of the elements of this philosophy of administration:

1. *The control of nature.* With the properly structured government and the appropriate administrative principles, man will be able to successfully govern the social and physical universe. The application of scientific principles to administration will achieve this end.

2. *The good society is the planned society.* Science now permits planning, and planning can be used by government to promote the good life. Some early public administrators were especially taken by the notion of urban planning and zoning; these were means by which

the entire urban scene could be transformed and new civic and political forms introduced. In local politics, public administrators were reformers, and planning was a key item on the reform agenda.

3. *The good life is a materially abundant one.* Waldo argues that planning was to attain the good life and that this was interpreted in material terms. Thus, slum clearance was both aesthetically pleasing and ethically commendable. The political philosophy on this point was one of this life: the ends included good housing for all, plenty of leisure time, a good supply of clothing, and the full range of social services.

4. *Peace is the aim.* Planning was conducted to achieve peace; war as a way of life is rejected. When governmental administration is called upon to fight wars, the task is undertaken to secure the blessings of peace; the military life is hardly the highest one.

5. *The good life is an urban life.* Jeffersonian agrarianism cannot be supported. The city is superior; it is where man can achieve his collective ends. The city permits industrialization, and industrialization allows material progress. Greater production is a healthy goal.

6. *Equality is a key value.* The early literature on public administration favored both equality and liberty, but equality was given the greatest play. Administrators are to distribute goods and resources as fairly as possible. Freedom for its own sake is not meaningful; it must be freedom to acquire, to spend, to produce. Equality, in fact, seemed to structure the conception of justice or, at least, was an important aspect of it.

7. *Administrators will rule.* The basic political philosophy is that government must rule and that, within government, administrators must control. The administrative branch is the rational branch, the one composed of the experts, the technicians, the skilled leaders. Not that public administrators rejected political responsibility; they were inclined to equate this with administrative rule. The administrative class will constitute a kind of Platonic guardian class; it will be the equivalent of Machiavelli's prince and Hobbes' sovereign; it will represent the new aristocracy; it will be like the gentlemen of Federalist vintage. This is where the fundamental power must reside. This class will be recruited democratically and will rule in the public interest.[1]

IMPLEMENTING THE EARLY PUBLIC ADMINISTRATION

The principles and philosophy of public administration were meant to be applied; they were assumed to have practical value and relevance. A

[1]See Dwight Waldo, *The Administrative State: A Study of the Political Theory of American Public Administration* (New York: Ronald Press Co., 1948), especially Chapters 4 and 6.

number of efforts directed to government reorganization were launched in the 1930s (and later) in order to carry out the basic principles of early public administration. In fact, the influence of these principles can even be felt in the 1970s, as many of the assumptions of early public administration are still accepted as an article of faith in the United States, particularly at the state and local government levels.

The President's Committee on Administrative Management, for instance, called for the extension of the merit system "upward, outward, and downward" to include virtually all nonpolicy posts. This recommendation was consistent with the teaching of the high noon of orthodoxy principles, specifically the politics-administration dichotomy and the career civil service notions. The Committee also made the following recommendations: that the Civil Service Commission be replaced by a civil service administrator, a single executive (based on the coordination and staff concepts); a simplification of the organizational structure be effected by reducing the 100 or so agencies, boards, and commissions to 12 major departments (unity of command, span of control, and coordination-single executive concepts); and staff aid be provided to the President (staff assistance principle).

Following the issuance of the Committee's Report in 1937, several actions were taken. The Reorganization Act of 1939 was passed by the Congress of the United States, and this had the effect of facilitating the reorganization process, consistent with a key recommendation of the President's Committee. In addition, the Hatch Acts of 1939 and 1940 became law; their purpose was to eliminate political activity on the part of federal employees and state and local government agencies assisted by federal grants. Hatch Act legislation prohibits active employee involvement in political party campaigns, including running for office on a partisan label. It does not, of course, restrict registration by party or voting for partisan candidates. Partisan and political party are interpreted to mean Republican and Democratic.

Two commissions were formed at the national level in the 1940s and 1950s to study governmental organization. These were both chaired by former President Herbert Hoover and known as the first and second Hoover Commissions. Following this pattern, a number of states also established government organization and administration study groups, and these were known as "little Hoover Commissions." The Hoover Commissions at the national or state levels generally adhered to conventional wisdom in public administration. It also seems that business values may have played a key role on some of the panels, particularly since businessmen were commonly appointed as members. Yet, it does not appear that business and public administration views were at all incompatible; in many respects, they seemed to reinforce each other. The business community could be expected to support the principles of efficiency, rationality, science, and expert rule that run through so much of the early public administration literature.

The Commission on Organization of the Executive Branch of the Government, the first Hoover Commission, reported in 1949. While the Brownlow Committee was composed of political science or public administration experts, the first Hoover Commission's membership included a sizeable contingent from the business community. Most of the Hoover Commission's members were appointed by a Republican controlled Congress; a minority was picked by the President. The first Hoover Commission issued 19 reports; the main one was *General Management of the Executive Branch* (1949).

The first Hoover Commission made the following recommendations:

1. The reduction of the number of departments and agencies from the existing 65 to about one-third of that number. The Hoover Commission, like the Brownlow panel before it, found too many agencies, a lack of coordination among the various agencies, and an unnecessarily complex administrative system. The Commission urged a more orderly grouping of departments, agencies, and bureaus; this required a reduction in their number. The Commission noted that the system as they found it led to executive irresponsibility. It was critical of Congress for breaking the executive line of command by legislating important functions at the bureau level, beneath the departmental or cabinet level.

What the first Hoover Commission saw, and what is still evident, was the development of more or less independent bureaus and agencies with separate legislative bases and statutory authority, a separate political clientele, and direct links with key Congressional committees and spokesmen. The Hoover Commission found that these practices interfered with efficient and effective administration, and it wanted greater central executive control over these bureaus. This recommendation did not apply, however, to the independent regulatory agencies. (The Report's basic premises were consistent with several principles from the high noon of orthodoxy; this was especially so in the case of the span of control and hierarchical structure doctrines.)

2. Continued independence of the federal regulatory commissions, but the creation of an office of chief administrator in each. In American government, key regulatory functions, in such areas as airline, communications, securities, trade, trucking, and railroad regulation, have been assigned to independent agencies, agencies that are broadly part of the executive branch but not directly responsible to the President or any department under him. The theory is that this pattern keeps politics

from interfering with the regulatory agencies, giving them a free hand to regulate in the public interest; political influence is assumed to stem mainly from the White House. This system, however, has been sharply criticized by some because it often results in a close relationship between the government officials doing the regulating and the industries being regulated.

The Hoover Commission did not disapprove of the independent regulatory agency process and wanted it continued. It found significant advantages in this practice, including the protection it afforded the independent agencies from pernicious political pressures. It suggested only that a more efficient administrative system be developed inside the agencies. The agencies should have a chief administrator, and the person holding this office should also be chairman of the regulatory commission. The Hoover panel argued that the boards that head the regulatory agencies could not perform the administrative tasks and that administration be placed in the hands of a single individual who could be held accountable for this activity. (The recommendation for internal restructuring is consistent with the coordination-single executive and unity of command ideas.)

3. The provision of more staff services to federal departments. The Hoover Commission discovered that staff support in the various federal departments was inadequate. It urged that more staff assistance be made available to each department in the areas of law, supply, management research, and congressional liaison. This recommendation is of course consistent with the staff assistance principle of early public administration thought.

4. Presidential responsibility for reorganization. The Hoover Commission believed that the President should have the responsibility for organization of the executive branch. It was the chief executive who was held accountable for the administration of public policy and government affairs, and the chief executive should have the reorganization authority. Federal agencies are commonly established by congressional enactment, and such laws may be rather specific and cause rigidity in the administrative structure and agency assignments. The Hoover Commission wanted the President to have the power to change the organizational structure and functional assignments. (As effected in practice, this recommendation might well be consistent with the coordination-single executive, unity of command, span of control, and hierarchical structure principles.)

5. Adoption of the performance budget. The Hoover panel urged a revamping of the budgetary process, suggesting that existing techniques be scrapped and the performance budget concept adopted. Un-

der performance budgeting, results rather than detailed, itemized costs
are stressed; performance budgeting permits the measuring of unit costs
on a performance basis (units of labor or material inputs required to
achieve particular objectives). Traditionally, government has used the
line-item budget, under which costs for each agency or department are
listed line by line (salaries, wages, supplies) and not related to particular objectives. The Hoover Commission felt that the performance
budget would promote efficiency and add an element of rationality to
the budgetary process. Through performance budgeting, congressional
and executive officials would be better able to judge program results
and evaluate alternative courses of action. (This recommendation is
compatible with the planning, goals, control and reporting, and efficiency notions.)

Following the first Hoover Commission's report, several actions
were taken. First, Congress passed the Reorganization Act of 1949; this
legislation gave the President the power to reorganize by executive
order until June 1959, at which time the authority was extended. Specifically, the act provided that the President may draw up a reorganization
plan, which was to be submitted to both houses of Congress. Unless a
majority of either house disapproves within a 60-day period, the plan
becomes law; other laws to the contrary are superseded.

Second, an attempt was made to reorganize certain government
activities on a more logical basis. The Bureau of Public Roads was transferred to the Commerce Department (the Bureau of Public Roads,
under a new name, is presently in the Department of Transportation),
and the United States Employment Service was moved to the Department of Labor; somewhat later, the Department of Health, Education,
and Welfare was formed, bringing together under one roof various agencies previously operating in more independent administrative roles. Also,
the chairmen of some regulatory commissions were given the administrative authority, compatible with the spirit of the Hoover unit's sug-
gestion. Finally, in 1949, performance budgeting was introduced in the
federal government.

The second Hoover Commission was also known as the Commission
on Organization of the Executive Branch of the Government; its report
was issued in 1955. This Hoover panel recommended:

1. the elimination of certain federal programs;
2. the establishment of a senior civil service; and
3. the judicialization of the regulatory commission process.

The Hoover group contended that certain federal functions and programs could be better handled by private enterprise and that the federal
government should not be in competition with the private sector. It,

therefore, urged the elimination of certain federal activities and corporations that met this criterion. Although based more on policy preferences than administrative principles, this recommendation is generally compatible with the efficiency principle of early public administration, which held that goals should be attained with the minimum expenditure of resources and manpower; if specific federal programs did not appreciably help attain government goals, they should be dropped. At the same time, the recommendation seems to conflict with the political philosophy of the early public administrators, under which government and government executives are the keys to a fuller life and a better society.

The Commission also suggested the development of a senior civil service. Under this plan, one group of executives would not have permanent job assignments and their rank would be based on *them*, as individuals, not the job they may hold. These executives could be moved from place to place as conditions required. They would not be identified with the policies of any particular administration or political party—and would be neutral in this sense—serving to carry out whatever policies were decided upon by political leaders. Those serving in the senior civil service would be distinguished from political executives, whose appointment and administrative actions would depend on the administration and party in power. The senior civil service would operate largely at the bureau, or just below the departmental, level.

It should be pointed out that this idea runs somewhat counter to Max Weber's legal-rational bureaucracy model, which stipulated that officials hold particular jobs; the whole nature of bureaucracy to Weber was that of a hierarchy of official functions and the appointment of persons to specific offices or positions. Others, such as the Committee for Economic Development, a group of private business executives, have proposed comparable plans, in which rank would be in the person, not in the job.[2] One of the assumptions behind this plan is that, at the higher levels, it is the administrative and not the technical (or substantive) knowledge and skills that count most; besides, general program and technical knowledge can be readily acquired by most administrators.

To the extent that the senior civil service would contribute to efficient government operations, this recommendation is naturally consistent with orthodox principles. In a broader sense, the idea seems to reflect the political philosophy of traditional public administration be-

---

[2]See Franklin P. Kilpatrick, Milton C. Cummings, Jr., and M. Kent Jennings, *The Image of the Federal Service* (Washington, D.C.: The Brookings Institute, 1964), p. 263.

cause of the increased prominence and perhaps power it would give to administrators. The plan was never approved.

The independent regulatory agencies perform many, if not all, of the basic government functions; they make policy, administer policy, and serve in a judicial capacity as well. The Hoover Commission suggested that the judicial role of these independent bodies be given greater attention. It was recommended that the investigatory function inside these agencies be separated from the adjudicatory function, that the basic judiciary functions of the agencies be transferred to the courts, and that the right of judicial review (review by courts) be more broadly applicable to agency determinations. These changes would be helpful for administrative reasons, serving to clarify functions and operations, and would work to define and protect the rights and liberties of those affected by the independent regulatory bodies. This recommendation goes somewhat beyond the major emphases of orthodox public administration.

Little Hoover commissions in the states followed the same general pattern. They usually provided ample representation of the business point of view, and their objective was to improve the efficiency and administrative operations of government. The members of the state commissions could be appointed by the governor, the legislature, or both. The task at the state level may have even been greater than that in Washington, because of the typically wider range of state agencies, boards, commissions, and officials, all technically part of the executive branch. Also, the blending of legislative and executive powers is greater at the state than at the national level, and it is often hard to identify whether a decision or policy determination is in reality a legislative or executive one. Some states have special boards composed of key legislative and administrative officials which make major executive type decisions (ultimate release of appropriated funds, approval of significant projects for which money has already been appropriated). In addition, a number of executive officials in states may be elected directly by the people including, in addition to the governor, the lieutenant governor, the secretary of state, the comptroller, the auditor, the attorney general, and others; this adds to the administrative complexity in state capitals.

Typically, the little Hoover commissions conduct extensive studies of the state government organization structure, examining the history of administrative operations and the relevant laws and administrative regulations. Their recommendations normally call for the reduction in the number of agencies, boards, and departments reporting to the governor; the more orderly grouping of state administrative agencies; the delegation of reorganization powers to the governor or a department under his control; and, perhaps, the transfer of the administrative functions of the regulatory bodies to an administrative agency.

There has been a tendency in the states for study commissions to urge a grouping of agencies along functional lines, with each major functional area serving as an administrative category. Thus, labor might be a functional area; if so, the study group may recommend that all agencies in labor be put under one organizational roof. These agencies may formerly have been independent of any department or they may have been in another department. As an example, the group may ask that the department of industrial relations, the bureau of unemployment compensation, the agency that handles workmen's compensation, and the organization responsible for industrial safety and hygiene be placed in a single department of labor, under a single secretary; this secretary would then report to the governor, and the responsibility for all labor matters would be concentrated in one administrative office.

Another illustration of reorganization according to function would be a recommendation that all natural resources activities be put in one department. Agencies that might be affected by such a recommendation could be those responsible for state forests, parks, fish resources, wildlife, water resources, and soil and water conservation. The effect of such a recommendation would be the reduction of the number of agencies in the natural resources field and the assignment of natural resources authority to a single office. Some state study commissions have stressed the importance of developing an executive budget (coordinated, unified budget under the direction of the governor) and curtailing the direct power of the legislature over administrative affairs.

Hoover type study commissions have also been active in *local governments*. These commissions have been guided by the principles of: concentrating administrative power in a single office, a mayor, a city or county manager, a chief administrative officer, or a county executive; the more logical categorizing of administrative agencies; the use of agency boards and commissions for advisory purposes only, not policy making or administration; the use of the executive budget and the adoption of advanced budgetary concepts; and the restriction of the legislative body to legislative decisions, or the limiting of the administrative and appointment powers of legislatures. Local governments, like states, are characterized by large numbers of administrative agencies and independent or semi-independent administrative commissions, boards, and officials. Invariably, local study groups urge a simplification of local government structure. (Their recommendations may include the creation of a single metropolitan area wide government. Only a few areas of the country have such governments.) Local governments include municipalities (city governments), counties, townships, towns, boroughs, special districts and authorities, and school districts.

The implementation of the principles of public administration orthodoxy is probably a more difficult task at the local than at other levels in the political system. In the locality, it is not only necessary to examine local actions but actions of the state and national governments as well. All local functions are, at least broadly, subject to state authority, since local governments are legally part of the state system.[3] In some areas, local governments are directly controlled by states.

Many local functions also exist or are funded to the extent that they are because of federal laws, incentives, and programs. Examples of the latter are urban renewal, public housing, airports, community action agencies, model cities, and soil and water conservation districts; in fact, it is hard to point to any local function that is not in some way assisted under some federal program. Local reorganization groups have to take into account state and federal requirements, regulations, and policies in recommending organizational and functional changes. Furthermore, acting contrary to the personal feelings of state or federal, higher level administrators may well jeopardize the funding of local programs.

ASSESSMENTS OF IMPLEMENTATION EFFORTS

The attempts to implement the principles and philosophy of early public administration represent the efforts of practically minded people to improve the operations of government. These people were given a mission, and they sought to carry it out in the most feasible and imaginative manner possible. Even today, it is likely that most of those concerned with the practice of public administration "believe" in the principles of the orthodox period. The reason for this is that these principles seem reasonable to most, and they are usually accepted on *a priori* grounds. It is unlikely that much thought will go into the examination of the principles; most serious reflection is likely to be directed toward the more specific and detailed matters in the administrative process. The author's impression is that the old principles are hardly unfashionable, although they are considered outdated by most public administration experts in the academic world.

---

[3]This point is common knowledge, but it is made most emphatically by Daniel Elazar in *American Federalism: A View from the States* (New York: Thomas Y. Crowell Co., 1966).

Traditional public administration is probably most vulnerable in its somewhat blind acceptance of "principles." Little time has been spent on the development of standards by which principles could be tested and made more certain and specific; even less time has been spent on testing the principles to verify their validity empirically. Probably in no other sphere of American life are broad generalities accepted with so much faith as are the traditional principles in public administration. A notable lack of application of scientific techniques and knowledge is reflected in efforts to improve the administrative process in government. In recent years, much scientific study of administrative structures has been carried out, and many valuable scientific principles have been advanced.[4] However, these principles do not do what traditional public administration attempted and purported to do: make the administrative process better.

It is in this light that public administrators are left to the orthodox principles. Many behavioral scientists will not even touch "ought" or "should" questions; they will not explain what action should be taken or what organizational structure is best, claiming that such questions are "relative" and, therefore, not subject to scientific investigation. As the newly trained scientists back away from such matters, the traditionalists are the only ones that remain; no other choice may exist.

The author does not intend to let this question hang. We return to it in the next section, which examines some of the reactions to public administration orthodoxy and some of the most recent trends in public administration thought and organizational theory.

NEW VIEWS ON PUBLIC ADMINISTRATION

Not everyone accepted the traditional view of public administration; not everybody agreed with the high noon of orthodoxy principles. As times change, so do views, and public administration is no exception to this. Yet, it should not be assumed that, in any given period, all experts were in full agreement. To the contrary, at any given time, there are likely to be a variety of views expressed, a variety of approaches to an understanding of public administration. What we are discussing here are general tendencies, broad patterns, which can be detected for particular periods. The high noon of orthodoxy persuasion in public administration was most popular in the 1920s and 1930s, particularly in the latter years; however, some dissented even in this period. Nevertheless, even since then, the high noon principles have continued to prevail in some quarters.

---

[4]See, for example, Anthony Downs, *Inside Bureaucracy* (Boston: Little, Brown and Company, 1967).

The Postwar Assault

Wallace Sayre has described the main elements of the post-World War II position on the high noon teachings.[5] The postwar assault on public administration orthodoxy took the form of skepticism about:

1. The politics-administration dichotomy.
2. Claims that science had produced universal principles of administration.
3. Claims that administration was value free.

Sayre pointed to literature in the postwar period that brought into serious question the separation of politics and administration. Work by Paul Appleby (*Policy and Administration,* 1949), Philip Selznick (*TVA and the Grassroots,* 1948) and others suggested that the dichotomy could not stand up in practice. The scientific and universal principles of public administration were found by Waldo (*The Administrative State,* 1948) to be neither scientific nor universal, but unscientific and culture bound; sociological studies also discovered public bureaucracies and supposedly value free administration to be deeply embedded in politics and to represent power sources in and of themselves.

Sayre noted a new consensus developing in public administration, formed around the notions that public administration doctrine is relative (to different conceptions of the public interest, for example), that public administration is a key political process, that administrative theory is a matter of political strategy (serving different interests differently), that the enforcement of management principles have their costs (strengthening the hand of administrators) as well as benefits, and that public administration is fundamentally a question for political theory (how to make the administrative processes democratically responsive).

Herbert Simon labeled key orthodox principles "proverbs" and urged the construction of a new science of administration, one which separated facts from values. Simon's new science placed a high priority on studying rationality in administrative behavior, administrative decision-making processes, group activity in public and private organizations, and the psychology of organizations.[6] Simon's approach itself was later said to be value laden and to represent just another political theory.[7]

---

[5]Wallace S. Sayre, "Premises of Public Administration: Past and Emerging," *Public Administration Review* Vol. XVIII, No. 2 (1958), pp. 102–105.

[6]Herbert A. Simon, *Administrative Behavior,* 2nd ed., (New York: Free Press, 1957); Simon's criticism of orthodox principles is in Chapter 2. See also Herbert A. Simon, Donald W. Smithburg, and Victor A. Thompson, *Public Administration* (New York: Alfred A. Knopf, 1950).

[7]Herbert J. Storing, "The Science of Administration: Herbert A. Simon," in Herbert J. Storing, ed., *Essays on the Scientific Study of Politics* (New York: Holt, Rinehart and Winston, 1962), pp. 63–150.

WHAT WAS WRONG WITH THE EARLIER DOCTRINE?

In the first place, nothing was wrong. That is, nothing was wrong in the absolute sense. The old public administrators, the old scientific management advocates, were practical men with practical objectives. They felt a responsibility for improving administration, for increasing efficiency; they sought theories and principles to help them, and they used what was close at hand and what seemed to "make sense." Those who presently draw on orthodox views in public administration simply do not have minds that work in behavioral channels. They believe in and act on broad generalities which the modern scientist would find too vague to be practically meaningful, of questionable validity, or downright inaccurate. By and large, proponents of the orthodox view are the people that today sit in our state legislatures, man most local governments, and head many a bureaucracy across the land.

The "change" that took place in public administration appears to be less one of ideas, pure and simple, than it was a change in the sort of person concerned with public administration. Public administration took on a new outlook after the war not primarily because students "saw the light" but because new people were coming into the field. Also, new studies, some done years before, and new disciplines were consulted. The result was a new public administration, a public administration that had an academic cast, a public administration directed by a new science.

Objectives also changed. The new students were more interested in *describing* the administrative process—in learning about it, in developing theories about it—than they were in "making it work better." Many had no interest in such improvement, considering such matters to be beyond the scope of scientific inquiry. They were closer to Max Weber than to Frederick Taylor or Luther Gulick. After the war, public administration was no longer the exclusive property of the practitioners; it was shared with scholars.

Much was wrong with the early public administration, and the orthodox principles are no more applicable today than they were in the past. Much research had begun to show that the old public administration was unacceptable. What "seemed" reasonable was, in fact, not. What appeared to make "good sense" did not. What was "assumed" to work did not. In short, to paraphrase Simon, the earlier doctrine was in full rout.

We can discuss the discontent with public administration orthodoxy and the development of new views in public administration by focusing on the following:

1. inconsistencies in the old public administration;

2. the difference between power and authority;
3. the role of politics and interests in governmental administration;
4. the sociology and psychology of bureaucracy; and the
5. advantages of "deviant" organizational structures.

Inconsistencies in the Old Public Administration. Public administration orthodoxy was not entirely consistent. As an example, it held that the span of control in administration should be limited, say to six subordinates. At the same time, it insisted that the number of levels in the organization be kept to a minimum. It follows that the more the span of control is limited (especially down to as small a figure as six), the more levels will be needed. In fact, a limited span of control of this variety would require unlimited levels within the typical large bureaucracy.

Second, public administration grew up in a democratic environment; no public administrator argued that democracy should be abandoned. Yet, the traditional doctrine believed that administrators should rule; administrators in government should work to promote the good life and for a more equitable distribution of the world's goods and resources. The administrators should set goals and engage in extensive planning for the benefit of the population. The idea that the administrator, the technician, knows best, that scientific knowledge is superior to hunches runs through the early literature of public administration. Now, the question is, what happens if "the people" don't agree? What happens if the elected representatives don't want to be "planned for"? Or receive a "more equitable" distribution of resources? In Houston, the people voted down zoning, and that city has no zoning to this day. What do we do in a situation like this? In a Delaware community, the citizens, by referendum, recently turned down public sewers. The citizens found no "need" for these sewers, notwithstanding the fact that thousands of dollars were spent on demonstrating the need and that government technical experts testified to the need. How does public administration handle this? It provides no direct answer. Modern behavioral science has an answer: it refuses to get involved, for these are value questions.

Traditional public administration says that administration is impartial and neutral; yet, it insists on an active role for administrators in the governance process. What happens when administrative activism ceases to be impartial, when it supports particular policies, presses for particular legislation? Ultimately, it would seem that neutrality and activism would have to come in conflict.

Power and Authority. The old public administration acted as though power did not exist or that, if it did, it was the same as authority. It tended not to distinguish between the two or, more important, to suggest the existence of two different matters in administrative organizations symbolized by these terms.

Mary Parker Follett (*The New State*, 1920; *Creative Experience*, 1924) early brought "power" into the literature of administration. Since then, many have pointed out the difference between power and authority. Power is the ability to make things happen in accordance with some goal that is desired; it is the ability to establish control. Authority is a more formal matter; it is associated with particular positions, jobs, organizations. The exercise of power may or may not be legitimate; it may or may not be legal. In the final analysis, little action could take place without the use of power, although power in any given situation may be simply a matter of authority.

The early public administrators wrote as though power and authority were synonymous. They seemed to assume that, if a proper organization were established, proper actions would follow. They appeared to believe that the formal would equal the informal, that the organization would operate according to formally ordained principles. The question of power concerned them little.

In analyzing administrative organizations, it is necessary to take into account both authority and power. Both are likely to play a role. Both are likely to be important. It is possible that they work together, in the same direction, reinforcing each other. Or they may be working at odds with one another. In the first case, the organization is apt to be more stable than the second.

Power can be used synonymously with influence. Power and influence should not be considered "evil" or "bad." They should be interpreted in a more neutral sense. Power and influence may be used for "good" or "bad" ends; they can be used to promote the public interest or to subvert it. In all organizations, there are patterns of control; in all organizations, there are structures of power; in all organizations, some people will have power and others will not or, more accurately, some will have more power than others. Power is part and parcel of organizational life; there is no way of avoiding it. However, we can attempt to shape it to healthy ends.

Politics and Interests in Administration.   The politics-administration dichotomy pervades the early literature in public administration. Politics can be understood as policy making and the various processes and activities surrounding the policy making function. Politics is something that was to be kept separate from administration; in fact, it was separate. Politics and administration represented two different spheres, with two different sets of operating premises. The career civil service was supposed to be neutral and impartial; it did not serve political or partisan ends.

Political interests were found in and, impinging on, legislative bodies; they had nothing to do with administration.

Hard experiences and dozens of studies have proved the politics-administration dichotomy false. It is not true now; it was not true then. In the first place, administrators, or particular segments of administrators, represent interests, most notably their own. Additionally, they may represent the interests of their professional group (public works administrators; highway administrators; city planners) or the interests of departmental clientele groups. They may also represent the public interest; however, the point is that, even though this is true, administrators have other interests as well.

Administrative organizations serve public ends; they may improve rivers and harbors, or build highways, or operate mass transit systems. They may work to preserve the environment, to curtail air and water pollution. They may provide parks, forests, public housing, or welfare assistance. However, this is not the entire story. Administrative organizations, public bureaucracies, seek to survive. They seek to expand their budgets, to add to their staffs, to extend their powers. They wish to maintain themselves, to build their political bases, to increase their support in the community, to enhance their public position. In so doing, they may form coalitions with other bureaucracies, or with private interests. In the national government, they may develop alliances with key congressional committees, powerful committee members or factions, and important interest groups. In other words, government agencies have political ends; they serve political purposes. The administer policy, but they also help make it.

Government agencies are in politics in another way. They may well serve as spokesmen for particular interests in society. Labor departments in national and state government, for example, are commonly close to unions, and they may represent the union viewpoint in policy councils. The same is true of agriculture departments (representing farm interests), education departments (public school interests), housing agencies (housing interests), and planning commissions (real estate or citizens interests). When there is important conflict within any of these interests, the public agency may play the role of a judge or resolver of differences. And, it is possible that different sub-bureaus or divisions in a given bureaucracy are more sympathetic to this or that faction of the particular interest involved. This is especially so in the larger of the government administrative organizations. Of course, it is possible that the government agency may not be able to resolve differences within a particular interest grouping, that is, to the satisfaction of all. In such a case, it may be that one faction will become disaffected and work for the creation of a new public agency with comparable functions, or urge the transfer of powers from the present agency to another one in which it has more influence.

The specific location or assignment of functions and authority in government is often a political question. Hardly any major department of government is without some identifiable and organized political support. Hardly any major department of government does not have associated with it in some form a private interest group, a group that provides it with political assistance and that may serve as a source of pressure on it. This group may represent profit making private businesses; it may represent nonprofit organizations; it may represent other government organizations and bureaucracies; it may represent concerned citizens; or it may represent other clients that have some stake in its operations and decisions (social workers and teachers are examples).

Interest groups generally are not neutral in matters of government organization. Sometimes, this is difficult to discern, the reason being that all figures publicly involved in organizational or reorganizational decisions will likely discuss the matter in only the most general of terms. Advocates of one organizational pattern may argue that their proposal "increases public responsibility," "makes coordination more likely," or "promotes efficiency." Advocates of a differing plan may contend that their's "increases effectiveness," permits the representation of "broader points of view," or makes "more economical operations possible." Seldom can one detect in the language the fact that different interests may have more to gain by one organizational pattern and others by another.

Access to administrative decision-makers is an important concern of interest groups; moreover, not all organizational arrangements are equally accessible—that is, to a particular group. Reorganization plans are apt to be politically motivated, and nearly any reorganization will have political implications. This was commonly overlooked in the early literature of public administration.

Interest groups have opposed recommendations of government organization study commissions. And it seems that these study commissions have commonly made their proposals on the grounds of administrative efficiency, not political feasibility. Interest groups use different strategies in blocking the implementation of reorganization plans, depending on the process by which these plans are to be approved (or defeated). In some cases, by simply making their position known, powerful interest groups can inhibit implementation efforts; in others, lobbying among legislative and executive officials is the best tactic. If a popular vote is required (as it may be at the local level), interest groups may campaign publicly. Interest groups have also favored reorganization, in which case the same techniques are used to gain approval of the reorganization plan.

In addition to access, interest groups are concerned with public policy; in fact, this is usually their greatest concern. The nature of government organization and the location of powers in the government structure may well have policy consequences. Interest groups favor one organizational pattern over another, in part, because of public policy. Interest groups want certain policies enacted and carried out, and particular government organization patterns may facilitate or impede the development of certain policies. This can perhaps best be seen at the local level, because of the large number of local governments (80,000), and the large number of reorganization plans considered at that level.

In local politics as elsewhere, citizens differ on government and policy questions. Citizens and different interests commonly organize; they form interest groups. These interest groups take stands on matters of public concern, including government organization. Certain patterns have emerged. Organized business can normally be expected to support a change in government organization from a mayor-council to a city manager plan; organized labor frequently opposes this change or gives it only lukewarm endorsement. Why? Banfield and Wilson give this reason: to the supporters of city manager government, the plan has meant cutting into the power of labor unions and ethnic minorities.[8] City manager government encourages a more "businesslike" approach and "eliminates politics" from government; at least, this is what its defenders contend.

In upper-middle and middle-income suburbs, changes in government organization and structure have commonly been demanded by new residents. These residents, who began moving to the outskirts of the metropolitan area after World War II, often found the existing government inadequate to their needs. Through their citizens' associations and other interest groups, they lobbied for city manager government or, in counties, for the county manager or county executive plan; in some cases, they urged a restructuring of the planning function, their key policy concern. Why? The philosophical answer is that they wanted "good government." Practically, however, they wanted new policies and they wanted government structure to represent new influence patterns. In the past, the government (commonly commission government or a decentralized "rural type" government) was in the hands of the old

---

[8]Edward C. Banfield and James Q. Wilson, *City Politics* (New York: Random House, 1963), p. 171.

guard, the landed interests, the business community; reorganized government would be more centralized, more responsive to "citizens'" interests. What were the policy payoffs? First, a land-use policy that shifts control over physical development from the private marketplace (old government) to government planners (new government). Second, planning policy that discourages high density and commercial development (old government supported such development) and requires low density, single family land-use (new government). Other policy shifts of less significance have also accompanied government organization changes (for example, the change from a volunteer to a paid, professional fire department). Incidentally, business and real estate interest groups often opposed these changes in government organization.

In some suburban areas on the east and west coasts, the government organization question has pitted real estate interests against citizens' associations. Real estate groups have supported placing important land development powers in special districts, suggesting that this will take such powers "out of politics." Special districts, they note, also permit greater "flexibility," since they are not subject to local geographical boundaries. As previously noted, special districts are local governments that are independent of general-purpose government (city, county); they usually have one function, are run by autonomous boards, and operate much like private corporations.

Citizens associations, however, have favored putting land powers in general-purpose governments, governments whose officials are popularly elected. These groups argue that this will make the land-use process "more responsive" and more democratic. One of the basic concerns of each set of interests is the extent of influence it can exercise over one, as opposed to the other, organizational pattern, and this is a concern because each wants public policy to reflect its values and interests. If government functions are assigned in the way the citizens groups want it, that policy will likely serve to limit future development, perhaps stop it, or keep it in the low-density residential category; if they are assigned the way the real estate groups want it, that policy may serve to stimulate further development. Government organization and public policy outcomes are closely intertwined matters; they cannot be easily separated.

In addition to interest groups, there are other actors in the government organization and reorganization process. Government bureaucracies themselves are often a key force. Few government agencies want to be abolished or shifted from one department to another; independent agencies are particularly resistant to this sort of change. Such organizations may lobby against reorganization plans that they believe will adversely affect them and their interests. This opposition may be manifest directly or indirectly through interest groups.

Legislative bodies, political parties, and voters may also be active in the "politics of reorganization." Legislative bodies may have to approve reorganization plans, and they are generally responsible for the establishment of new administrative agencies and the assignment of new government powers. Legislatures are subject to pressures from the outside (interest groups and government agencies, for example) and to internal pressures (legislative factions, committees, party caucuses); either may be involved in government organization questions.

Political parties may control the legislative or executive branches. They also have interests at stake in government organization matters. To the extent that parties represent key interests (labor or business, for example), they can be expected to side with organization proposals that these interests support. Parties may also find their own, independent, interests served better by one organization plan as opposed to another. Where the citizens have the right to vote on such questions, they may determine the fate of government organization.

The early students of public administration wrote as though politics and interests were not part of the administrative process. Yet, facts dictate otherwise. Attempts to translate public administration principles into practice will have to take into account the politics of administration or be doomed to failure. This does not suggest that the attempts should not be made to approach political neutrality in administration, only that politics will be encountered along the way; pragmatism requires the consideration of political factors. Furthermore, there is no reason why politics cannot serve idealistic ends in the same way that it serves private interests.

Sociology and Psychology of Bureaucracy. Traditional public administration sidestepped key sociological and psychological questions. So did scientific management. The old public administration emphasized the importance of fitting people into impersonal structures; the structures came first, and people were to be found to man them. To both traditional public administration and scientific management, workers seemed to represent the "raw materials" or the means to the accomplishment of greater ends. The early public administration also insisted that organizations be hierarchically structured and subject to executive command; it emphasized the "boss," required a single superior, and held that authority should flow from the top down. Employee control techniques were to be instituted, workers were to report what they were doing to management, and efficiency was to reign supreme. Scientific management was based on similar logic. It could be argued that this was a philosophy not for organizations as a whole but for top executives.

In any event, much research has served to challenge this conception of organizations. It is not so much that this conception is no good or wrong, only that it will not work; it simply does not accord with reality. It overlooks the sociology and psychology of the situation. It overlooks the key role of groups, the important informal or less obvious motivating forces. The Hawthorne studies, for example, illustrate the myopia of the orthodox position.

The Hawthorne studies refer to the research done on the Hawthorne plant of the Western Electric Company; the plant is located near Chicago. The studies were conducted in the 1920s, and they were sponsored by the Harvard Graduate School of Business Administration, under the leadership of Elton Mayo. The studies were publicized somewhat later, in several reports, the most prominent of which is *Management and the Worker* (1939), by Fritz Roethlisberger and William Dickson.[9] Roethlisberger was Mayo's research assistant, and Dickson was with Western Electric.

The Hawthorne experiment found that social pressures were highly significant in determining worker behavior. It also pointed to the importance of informal groups in organizations. The research suggested that employees cannot be easily manipulated and that much of what was done at work was based on an informal network of social relations. In fact, this network may prove decisive in affecting worker habits and worker production levels. There was, in effect, a "power overlay" which was as important or more important than the formal organizational structure. This pattern gave significant influence to the workers collectively and had its effects on management. Lower-level administrators did not interfere with it; in fact, they sanctioned it, presumably having little choice in the matter.

Satisfactory production levels were set socially, and what was a satisfactory output was not determined by management, but by the workers. All workers were expected to conform, to neither exceed nor fall below the standard. Most workers accepted this. Those that produced too much or worked too hard were termed "rate-busters" and socially ostracized, which seemed to cause them to produce even more (as a way of "getting back" at the group). Those that did not produce up to the set level were termed "chiselers" and punished socially.

Other social norms were found to be operative in the work environment. For example, work records were "faked" with the goal of making

---

[9]Fritz J. Roethlisberger and William J. Dickson, *Management and the Worker* (Cambridge: Harvard University Press, 1939).

the workers look good. Workers were expected to "keep their distance" from management and not to "squeal" on their fellow employees. Output was retricted in order to show dissatisfaction with management directives. Adhering to informal social pressures appeared to be a considerably more important motivating factor to employees than money, high production, success, personal ambition, or approval of management. Different cliques were discovered among the workers, and they seemed to be in competition with each other over which could most closely approximate group norms. But it was group norms and social considerations that counted, not independently developed individual motivations.

The lessons from Hawthorne are clear. And they do not apply only to factories but to other organizations as well, including government administrative agencies. In the first place, the studies show that the view of administration as a purely hierarchical and formal structure is too narrow. Second, they show that groups inside organizations have much to do with directing behavior. Third, they show that employees are motivated by a variety of forces, and that social pressure is a key one of these. Fourth, they indicate the importance of understanding organizations from differing vantage points. Sociology and psychology have much to contribute in this sense. The Hawthorne studies represent the beginning of the "human relations" approach (or school) in management thought. They also represent a historic landmark in the unfolding of administrative thought.

After Hawthorne, management writers began to urge a new tact in administration. Less emphasis was placed on authority, more on "working with people." Less emphasis was placed on command, more on bargaining, reconciliation, compromise. Less emphasis was placed on formal factors, more on informal ones. In short, a new trend was under way in administration, a trend that carried over into public management; this trend still represents an important strand of public administration thought.

There was nonetheless a reaction to Hawthorne. Some found the studies and their implications "hogwash." It was not that they challenged the validity of the inquiries in the technical sense; they simply believed that many drew the wrong conclusions from them. They rejected the human relations school because it was "going soft" on workers. They demanded new methods of dealing with employees, the development of harsher techniques; they wanted to bring employees to heel, and they proposed the adoption of Machiavellian strategies to this end. They would not accept the point that administrative operations were not controlled by management; they would not relent in the search for means to carry out the traditional conception of proper administrative operations.

The Hawthorne studies and others like them (especially research in social psychology) also had important implications for political theory. If internal social and psychological forces determine actions inside organizations, how is it possible to make administration democratically responsible? According to the conventional democratic model, the people elect the legislature, the legislature passes the laws, and the bureaucracies carry them out. Administrators and employees are to execute policy. Attempts have been made to answer this question, but the answer may not be thoroughly satisfactory to all.[10]

The Hawthorne studies raise other questions. Does the board of directors really control the corporation? Do the owners of corporations (the stockholders) really direct these corporations? Do political party members really control political parties? Do interest group members really control interest groups? The idea is that "external" authority can be exercised over internal operations. But can this be so? Or, to what extent is it so? The Hawthorne studies seem to suggest that we address ourselves to the matter of legitimacy, not only in public administrative agencies but in other organizations as well.

The stress on the informal or the real influences in organizations led to an assault on another traditional doctrine. Early public administrators argued that staff positions be created and that they be dependent on executive authority; staff officers were to work within the authority of the line executive or to be advisory to line executives—in either case they would possess no independent power. Again, early public administration proved defective in its concentration on formal requirements. Staff people and staff offices often exercise independent power within organizations; staff personnel in some technical fields, in fact, have been able to translate their professional expertise into political power, power that has important implications both inside and outside the organization. Budgeting and planning staffs have been particularly notable in this respect. The role of Sherman Adams under President Dwight Eisenhower suggests the influence that a staff officer can have, in this case a general staff officer. Adams was generally considered to have independent power when he served in a staff capacity under Eisenhower.

Advantages of "Deviant" Organizational Structures. Not all organizations have followed the earlier principles in structuring their opera-

---

[10]See Emmette S. Redford, *Democracy in the Administrative State* (New York: Oxford University Press, 1969). See also Charles S. Hyneman, *Bureaucracy in a Democracy* (New York: Harper & Row, 1950).

tions. Yet, by all standards, they have been successful. Some government and private organizations do not adhere to the span of control concept as advanced by the earlier theorists; some do not use the unity of command doctrine. There would be no way of knowing for certain just how many organizations in or outside of government do acknowledge the validity of the old principles and apply them in practice; nevertheless, it is clear that many neither acknowledge or apply the old practices.

The broader point here is that recent scholars in public administration and business management have suggested that the only way to know whether a principle is valid is to apply it, or to study it in operation. The idea is that principles should spring from practice, not vice versa. Principles cannot be decided upon on *a priori* grounds. Only empirical research through the use of systematic study techniques can provide insight into the relative effectiveness or ineffectiveness of different principles and doctrines.

Herbert Simon and his study group at Carnegie Tech discovered that breaking the unity of command may help achieve organizational objectives. It is not necessarily true that it would, but the goal was to attain organizational ends, not to stick rigidly to some principle. The Simon researchers concluded that it was entirely possible for one man to serve two masters, provided the "masters" are not working at cross purposes. When organizational goals so require, the unity of command principle may have to be discarded.

In the private sector, Sears and Roebuck and the Bank of America, for example, have notably "flat" organizational structures; they do not follow the concept of a limited span of control for their supervisors and executives. In fact, in Sears, the organization was deliberately structured this way to prevent executives and central office personnel from interfering with the day-to-day operations in Sears stores. Sears had found that, under a restricted span of control, central executives were exercising too much control over the individual stores and contributing to inefficient operations. The theory is that since central administrators have so many people reporting to them it is not possible for the central office to spend too much time on any given store. Sears feels that this decentralized organizational pattern has paid dividends.

The Bank of America operates in a similar fashion. It has over 600 branches throughout California, each of which reports directly to the San Francisco headquarters. No intermediate level or levels exist between the central office and the field operations. In this way, each bank is able to have a greater voice over its internal policy and to adapt to local conditions; it also has the advantage of permitting the greater development of entrepreneurial talents and skills among its executive ranks. Also, higher level administrators have less opportunity to "meddle" in the affairs of the individual banks.

RECENT DEVELOPMENTS IN ADMINISTRATIVE THOUGHT

Recent developments in administrative thought can be summarized under two categories: organizational theory; and the search for administrative efficiency.

It has only been relatively recently that organizational theory has attracted much attention in public administration. Organizational theory has risen with the growth of the behavioral sciences. The two stress empirical research, the separation of facts and values, and the construction of operationally testable hypotheses and models. Organization theory applies to all organizations and is not limited to public agencies or private business firms.

Examples of ideas drawn from organizational theory are as follows:
1. Organizations tend to become more conservative as they age, except under rapid growth or internal takeover conditions.
2. A hierarchical organizational structure is required to coordinate activities in large scale enterprises without markets.
3. Coordination at the top is more difficult in larger than smaller organizations.
4. The greater the effort made by the hierarchy to control subordinate officials the greater the evasion or counteraction tendencies found among lower officials.
5. All organizations are in conflict with any social agent dealt with.
6. Organizations that do not charge money for services develop nonmonetary costs which serve to ration outputs among clients.[11]

The search for administrative efficiency has taken on a different cast depending on the period. One of the current ideas in public administration is Planning-Programming-Budgeting-Systems, known as PPBS or simply PPB. When it was introduced widely at the national government level, President Johnson called it "a very new and very revolutionary system . . ."[12] The President explained that the goal of PPBS was to draw upon the most modern management techniques so that "the full promise of a finer life can be brought to every American at the least possible cost." Using sophisticated analytical tools, PPBS will permit the nation to:
1. identify national goals;

---

[11]Anthony Downs, *Inside Bureaucracy* (Boston: Little, Brown and Company, 1967), pp. 262–63.
[12]President Lyndon B. Johnson, "Statement to Members of Cabinet and Heads of Agencies," August 25, 1965.

2. select among the goals the most pressing ones;
3. search for the most effective and economical alternative means of achieving goals;
4. inform ourselves not only of the coming year's costs but those of subsequent years; and
5. measure the performance of national programs to assure service levels equal to the resources allocated.

To carry out the system, each federal agency was to: prepare a five year program and financial plan, which would show money needs and program outputs year by year; develop a memorandum for each program category indicating the objective of each and finding that alternatives to present programs are unavailable, or available and desirable, or available but undesirable; and establish a program evaluation staff.

PPBS was first used in government in the Defense Department, where it was promoted by Secretary Robert S. McNamara and his staff. Attempts have also been made to have it introduced in state and local governments, and it is presently used by some subnational governments. Every indication is that PPBS has been effective, although there has been only limited discussion of it as of late. In the final analysis, PPBS represents another in a long series of efforts to bring an added degree of efficiency and rationality to bear on government operations. The search for new and improved methods will no doubt continue.

SUMMARY (Chapters 7 and 8)

This chapter completes the treatment of administrative thought. We have sought to examine the wide range of theories and philosophies that have influenced administrative thought. This has taken us into a number of different fields. Public administration was found to have roots in political science, scientific management, and sociology; it was found to have drawn on work and thinking in business administration and psychology. And it was found to have a rich heritage of its own.

Administrative thought, like public administration, is not static; it has changed as conditions have warranted and it moves with the times. Administrative thought was discovered to have both practical and academic value. We noted that, in recent years, there has been a tendency for it to build on a more empirical base. We have attempted in the two chapters on administrative thought to suggest the relevance of public administration to public policy, expanding on the earlier treatment.

9

APPROACHES IN PUBLIC ADMINISTRATION

REASONS FOR CONCENTRATING ON ADMINISTRATION

There are different reasons for concentrating on public administration and government administrative organizations. One is to change existing administrative practices, structures, or decisions. Many people are not satisfied with the output, performance, and operations of government agencies. Usually, this concern is directed to particular levels of government and to particular bureaucracies or policy areas, although the concern may be broader.

The concern may be that of individuals who are simply interested in better administration or perhaps something more concrete, or it may be that of organizations, especially interest groups, who "want something" or who have something quite definite in mind. The concern may also be that of governors, the President, or other chief executives (Chapter 6). The concern of interest groups and most public officials will have much to do with politics, interest, power, influence, and decisions. That is, their goal will be to restructure political, group representation, power, and influence patterns. The means will be administrative (organization) change. It will be assumed that the change will result in greater power for some groups or officials and less for others, and that the shift in power will produce different decisions and policies. Although these points may not be discussed by the participants they, nevertheless, represent the pertinent motivating forces.

It is also possible that one might be interested in public administration for scientific reasons. The concern may be with empirical study, for its own sake and not to "improve" administration or change power and influence patterns. The interest might be with understanding how administrative decisions are made, the foundations of administrative growth or decline, the motivations of government executives, the influence of different patterns of administrative organization on decisions or policies, the bases of administrative actions (personality, power, laws), or the role of clientele groups in shaping administrative behavior. This interest may have nothing to do with changing administrative organizations, decisions, policies, structures, and actions.

TRADITIONAL AND BEHAVIORAL APPROACHES

Two current approaches in public administration are represented by the traditional and behavioral schools. Even though they represent different tendencies, the two are not in diametric opposition to one another, and they are not in conflict on all matters.

For example, in studying government administrative organizations, traditionalists focus more on formal matters, such as laws, regulations, constitutions, authority (not power), legal functions, and administrative structure as pictured in organization charts. Behavioralists, on the other hand, see this concentration as overly narrow and also call attention to such informal factors as personalities, group pressures, power drives, political motivations, and role perceptions.

Behavioralists strongly emphasize the human element in organizations, the quantification of objects of study, and scientific research. They insist on the separation of facts from values, systematic inquiry, the elimination of moral-ethical considerations in research, the verification of generalizations, precision in methodology, and an integration of the social sciences. Behavioralists believe that there are certain regularities in human behavior and that these can be uncovered through systematic research. Consequently, they place little stress on public organizations as such, preferring to deal generally with organizations and administrative behavior, whether public or private.[1]

---

[1]For a criticism of behavioralism in public administration, see Herbert J. Storing, "The Science of Administration, Herbert A. Simon," in Herbert J. Storing, ed., *Essays*

Behavioralist principles can be drawn only from empirical observation and scientific testing, not hunches, conventional wisdom, or nonsystematic research. Contemporary behavioralists reject the orthodox principles of public administration, for they were not subjected to scientific investigation and analysis; in fact, as noted in Chapter 8, research has invalidated some of them.

SPECIFIC APPROACHES

We may study administrative agencies and organizations through the following approaches:
1. Legal.
2. Theoretical
3. Formal (organization chart).
4. Systems analysis.
5. Group.
6. Power.
7. Historical.
8. Elites.
9. Change.
10. The Individual.
11. Function.
12. Decision.
13. Action.
14. Communications.

We may consider these categories as concepts that help structure the way that we "get into our material" and that also determine how we treat our subject. In the context of this book, they are the means that represent a particular orientation to the examination of government administrative agencies and activities. They are the special vehicles that assist us in mastering the government administrative organization, its internal operation, and its external relationships. A wide variety of approaches is presented; others or combinations of the ones listed above could be mentioned as well.

It should be noted that none of the classes is perfectly "watertight." The line that differentiates one from another may not be entirely clear, and a certain degree of overlap can be expected. Some may conclude,

on the Scientific Study of Politics (New York: Holt, Rinehart and Winston, 1962), pp. 63–150. For a general discussion of the matter, see David Easton, "The Current Meaning of 'Behavioralism' in Political Science," in James C. Charlesworth, ed., The Limits of Behavioralism in Political Science (Philadelphia: American Academy of Political and Social Science, 1962), pp. 1–25.

after a review of all of them, that the chief difference between them is one of terminology. Yet, the differences, no matter how subtle, are there.

Although our interest is in public administration, these concepts apply to disciplines and fields in addition to this one. For instance, the group and power approaches are useful in economics and sociology; the functional approach is useful in anthropology; and the systems concept can be used in virtually any of the social sciences.

Some scholars, however, have sought to adapt some of the approaches to public administration per se, and we shall present these contributions where possible. In addition, all of the approaches listed have been used in one way or another in the study of public administration and government administrative organizations. Some are emerging at the present time as valuable tools by which to examine government administrative institutions.

The legal approach refers to legislative enactments of government, government constitutions, municipal charters, public ordinances, judicial decisions, and administrative regulations. The idea is that these are the means used to study and analyze the operations of government executive branches.

Many of the early investigations into government administration focused heavily on the legal aspects of bureaucracies, their structures and functions, and accepted the results as reflecting the reality of public administration. The recommendations of the first study commissions set up to examine administrative structure were founded on an essentially legalistic understanding of public agencies and their missions. (See Chapter 8.)

An advantage of this approach is that it provides a good idea of what was expected, at least in the minds of the drafters of the laws, constitution, charter, ordinances, or regulations. It also provides an indication of the general constraints on administrators, such as those reflected in judicial decisions. Without this knowledge, one may not gain the proper insights toward administration, which this approach assumes to be directed by certain legal imperatives.

A danger in this concept is the belief that law is fact and constitutions practice. Overreliance on legal matters may lead to an unjustified depreciation, if not a total neglect, of the human element. It may also lead to the conclusion that new and more laws alone can fundamentally alter government and administrative actions, decisions, and behavior.

The theoretical approach is frequently associated with the legal one, and it is often difficult to disentangle the two. They seem to have a common root. Theory is used here in the normative sense, and includes abstractions that purport to explain or promote the understanding of political activity, including basic processes in public administration. In reality, they serve more as socializing forces, with little or no scientific base; perhaps they are not subject to systematic testing.

An example of this theoretical orientation is the belief that all government power derives from the people. Another is that government administrators represent the public interest. By consulting such theory, one is apt to gain a better idea of the broad goals of a society, but this may provide him with little indication of the actual functioning of government and administrative bureaucracies.

Such theory is generally so broad, vague, and imprecise that it can scarcely provide meaningful standards by which to judge or advance an understanding of actual behavior. Besides, this theory is commonly used to justify whatever decisions officials make.[2]

Most studies of the executive branch in national, state, and local governments have been based, to a considerable extent, on the theoretical approach. These would include the President's Committee on Administrative Management, the two national Hoover Commissions, and the numerous "little Hoover Commissions" in the states. At the same time, they have almost uniformly overlooked the sociological, political, and psychological forces, which are found in all government administrative organizations.

The formal approach refers to the organization chart. Government bureaucracies typically use organization charts as a means of depicting the key interrelationships among officials, offices, and levels within their structure. Organization charts are based on the principle of hierarchy, which shows a single official, office, or board at the pinnacle and other units in subordinate positions. (Examples of organization charts are found in Chapters 4, 5, and 6.)

Organization charts of entire administrative branches will show the chief executive at the top. Thus, the President will be pictured presiding over the federal departments and agencies, the governor over state offices, boards, and commissions, and the mayor, city manager, or county executive over local bureaucracies. The legislative body—the Congress, state assembly, or local council—may be placed at the top of the chart, as may "the people." Organization charts may also be prepared for particular departments or other administrative subunits.

One of the principles behind organization charts is that no position has more than one superior. The assumption is that the organization chart should demonstrate the nature of the basic flow of decision-making power, administrative authority, and executive responsibility within the

---

[2]See Joseph A. Schumpeter, *Capitalism, Socialism and Democracy*, 3d Ed. (New York: Harper & Row, Publishers, 1950), especially Chapters XXI and XXII.

agency. The organization chart will show only the more "important" posts, not the minor ones. It covers both staff and line offices.

The most glaring defect of the organization chart approach is that it may not reflect the reality of decision-making and the interrelationships among the different offices in the organization. It is entirely possible that the organization chart simply portrays the objectives of top management, the ideal administrative picture as viewed by those with key formal responsibilities; the organization chart may, in short, present what management thinks "should" exist, and this may have little to do with what does exist. If the organization chart does not adequately explain administrative patterns in a particular case, it is unlikely that this will be pointed out to someone unfamiliar with the organization. This may well make it difficult for the outside observer to gain much insight into the actual operations of a government agency, and it certainly makes him heavily dependent on formal descriptions.

The following are the weaknesses of the organization chart approach:

1. The organization chart shows patterns of authority, a formal matter—not power, a practical consideration. Both authority and power refer to control within the administrative structure; authority is formally assigned control, and power is practically exercised and empirically identifiable control.[3]

2. The organization chart tells one nothing about centers of influence; instead, it concentrates on individual offices and positions. Centers of influence may include several offices or may be found in a single office but not reflected in a diagram of the formal organizational structure.

3. The organization chart does not depict horizontal relationships, focusing almost exclusively on the vertical variety as found in the single headed hierarchy.

4. The organization chart is not likely to give the observer any indication of the relative importance of any functional area or office, and this is true no matter how "importance" is to be defined. In government, "importance" may be viewed in terms of appropriations (the larger, the "more important"), number of employees (the more, the more important), or character of the mission (diplomacy may be considered more important than waste disposal, both functions of government).

---

[3]As briefly noted in Chapter 8, Mary Parker Follett was one of the earliest scholars to use the term power in the study of administration, and to distinguish it from authority. See Mary P. Follett, *Dynamic Administration: The Collected Papers of Mary Follett,* Henry C. Metcalf and Lyndal Urwich, eds. (New York: Harper & Row, 1942). For a discussion of the difference between power and authority, see John M. Pfiffner and Frank P. Sherwood, *Administrative Organization* (Englewood Cliffs, N.J.: Prentice-Hall, Inc., 1960), pp. 24–5.

"Importance" may also be understood in the power sense and, again, the organization chart does not necessarily characterize the relative power positions of the different offices.

5. Decisions vary by type and the urgency or immediacy associated with them, and the organization chart represents a more static or single dimension process, neglecting such variances.

6. Organization charts may overlook boards, commissions, and positions that for one reason or another do not fit neatly into the administrative agency or executive branch diagram of offices and their interrelationships. This is particularly so in state and local government, where organization charts of the administrative structure may not consider the numerous independent commissions and elected officials that are technically part of the executive branch of government. Thus, the organization chart may not reveal the nature of the entire administrative operation, tending to give the impression that more power resides in the chief executive and posts subordinate to this executive than really does.

7. Governing bodies and boards in government may be active participants in the administrative process—other than through formal channels—and this activity is not normally shown on the organization chart. The nature of this participation may well be informal and may be based on tradition and past practice or on personalities or present power relationships. The participation may also be rooted in statutory law or other written rules but, nevertheless, is not reflected on the chart. In some governments in the United States, the legislative body appoints certain key executives and, as a result, establishes continuing and close ties to the administrative bureaucracies ruled by these executives. While an organization chart may show this appointment power, it does not portray the ensuing administrative links.

8. The organization chart entirely overlooks interest groups and their involvement in the administrative affairs of government. The dominant characteristic of organizational behavior in advanced stages of administrative development is the key role that "clients" of governmental bureaucracies play in shaping the general political process in the direction favored by particular bureaucracies and supporting interests and in molding (broadly) administrative decision-making in specific agencies. Interest groups "serve" government organizations in two ways: (1) by using resources to help get a favorable hearing for their agencies among general political actors (chief executive, legislature, etc.)—an example would be an association of hospitals testifying before a legislative panel for an expanded public hospital budget; and (2) by influencing particular decisions in the governmental agency in

which they have a stake or by structuring the decision-making process in that agency. The term interest group is used here in a rather broad sense; it includes the organizations traditionally considered to fall in this category such as labor, business, and farm groups as well the more recently identified pressure units such as employee associations, social welfare, housing, planning, and health groups, organizations of minority citizens, professional associations, citizens groups, and public interest organizations. These groups may well owe their existence to the presence of some administrative bureaucracy and, in any event, are likely to serve as both supporters of and an important source of pressure on governmental agencies. Incidentally, the tendency in the past decade or so has been for interest groups to splinter and to form around particular functions or agencies in government. The organization chart is then especially weak in its failure to recognize the presence and power of pressure groups.

9. The organization chart overlooks the often important influence of lower level personnel in executive agencies. Normally, the organization chart includes only the top office, officer, or bureau at any given level— thus, certain subordinate posts and administrative subdivisions are not apt to appear on the chart, and such posts or subdivisions may contain personnel or activities that determine the nature of an organization's behavior or operation.

10. The organization chart fails to treat interpersonal relationships not dictated by formal organizational arrangements. The power over decisions in any administrative agency may well stem from key interpersonal contacts which are not related in any discernible way to the formal administrative structure. Such interpersonal contacts may become institutionalized (but still formally unrecognized on the chart) or they may result from immediate circumstances and thus not be in any sense permanent; in either case, the contacts may become the basis of important activity in the agency.

11. The organization chart does not give any indication of the role of informal groupings in the agency, focusing exclusively on individuals or specific positions or units and formally constituted governing boards. These informal groupings are not to be confused with interest groups, as the latter operate openly even though they are not found on the organization chart. The informal groupings are essentially invisible, certainly not depicted on the organization chart, and they may be loosely organized. Often, organizations in government and business are split into competing factions, all of which profess allegiance to the general goals of the organization but which contest with each other for control of the internal administrative apparatus. Usually, one or another of these groups will be dominant, and sometimes only one such

group will be found in the organization, serving as the real power force and as the real bargaining agent with external units (in the case of government, an external unit might be a Congressional committee or an interest group). Although most employees in any government agency or other organization will not be aware of the presence of these contesting groups, they are still affected by them.

12. The organization chart gives a false sense of unity in an agency when, in reality, perpetual conflict will typically characterize any large agency. The impression that we get from the organization chart is that decisions are made in a hierarchical fashion, with authority ultimately resting in the top office and with all levels working toward common objectives that are determined at the highest point in the structure. This suggests a unified organization, one working toward a single goal. However, this impression is usually an incorrect one. In organizations, public and private, much disagreement exists among different units and personnel; this disagreement may stem from personality conflicts, varying views of organizational objectives and means, ambition of certain persons or groups in the agency, and a variety of other factors, such as the race, religion, or nationality backgrounds of individuals. Internal struggle seems to be more intense in private business firms, but it is equally common in public agencies. Significantly, this type of conflict is seldom stressed and sometimes not even mentioned in the literature. To overlook its presence is, nevertheless, avoiding a key practical matter in administrative behavior.

The fourth approach to organizations is by means of systems analysis. Applied to our topic, the government agency is viewed as part of an administrative system, affected by various forces in the environment and in turn making decisions and taking action that have an effect in the environment. The administrative system is depicted in Figure 9.1. The administrative system has inputs, the administrative organization itself (structure and personnel), and outputs. It also contains a general

FIGURE 9.1: The Administrative System

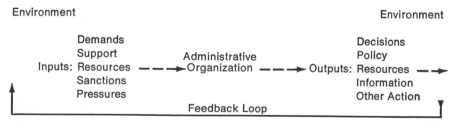

environment from which inputs are transmitted and into which outputs are sent. Another important feature is the feedback loop, by which outputs may shape the nature of the inputs.

⟨ Inputs from the environment affect the administrative organization and help shape its operations. These inputs include demands made by various groups and forces that have an interest in the agency's programs and a stake in their administration; they also include support, resources, sanctions, and a variety of pressures which may come from a number of environmental sources, including public and private interests who may wish to influence the decisions of the particular organization. The administrative organization itself—that is, the structure and personnel—"receives" these inputs from the environment and makes determinations based in part or in whole on the nature of and the intensity of effort associated with the inputs. These determinations are reflected in agency decisions, policies, resource expenditures or allocations, information dissemination, and other actions—all of which "come out" of the organization in the form of outputs. ⟩

Outputs move in two interrelated directions: (1) they are sent into the general environment where they may affect social behavior or the utilization and distribution of resources of various sorts; and (2) they may be "fed back" into the input side of the ledger, in most cases serving as sources of support for the agency and its programs or otherwise affecting the character of the pressures put on the organization. As an example of each of these uses of outputs, the federal road building agency develops standards and criteria that help administrators determine the allocation of certain highway funds; the particular decision made in this area will have a different effect on different states and communities throughout the nation, and it will result in a certain pattern of resource utilization and distribution wherever money is spent. One of the informal criteria going into a highway spending decision may be building support for the agency and, thus, more funds than might be expected could go into a state with a congressman or senator whose help is needed to expand the general roads budget. In the latter case, the output (decision to spend in a particular state) is actually tailored to shape the nature of the inputs (to strengthen the support base for the highway agency) and presumably would objectively have the desired effect on the inputs. The route followed by the outputs in the latter case can be called the "feedback loop."

Ira Sharkansky views the middle portion of Figure 9.1—the administrative organization—as representing "withinputs," or the internal agency features which may independently affect decisions or other outputs.[4] However the administrative organization is labeled, it has become clear that the public agency or bureaucracy itself should be considered as a force in the decision-making process, a force to some extent independent of other forces with an interest in the agency and its activities. In other words, the personnel in any type organization do not exist in the abstract, awaiting impulses from the outside before forming judgements or taking action; the personnel, their rules, and the structure that surrounds them may well constitute an independent interest in the administrative system, an interest whose objectives do not necessarily have to be consistent in every way with various input forces.

Inputs for a governmental agency may come from a wide variety of sources. Assuming that we are talking about a specific unit (for example, a federal department) as opposed to the executive branch of a government in general, this organization will be affected through inputs supplied by the chief executive of that level of government (the President at the national level); the legislature and legislative committees (at the federal level, Congress and its committees); other departments, bureaus, and administrative organizations; public (governmental) and private interest groups; departmental contractors and consultants; individual clients (as opposed to organized interests) of the agency; key political parties; public opinion; and other forces (such as a study group that makes recommendations about the administration of the agency's programs). Any one of these actors in the administrative system may apply pressures on the agency by making demands on it (a legislative committee may direct the agency not to spend any more money in a particular metropolitan area); by providing support (the chief executive may request larger appropriations, favored by the agency); by expending resources (an interest group may spend money to get an agency to change a policy stand); and by using sanctions against the agency (the legislature may transfer an agency function if displeased with the agency's administration of it).

Nevertheless, even with all of these inputs facing the administrative organization, it is likely to have considerable discretion in making decisions and taking action. Because of this factor, the input forces, in all probability, will not determine the precise nature of the outputs. For instance, legislation has to be enacted which provides the legal base for the agency's general activities, and this legislation is brought into the organization through the input side. However, legislation is normally couched in broad language, and it is the responsibility of the

---

[4]See Ira Sharkansky, *Public Administration, Policy-Making in Government Agencies* (Chicago: Markham Publishing Company, 1970), Chapter 1.

administrative agency to decide what that language means in a practical setting.

Outputs, incidentally, may include not only the major decisions that all agencies make but the minor ones as well. For instance, minor decisions such as the formulation of administrative regulations may have an important bearing on the ultimate distribution of the agency's resources because they are likely to contain the specific elements which form the basis for major administrative decisions.

It is also worth noting that outputs of one agency may serve as inputs in another administrative organization (or other type of organization, for that matter). For example, during the heyday of the community action program (CAP) in the middle 1960s, numerous local community action agencies, funded largely by Washington, were spending funds to educate the poor and blacks in cities on how to reshape the political climate of the locality. Poverty class representatives, trained by the community action agency, brought pressure to bear on conventional health and welfare bureaucracies in the community and engaged in a variety of tactics designed to influence public officials on different policy matters. The decision to allocate resources in this manner was an output of the community action program and its administrative unit, the community action agency; once the decision was made and implemented, it often became an input for another agency or other organizations, such as a local health or welfare department. In some cases, in fact, the output of the community action program became an input into another unit and was translated into a new decision by this unit, presumably more favorable to the poor than earlier policy.

Although systems analysis can be a tremendously useful tool in understanding the general operations surrounding administrative organizations, it has certain limitations, particularly if its potential is not fully understood. Anyone seeking to use it to explain administrative behavior should be aware of these points:

(a) All influences acting in any significant way on the administrative organization should be considered as inputs. A common shortcoming of traditional administrative analysis has been the exclusion of distasteful or "evil" forces in the description of administrative operations. The best example of this has been the tendency to play down or overlook the role of interest groups in the administrative process; often, when interest groups have been recognized, they have not been pictured as a normal part of this process but as a deviant phenomenon to be expelled. Systems analysis allows us to take into account the important part played by interest groups and to view such forces along with others affecting the administrative agency. This approach permits us to consider both those inputs traditionally seen as legitimate and those inputs seen in a less favorable light.

(b) Systems analysis can tell us little or perhaps nothing about the exact nature of the relationship between a specific input and a specific output. That is to say, one cannot determine through the systems method whether "Input A" caused "Output A," although certain inferences can be made in this regard. The reason for this is that, under typical circumstances, a variety of forces act on the administrative agency and its decision-making process; and, what may superficially appear to account for a specific decision may not. For instance, many have held Mayor Richard Daley responsible for the actions of the police against dissenters at the Democratic National Convention in Chicago in 1968; however, if the Chicago police department were analyzed through the systems approach, it would be likely that a number of considerations went into the department's decision to handle demonstrators the way it did, Mayor Daley's general instructions being but one of several forces shaping the decision.[5]

(c) If it is to be viewed in any sort of specific sense, the influence of public opinion on administrative operations is a difficult matter to gauge. One reason for this is that the public is not organized as an interest group and seldom takes stands that can be clearly translated into particular administrative decisions. At the same time, the portion of the public that feels its resources or interests can be significantly affected by an agency or program of government may well be represented in the administrative decision-making process through a lobbying group, and the positions of this group toward administrative action may be quite specific and able to be translated into administrative policy. Even if the public is asked to take a stand on a particular matter by an opinion pollster and this stand has relevance to an agency's programs and policies, the administrative bureaucracy is unlikely to take the poll too seriously (one reason being that polls may reflect casual or even irresponsible opinion); if it does, it will usually intepret the public's views on its own terms and in the light of its own interests.

(d) Systems analysis does not explain the internal power distribution in administrative organizations or the relative influence of the various forces inside the agency on the organization's decision-making

---

[5]Mayor Daley may be inclined to take credit for decisions that are not really his, thus boosting the stock of the Left. Liberal former Mayor Carl Stokes of Cleveland shed some light on police-mayor relations recently when he questioned how much control mayors have over "their" police departments, viewing the latter as essentially autonomous bureaucracies not entirely responsive to the chief executive.

process. As has been suggested, not all forces within an organization are likely to be in agreement on how the agency should be run, what decisions should be made, and who should make them. In other words, the organization is not a monolith, composed of like-minded individuals who are united on questions of specific goals, strategies to achieve these goals, the allocation of resources inside the organization, and the like. In addition, systems analysis does not help us delineate the extent to which the administrative organization, when taken as a single element, may independently affect the character of outputs. In fact, when systems analysis was first introduced into public administration, there was a distinct tendency to overlook the administrative organization as a force in and of itself.

Groups and organizations are the focal point of some students of the administrative activities of government agencies; this seems understandable enough in view of the increased attention given today to behavioralism in political science. In public administration, the concern with organizational behavior has led some to stress the significance of social psychology as an analytical tool, a tool that recognizes the crucial role of organizations and groups and their values in the administrative process and in shaping individual attitudes and actions. For example, Simon, Smithburg, and Thompson are convinced that the "only" way to learn about key aspects of organizations is through an "analysis of the basic psychological processes . . . in administration."[6] This trio believes that the basic psychological processes have their roots in situations which are largely interpersonal in nature and suggest the group orientation. The group focus, like behavioralism more generally, tends to move students of public administration toward an inquiry into organizations broadly (not public agencies in the narrower sense) and toward the interdisciplinary school.

The history of the group approach runs deep in American political science, and, at the academic level, the names most commonly associated with "group theory" are Arthur Bentley and David Truman, authors of *The Process of Government* and *The Governmental Process* respectively.[7] Earl Latham's *The Group Basis of Politics* and Bertram Gross's *The Legislative Struggle* are among the somewhat more recent works pre-

---

[6]Herbert A. Simon, Donald W. Smithburg, and Victor A. Thompson, *Public Administration* (New York: Alfred A. Knopf, 1950), p. vi.

[7]Arthur F. Bentley, *The Process of Government* (Chicago: University of Chicago Press, 1908), and David B. Truman, *The Governmental Process* 2nd Ed. (New York: Alfred A. Knopf, 1971).

senting the general group theory point of view.[8] Not all group theorists are in agreement as to the precise definition of "group," its most common foundation and elements, and its implications for the body politic; nevertheless, they all support the proposition that interests and corresponding groupings shape the direction of the political system and account for the public policy enacted by government and the basic patterns of public policy execution. The most obvious unit of analysis to the group theorists has been the traditional interest group, which this school finds lurking behind governmental action of all sorts.

The student of administration's concentration on power is not new in political science, although it was somewhat late in being introduced to public administration. Prominent among the great theorists of the past who stressed the importance of power are Thucydides and Machiavelli (see Chapter 7). In American political science, Charles Merriam and the Chicago School are most clearly identified with the power concept. In the past few years, power as an approach has been successfully used in the dissection of relationships and interpersonal activity in large corporations in American society.[9]

Power can be considered the ability to control or influence the actions, attitudes, and decisions of others, and power can be seen as an attribute of an organization or an individual. The conception that some hold of power as an evil method of ruling or achieving objectives is not what we are discussing here, for power is an amoral consideration and can be employed for whatever purpose its possessor wants, whether compatible with conventional morality or not. Neustadt uses power in this sense in his in-depth examination of the presidency and the chief executive's relationships with the administrative bureaucracy and other participants in the American political system.[10]

Power is about as useful a technique for investigating administrative operations as any, although its value is probably enhanced when it is used in conjunction with other approaches. It is an unwritten law of administration that major action with long-range implications cannot be taken by administrative agencies unless they have a power base. Much organizational activity can be explained through power and power is equally applicable in analyzing individual behavior in public agencies. Experience has demonstrated that, no matter what formal

---

[8]Earl Latham, *The Group Basis of Politics* (Ithaca: Cornell University Press, 1952), and Bertram M. Gross, *The Legislative Struggle* (New York: McGraw-Hill Book Company, 1953).

[9]Antony Jay, *Management and Machiavelli* (New York: Bantam Books, Inc., 1967).

[10]Richard E. Neustadt, *Presidential Power* (New York: John Wiley & Sons, Inc., 1960).

or legally based authority an agency or administrator may have, this authority has little meaning unless it is backed by the power to act.

A concentration on power requires the researcher to look well beneath the surface of administrative behavior, to inquire about the links with clientele of public organizations and their officers, and to examine the psychological, political, and sociological aspects of administrative operations. Power has become a particularly useful concept in studying reorganization attempts at all levels of government in the federal system; this is because administrative agencies with important political ties to key private and legislative interests have commonly successfully fought off merger and consolidation efforts, while the least powerful units have fallen victims to the efficiency experts.

Leonard White has effectively used the historical approach in his attempts to document the main patterns of administrative activity in several periods in the development of American political institutions.[11] This method can add a dimension that is sometimes overlooked in administrative research: the role that different philosophies of government play in shaping the administrative process. For example, White found significantly contrasting strategies of administration in his study of regimes in power in the early decades of the formation of American government; furthermore, these strategies could be traced to the views of the party in control of the executive branch at the time. Most notable in this respect were the differences between the aristocratic Federalists and the democratic Jacksonians.

Some students of political life have concluded that social and organizational reality can best be understood through a concentration on elites, their behavior, their views, and their interests. The key thinkers in this school have not been found in public administration per se, although their general concepts and ideas are as relevant to governmental administrative agencies as to other political institutions. The elitist point of view is that all organizations, all societies, all governments are ruled by an elite of some kind, and that philosophies and theories that hold otherwise are simply untrue, that is, not consistent with reality. To elitists, the "people" in a democracy are not in control any more than the "proletariat" are in a communist state, such theories being a product of tradition and mythology or serving as a rationalization for the dominance of the existing ruling class.

The elitist position can be of value in public administration in that it causes us to recognize the possible importance of influential persons

---

[11]See Leonard D. White, *The Federalists* (New York: Free Press, 1948), *The Jeffersonians* (New York: Free Press, 1951), and *The Jacksonians* (New York: Free Press, 1954).

or groups in administrative agencies. For whatever reason, allegiance is frequently given to certain individuals in organizations, and such individuals are likely to build a following; this process may have little to do with formal authority assignments or may reinforce such assignments. Actions and rulings in such organizations are best seen in view of their relationship to the interests of the dominant individual or group in the agency. It would appear that the elitist approach could be most effectively used in conjunction with the group and power concepts, as the three tend to be founded on similar assumptions and premises.

Much research at the local level in American government has pointed to multiple elites as the key political forces.[12] Many studies suggest that governmental actions are the product of elites and that the naure of the elite changes depending on the policy area. In other words, decisions in various policy areas are often made by an elite, but the composition of the elite varies by policy. Clearly, different hierarchies have been formed around public functions and programs, and these hierarchies are ruled or significantly influenced by small groups (elites) with important economic and political interests. Incidentally, these elites may contain elements of political and popular responsibility; they may include an elected official, for example.

The idea of change has served as the central point of interest to some scholars in political science and sociology; as time passes, organization theorists studying administrative agencies in government can be expected to look with increasing frequency to this concept.[13] Few, if any, government agencies are static—maybe *status quo* minded, but not static—and none operate in a static environment. Contemporary public administrative organizations of all types are in a constant state of flux and are affected continuously by changing environmental forces. How public agencies perceive change (if, indeed, they do), how they react to it, whether change is consciously taken into account in administrative programming are vital questions that have much relevance in public administration.

Other units of analysis that can be used in the study of public administration include: the individual, employed recently in a study of American bureaucracy by Emmett Redford; function, a concept of considerable interest to anthropologists and sociologists and having to do with broad services performed or rendered within an organization or society at large; decision, a research and study tool used successfully in

---

[12]See Robert A. Dahl, *Who Governs?* (New Haven: Yale University Press, 1961); and Robert Presthus, *Men at the Top* (New York: Oxford Unversity Press, 1964).

[13]See, for example, Chalmers Johnson, *Revolutionary Change* (Boston: Little, Brown and Co., 1966).

administrative analysis by Herbert Simon; action, a concept tapped by sociologist Talcott Parsons; and communications, or communications networks, a key focal point of political scientist Karl Deutsch.[14]

A variety of additional approaches may be of value in public administration or, more broadly, in organizational research. These include game theory, role, authority structures, leadership, economic analysis, and "will."

SUMMARY

This chapter presented the different persuasions and approaches to the study of public administration. It examined two possible reasons for focusing on public administration and government administrative agencies, the differences between traditional and behavioral research perspectives, and a number of specific means or tools which may prove helpful in analyzing government administrative organizations.

[14]For "the individual," see Emmett S. Redford, *Democracy in the Administrative State* (New York: Oxford University Press, 1969); for "function," Robert K. Merton, *Social Theory and Social Structure*, Rev. Ed. (New York: Free Press, 1957); for "decision," Herbert A. Simon, *Administrative Behavior*, 2nd Ed. (New York: Free Press, 1957); for "action," Talcott Parsons, *The Structure of Social Action* (New York: Free Press, 1949) and Talcott Parsons and E. Shils, *Toward a General Theory of Action* (Cambridge: Harvard University Press, 1951); for "communications," Karl Deutsch, *National and Social Communication* (New York: John Wiley & Sons, 1953) and *Nerves of Government, Models of Political Communication and Control* (New York: Free Press, 1966).

10

PUBLIC ADMINISTRATION AND POLITICAL CHANGE

Bureaucracies operate in a changing society. They are affected by change and they may help shape change.[1] Many look to government to stimulate change. Government undertakes a wide variety of programs that may be instrumental in effecting change, and government administrators execute these programs. In fact, government administrators may be the chief force behind the programs in the first place.

We can accept the premise that government agencies may promote change without suggesting that they necessarily do so. Much evidence points to the conclusion that bureaucracies serve to inhibit change and that they become increasingly conservative with age. However, we need only look at the operations and effects of the community action program agencies in the mid-1960s to find support for the proposition that

[1]Louis C. Gawthrop, *Administrative Politics and Social Change* (New York: St. Martin's Press, 1971).

bureaucracies can and do foster change.[2] Nevertheless, change does not come any easier through bureaucracies than it does by other means; government agencies oriented to change may not always be successful and can expect to encounter opposition and resistance.

⟍ Increasingly, the country's political system seems to be primarily characterized by the interaction of different bureaucracies. These include government agencies at all levels in the political system and the public interest groups that directly represent government agencies in the political processes. These bureaucracies set the tone of public policy, administer billions of dollars of government programs (over $300 billion at all levels), have important regulatory authority, have substantial numbers of personnel working for them on a full-time basis, possess valuable documents and information, have access to considerable expertise in particular policy areas, and are the custodians of enormous amounts of political power.[3] Anyone interested in political change can hardly afford to overlook them.⏋

This chapter is devoted to an examination of some principles that help to explain bureaucratic behavior and also may help to structure the approaches of those who feel bureaucracies can be effective instruments of political and social change. Bureaucracies can be expected to "produce" in certain ways and not in others. Hopefully, this chapter will shed light on what these ways are.

PRINCIPLE OF BUREAUCRATIC CONSTITUENCIES

Chapters 2 through 6 showed that bureaucracies do not operate in a vacuum. They operate openly in the political process and are constrained by this process. The nature of politics in the United States seems to dictate the building of constituencies. In any event, this is the way bureaucracies behave: they build constituencies. In fact, as interests tend to form around them anyway, they may have no alternative; still, it is a two-way street: bureaucracies generate constituencies, and constituencies are attracted to bureaucracies.

Bureaucratic constituencies are as real as those of a congressman or a senator, in some respects more so. Bureaucratic constituencies are more or less permanent. They are not interested in public policy in general; their interests are narrow and are usually limited to one policy area. This has considerable meaning politically. Bureaucratic constituencies do not "waste" their influence on all matters of public concern; they

---

[2]Daniel P. Moynihan, *Maximum Feasible Misunderstanding: Community Action in the War on Poverty* (New York: Free Press, 1969).

[3]Francis E. Rourke, *Bureaucracy, Politics, and Public Policy* (Boston: Little, Brown and Company, 1969). Rourke views bureaucracies in a highly political light.

"save" their resources and strategically deploy them to achieve specific ends. This gives them much more influence over particular functions of government than any given person or group could expect to exercise generally.

Bureaucratic constituencies include: other government agencies that are dependent in some way on the bureaucracy in question (such agencies may be represented in public interest groups); private interests that receive material and/or symbolic benefits from the bureaucracy's programs and policies; and legislative interests, including legislators and their staffs, that have specific duties or concerns with the policy area that affects the bureaucracy in question. This is not a comprehensive list, but it includes the major constituency elements.

Bureaucratic constituencies may have formal representation within the bureaucracy, on administrative boards or advisory councils, for instance. In a number of states, legislation requires the representation of "affected interests" on administrative agency boards; these affected interests may take the form of interest groups. Interest group representation in administration is considered by some to be not only legitimate but healthy. Normally, bureaucratic interest groups are less formally recognized but, nevertheless, are an important part of the administrative process.

Bureaucratic constituencies may perform a number of useful functions. They keep administrators informed as to the feelings of affected interests; this may be an important source of administrative "feedback," serving to restructure administrative efforts in order to make them more effective in reaching intended beneficiaries or clients. Bureaucracy constituencies may also help explain government programs to others whose understanding may make the administrative agency's job easier. Perhaps most important, constituency interests may be especially knowledgeable in the policy area in which they are represented, and this knowledge may serve as a valuable input into administrative processes. The latter is often given as the reason for having special interests represented on administrative boards in government.

However, bureaucracy constituencies tend to reflect rather narrow interests. No matter how broad and open minded particular bureaucratic support groups may think they are, they normally work to advance their own interests, interests that may well be at odds with the greater good. In this light, the process of each bureaucracy building its own constituency does not at all assure the representation or the ultimate emergence of the public interest.

It does seem to be a political fact of life that it is the rare bureaucracy that can operate without an important constituency base—that is, one that is readily definable, one that can be distinguished in basic ways from the public at large, and one that is organized. The mere existence of an interest group connected to a bureaucracy does not necessarily spell a powerful constituency base; for such a base to exist, the interest must be influential. Experience has shown that the most effective interest groups have an economic base and receive tangible material and economic benefits from bureaucracies. As an example, the highway bureaucracy constituency meets these two criteria.

PRINCIPLE OF POWER CENTERS

Chapters 2 through 5 have demonstrated the importance of particular power centers in the policy and administrative processes. Power centers are found mostly in particular policy areas, and they include at least representatives of bureaucracies, interest groups, and legislative bodies. However, as pointed out in Chapter 6, power centers may be built outside specific policy areas, drawing perhaps on the resources of more than one policy power center. Such a power center would be the chief executive.

Power is an important instrument of politics. Little can be done without it. Individuals and groups tend to form around particular functions and offices, and these functions and offices may represent power centers. There may be differences among the different power centers—differences over the allocation of public funds, over public policy, or over administrative strategies.

Efforts to change politics and policy should take this principle into account. This will require the identification of those power centers most likely to promote change. In general, it would appear that chief executives—the President, governors, and mayors—are most concerned with change. It is the chief executives at the state level, for instance, who are calling for a single transportation trust fund, for the use of highway revenues for mass transit; it is the chief executives at the national and state levels who are the basic forces behind administrative reorganization, and they are sometimes opposed by particular bureaucracies and their supporting interests.

In addition, some policy power centers favor change. For instance, the urban mass transit policy center is just beginning to emerge in Washington; it includes representatives of the mass transportation bureaucracy in the federal government, organized urban mass transit bureaucracies, organized municipalities, organized municipal chief executives, organized private transit companies, organized manufacturers of mass transit equipment, and key legislators with urban transportation duties. The mass transit power center was responsible for the Urban Mass Transportation Assistance Act of 1970, a multibillion-dollar program. This policy power center favors change, and it is beginning to challenge the highway power center (see Chapter 4).

PRINCIPLE OF LIMITED STOCKS OF POWER

Power in American politics is rationed. No single actor, no single bureaucracy, no single body has unlimited power. Each seeks to use its power strategically and "rationally." Power has different sources, both economic and noneconomic.

Change will have to be effected, if it is, within a system in which a power center's stocks of power are limited. A chief executive, for example, can do only what his power stock will permit him to do; he cannot "spend" more power than he has. The same is true of the mass transit power center and all other power centers. Change can be effected though building the power stock of those centers most likely to work for change.

The power of a given center can be built in a variety of ways. It can be done in a "positive" manner: through publicity about the center's cause, through fund raising, through lobbying for more political resources. It can also be built by challenging other power centers, by raising their "costs" so to speak; this may cause other power centers to "relinquish" something or to support the challenging center on some important matter. This is one reason, perhaps the only one, why the highway power center supported the mass transit power center in the latter's effort to pry a multibillion-dollar funding bill out of Congress; the highway power center reasoned that this would get the mass transit lobby "off its back."

The nature of the American system is such that new groups and interests are more easily brought into the system than old groups and interests are phased out. In the final analysis, everybody seems to get something, but no one gets all it wants, particularly if this means cutting into another interest's power base. In the case of bureaucracies, it is much easier to create new ones and build around new interests than it is to eliminate old ones and their supporting interests. Little else could explain the proliferation of government agencies, bureaus, and departments. This phenomenon serves both to inhibit and facilitate change.

That various power centers have limited stocks of power helps explain why administrative reorganization may not always achieve substantive ends. The chief executive of the reorganized structure must still work with particular power centers within the administrative hierarchy; the reorganization may give him more power, but it does not give him all power, nor does it eliminate all power in subordinate agencies. Presidents, governors, and heads of departments may represent power centers but, even under the most streamlined and hierarchically structured of administrative organizations, they must deal with other bureaucratic power centers. No organization pattern could change this. In short, Presidents, governors, and department heads must "bargain" with administratively subordinate power centers; orders and decrees will not do, not because this is wrong but because it will not work. With their own stock of power, drawn from both public and private sources, these technically subordinate administrative centers serve as formidable and independently influential participants in the administrative and political processes. Furthermore, they have a special advantage over their superiors in that they are permanent, while particular executives come and go.

Ultimately, it would seem that those wanting change would have to work within particular policy areas—at least, one area at a time—and seek to form solid constituencies in each. Chief executives may be instrumental in developing this base, but it is possible that they cannot be counted on over the long run. Permanent power is built around policies, and this power can prove decisive in given policy areas. Power in this sense can be centralized in particular policy areas but not in the executive branch or the government as a whole. Chapters 2 to 6 all point in this direction, serving to challenge some of the assumptions of orthodox public administration (Chapter 8).

PRINCIPLE OF EXTERNALLY INDUCED CHANGE

Change, from a given vantage point, is nearly always easier "elsewhere." It is usually easier to support (less chance of risk), and it may be easier to achieve. Bureaucracies may be more effective in stimulating change in geographical areas remote from their location or their political base than in their own immediate environment. Risks (favoring change is risky) are minimized if change can be introduced from a distance; for a bureaucracy to work for change in its immediate environment is to invite reprisals and possible political "punishment" (reduced appropriations, for example).

Change is more likely to be effected by "external" bureaucracies than "internal" ones. For example, the federal Office of Economic Opportunity was quite effective in stimulating political change in cities through its locally established community action agencies. The federally funded community action agencies served as an external force, successfully challenging city bureaucracies and community power structures. In all likelihood, this could not have been done through purely local channels, and it was not. (The operations of community action agencies are discussed in Chapter 2.)

It is interesting in this regard that the heads of state bureaucracies —the governors—are presently lobbying in Washington to eliminate the Highway Trust Fund, to create a transportation trust fund, and to divert highway money to other transportation uses. They may be successful, but the fact is that most of them have trust funds in highways in their own states. It is clear that the governors either are not powerful enough or are unwilling to use their stock of influence in their own political environments to change this situation; thus, they favor change in Washington which they cannot attain at home. This change could ultimately bring about change in their states, and the governors would not have had to risk their power where it counts.

This principle has long characterized our system. It is doubtful, for instance, if many cities in the country would have public housing or urban renewal programs today if it were not for the influence of federal bureaucracies. Local interests who favored such programs sought allies in the form of key federal agencies and, together, they changed the complexion of housing policy in cities. Without this outside force, local interests would have been significantly disadvantaged and most likely would not have been able to muster enough community strength to push through an ambitious local housing program. By the same token, if we are to change restrictive building code, zoning, subdivision, and planning practices in communities, we cannot look to local or even state bureaucracies for support; both are subject to local discipline and sanctions, and cannot be expected to foster much change. It is too risky. The change will have to come from Washington agencies.

PRINCIPLE OF LIMITED IMPACT

This principle holds that change is easier to effect if it does not act unfavorably on existing interests. The change can be significant or minor; this is not crucial. However, its chances of success depend on the effects of the proposed change on present interests. It is the effects of change and not change itself that is important.

Administrative reorganization, for example, is more likely to be accepted if it does not disturb existing power relationships and distribution patterns. Highway bureaucracies do not oppose reorganization so long as it does not curtail their power over highway funding and highway programming. If it did, they would vigorously oppose it. Also, highway bureaucracies are not against, and may even support, expanded funding for mass transit—as long as the money does not come from highway revenues. To the extent that proposed changes impinge directly and unfavorably on existing bureaucracies, the chances of these changes being approved are lessened.

Again, this principle leads advocates of change in the direction of developing power centers for particular policy areas. Power centers in existing policy areas resist change and may be sufficiently strong to stop it; nevertheless, new policy power centers will be accepted if they do not adversely affect existing ones, that is, if they do not seek to deplete the resources of existing ones. Those wanting change might look to new bureaucracies, to new interest bases, and avoid cutting into or changing existing ones.

This is the strategy that the urbanists followed. Urbanists got their own cabinet-level bureaucracy in 1965, over a hundred years after the farm bloc secured a Department of Agriculture. The farm bloc is composed of: the Department of Agriculture and its state and local branches and committees; farm interest groups such as the American Farm Bureau Federation, the National Grange, the National Farmers Union, the National Farmers Organization, and others concerned with particular commodity, livestock, or other farm program areas; and agriculture committees in Congress. The agriculture bureaucracy, the interest groups, and the congressional committees constitute the agriculture policy power center. Because this power center was not affected by the creation of the new Department of Housing and Urban Development, the agriculture power center did not oppose the new agency. Now, urbanists have a bureaucratic representative in Washington, and the new department is the foundation of a separate policy power center, a center that is a respected and influential force in national political and administrative councils.

PRINCIPLE OF BUREAUCRATIC INTEREST

Bureaucracies represent interests. These interests are the programs and policies administered by the bureaucracy. Bureaucracies "believe" in their programs and policies, and they are convinced of the value and usefulness of these programs and policies. These beliefs and convictions may be proper and well founded. Bureaucracies normally form elaborate rationales to support their activities and this applies to all bureaucracies regardless of the particular program or policy area involved.

Many people outside of bureaucracies also support government programs and policies. They may receive subsidies from a particular bureaucracy or otherwise be favorably affected by a bureaucracy's programs and actions. They are also likely to develop or have beliefs that support the bureaucracy and its programs; thus, they may become special pleaders for the bureaucracy's cause.

It is futile to attempt to legislate against these interests and beliefs; they are perfectly natural and legitimate. Furthermore, they are far more important in determining bureaucratic behavior than any other force, whether outright corruption, bribery, or even favoritism. Interests form the substance of a bureaucracy, and beliefs its ideological base. No conflict of interest legislation, however strong, is likely to change this.

Bureaucratic interests, in this context, refer to all the resources controlled by the bureaucracy. These resources include money, jobs, and power. Bureaucracies receive appropriations, spend money, employ persons, and exercise power internally and externally. Bureaucracies have much discretion over their own actions, largely because legislation permits this; in addition, this legislation is often written by the bureaucracies themselves or by supporting interest groups. Final decisions over the use of bureaucratic resources are made at the administrative stage. These decisions include the determination of the specific recipients of government money, the determination of where particular public facilities and improvements should be located, and the determination of what a company or individual is permitted or required to do with its land (zoning) or resources (pollution control).

As time passes, most bureaucracies ask for more money, expanded programs, and added powers. Sometimes, this takes place on an annual basis. Highway bureaucracies ask for more resources to build more roads, antipollution bureaucracies to build more sewage treatment plants, airport bureaucracies to build more runways, natural resources bureaucracies to acquire more park and forest land, river and harbors bureaucracies to upgrade more river channels and harbors, school bureaucracies to build more schools, housing bureaucracies to build more houses, and urban renewal bureaucracies to undertake more urban renewal projects. These additions, if granted, serve to strengthen the interest base of the particular bureaucracy.

Because of the importance of bureaucratic decisions, and because of the impact of these decisions, interests form around bureaucracies and bureaucratic policy areas. Bureaucratic decisions can seldom be entirely impartial, if this means nonjudgmental. Such decisions nearly always involve judgments, no matter how precise the standards governing them may be (usually, the standards are general, not precise). That these decisions may well be judgmental serves to point further to the interest base of bureaucracy. Major bureaucratic decisions almost have to reflect the agency's interest base, at least to some extent.

PRINCIPLE OF OPEN OPTIONS

This principle holds that key actors in the political process desire to keep their options open. It applies to bureaucracies in two ways: (1) legislators, wishing to keep their options open, tend not to put specific, precise, and operationally meaningful standards into legislation; and (2) high-level administrators, wishing to keep their options open, tend not to provide specific, precise, and operationally meaningful standards to subordinates. The reason for this is that both legislators and high level administrators want to retain the right to use broadly based criteria to judge adequacy of administrative performance, a right that may be lost to some extent if specific standards are provided. If such standards are provided, the ultimate responsibility for administrative actions rests more clearly with the legislators or high level administrators; if such standards are not provided, legislators or high level administrators are free to shift the burden for "bad" decisions to others. Regardless of the standards provided, the legislators or high level administrators are free to take the credit for "good" decisions.

In addition, some argue that specific standards are undesirable on other grounds. They may inhibit experimentation with different administrative approaches; they may put administrators in a straightjacket; they may serve to limit or eliminate the judgmental contribution that administrators can make; and they may be costly if they are improperly set. Of course, the fact that many bureaucracies write their own legislation is relevant here. General standards serve to delegate decisional power to bureaucracies as well as to keep legislative options open.

Within this context, there are two types of standards: those that are broad and general; and those that contain a high degree of specificity, precision, and operational meaning. Examples of the first are: "Highway funds authorized in this act are to be spent to facilitate the movement of persons and materials and to improve the transportation system"; and "The zoning authority is to be used to advance the general interest of the community." An example of the second is: "This code prohibits the use of plastic pipes in construction." Highway and zoning administrators are given little concrete guidance with such broad standards; these standards do not contain a high degree of specificity or precision, and they cannot be easily translated into actual administrative decisions on such matters as the desirability of particular freeway locations or particular land uses. On the other hand, a building code administrator can readily make a decision on the basis of the plastic pipe standard. Because his standard is explicit, he has no discretion in the matter. In all three of these cases, the standards are legislative.

PRINCIPLE OF BUSINESS DISUNITY

Business is an important interest in America. Still, business is far from being a united, or a monolithic, force. To the contrary, business is split, and this has political and administrative meaning and effects. Rather than discuss "the interests of business," it is more appropriate, politically, to talk about the interests of particular businesses, of particular industries.

Particular businesses and industries tend to congregate around particular bureaucracies. Builders and developers form an important part of the interest base of planning bureaucracies and sewer agencies; road contracting companies, automobile manufacturers, tire makers, oil firms, and trucking companies form an important part of the interest base of highway bureaucracies; rail equipment firms, bus manufacturers, and transit companies form an important part of the interest base of urban mass transit bureaucracies. These businesses are in competition with other businesses, and they seek decisions of bureaucracies that not only promote their interests in a positive sense but disadvantage their competitors.

In this sense, government bureaucracies may become an extension of the economic system, and their rulings and actions may be decisive in determining which businesses or industries are to be given certain economic advantages. Government bureaucracies often determine the rules that govern the economic system, and these rules may decide the outcome of the economic "game." In fact, these rules may be the single most important factor.

This principle may have a bearing on administrative reorganization. Generally, each particular business interest wants a bureaucracy of its "own," an independent one, and it wants it in part for competitive reasons. For example, atomic power interests fear that the President's proposal to create a single Department of Natural Resources will permit coal and oil interests to have a veto over atomic energy programs; presently, atomic energy programs are administered in an independent agency.

The principle may also have a bearing on government funding practices. Some highway bureaucracy backers in industry, for example, see the railroads' support of a single transportation fund as a mask to divert highway subsidies to railroads; this support will serve to weaken the economic position of the railroads' competitors (truckers), who depend on public highways for transportation, and to add to the relative competitive strength of railroads.

Existing businesses of all kinds favor administrative rulings that discourage new business that may be competitive, and they form around particular bureaucracies and press for such rulings. New business means competition (for customers, in prices, and for labor), and it is often opposed by existing businesses in this light. For example, existing merchants may favor planning and zoning bureaucracy rulings that limit the prospects of new retail business coming into the community; they may oppose all zoning permitting new businesses that are competitive. Existing banks favor banking bureaucracy rulings that prohibit new banking interests from coming into the state or community, or they favor rulings that strictly limit the number of new banking businesses.

Those wanting change in public policy and administrative practices may find this principle helpful. What it means is that business interests that stand to gain from new policies and practices may well back these new policies and practices. This is what urban transit supporters discovered. Mass transit companies and mass transit equipment manufacturers joined with urban transit bureaucracies in substantially increasing urban transportation subsidies in 1970.

Another example might be found in housing. A big business that wishes to expand into housing construction may form the base of efforts designed to change restrictive zoning and building code practices. Present zoning and building code practices require expensive construction techniques, prohibit factory housing, and discourage large scale housing undertakings; a relaxation of these practices could result in a substantial reduction in housing costs and provide better housing for the poor. Present builders have formed around housing and zoning bureaucracies that favor such practices. It would make sense for new businesses interested in housing to develop their own bureaucratic base and press for new policies and practices; others who favor more housing for low-income groups could join them.

PRINCIPLE OF LIMITED UNIVERSE

The basic administrative power is in particular bureaucracies. In Washington, this has usually meant particular bureaus which represent the key level under the "department."[4] In new federal agencies, the basic power seems to be in "administrations." In states, this power is often in

[4]Ira Sharkansky, *Public Administration: Policy-Making in Government Agencies* (Chicago: Markham Publishing Company, 1970), p. 208.

particular boards or commissions. Federal bureaus and administrations and state boards and commissions may have only limited contact with chief executives. They do not operate in the chief executives' universe.

Basic administrative units tend to develop their own universe, their own conception of things, and this is apt to be a limited one. Bureaucracies are concerned with particular programs, specific goals, limited standards, and narrow horizons. They are seldom interested in "solving problems" in general, but confine themselves to particular program areas. This is the universe that they can understand, and it serves as the base of administrative decision-making. This may be an administrative necessity, and it is certainly a political reality.[5] It serves as a powerful decentralizing force in administration. Broader decisions cannot be expected from bureaucracies. Advocates of change may wish to consider the prevalence of this framework.

CONCLUSION

This book has presented neither an optimistic nor a pessimistic view of public administration. It has attempted to present a realistic one. Bureaucracies have significant potential for stimulating change, although they also serve as conserving and stabilizing forces. Properly shaped and considered as a whole, they hold the key to political and social change.

---

[5]Herbert A. Simon, *Administrative Behavior: A Study of Decision-Making Processes in Administration Organization,* 2nd Ed. (New York: Free Press, 1957), p. 69.

INDEX